D1584912

PARANORMAL
SCOTLAND

RON HALLIDAY has been investigating paranormal phenomena for over twenty years. He is currently chairman of Scottish Earth Mysteries Research, and appears regularly on television and radio to discuss all aspects of the paranormal. He is a frequent contributor to newspapers and magazines, and is the author of two books on the Scottish UFO phenomenon—*UFOs: The Scottish Dimension* (1997) and *UFO Scotland* (1998), and the editor of *McX: Scotland's X Files* (1997). Educated at the Universities of Edinburgh and Stirling, Ron is employed as a university administrator.

Also by Ron Halliday

McX (Ed.)
UFOs: THE SCOTTISH DIMENSION
UFO SCOTLAND

THE A–Z OF
PARANORMAL
SCOTLAND

RON HALLIDAY

First published 2000
by B&W Publishing Ltd
Edinburgh

Copyright © Ron Halliday 2000

ISBN 1 873631 56 1

All rights reserved.
No part of this publication may be reproduced or
transmitted, in any form or by any means, without
the prior permission of B&W Publishing Ltd

British Library Cataloguing in Publication Data:
A catalogue record for this book is available
from the British Library

PICTURE CREDITS:

Thanks are due to the following
for their invaluable assistance
with the photographs in this book:

The *Scotsman* Photo Library for the Bob Taylor photo;
The Arbroath Herald for the Flannan Isle lighthouse;
Hulton Getty for Aleister Crowley;
The Still Moving Picture Co. for
Boleskine House and Glamis Castle;
David Knott for the Royal Mile photo;
Adrian Cerrone for the Green Man;
Warner Hall for the *Bombardment of Algiers* photo;
Avril McGuire for the Boy and Shop photos;
Steven Wiggins for Rosslyn Chapel, Haunted Tower,
Greyfriars, St Salvator's Tower and St Rule's Tower;
Ron Halliday for Loch Morar and Iona;
Dr R Halliday for Callanish

All pictures are copyright

Cover Picture: *Milton Lockhart House*
Photograph: Simon Marsden

Cover Design: Winfortune & Co

Printed by WS Bookwell

Humble as my apartment may seem, it is a place of some little experience in the affairs of both this world and the other. It has seen three entire generations come into being and pass away, and it now shelters the scion of a fourth. It has been a frequent scene of christenings, bridals, and lykewakes—of the joys and sorrows, the cares and solicitudes of humble life.

Nor were these all. There is the identical door at which it is said a great-grand-aunt of the writer saw a sheeted spectre looking in upon her as she lay a-bed; and there the window at which another and nearer relative was sitting in a stormy winter evening, thinking of her husband far at sea, when, after a dismal gust had howled over the roof, the flapping of a sail and the cry of distress were heard, and she wrung her hands in anguish, convinced that her sailor had perished. And so indeed it was.

Strange voices have echoed from the adjoining apartment; the sounds of an unknown foot have been heard traversing its floor; and I have only to descend the stair ere I stand on the place where a shadowy dissevered hand was once seen beckoning on one of the inmates.

How incalculably numerous must such stories have once been, when the history of one little domicile furnishes so many?

Hugh Miller
1835

ACKNOWLEDGEMENTS

First and foremost, I would like to thank all those who have talked of their experiences of the paranormal in all its various forms. Many will be found mentioned in the text. If we didn't have this knowledge of encounters with the weird, strange and bizarre, we would be deprived of fascinating insights into other worlds and dimensions that may interact with our own. This thanks extends not only to those still living, but to those who have long since departed to other realms—and may even be watching us as we read!

I'd also like to express my sincere appreciation of those investigators into the paranormal whose research has done so much to extend our knowledge of the subject, particularly the work of Malcolm Robinson and David Cowan. And not forgetting those of a sceptical frame of mind—Steuart Campbell stands out—who provide an opposing perspective.

I would also like to thank Alex Hamilton and Russell Kyle of the *Evening Times* in Glasgow, Lorna McLaren and (from a long time back) Jim Crumley. I would like to thank Gareth Halliday for his research and editorial contribution, and my wife Evelyn, both for word-processing much of the material and her suggestions on the text. I would particularly like to thank Simon Cave for his editorial work, enthusiasm for the project and his constructive comments on the text. Finally, I would thank B&W Publishing for their continued interest in the subject of the paranormal in Scotland.

Ron Halliday
May 2000

A

ABDUCTION

It would be wrong to consider the abduction phenomenon as a development of the late 20th century. Hundreds of years ago individuals were regularly 'taken away'—or 'abducted' as we would say today—by strange entities.

In the past, however, the abductors were not seen as coming from distant planets, but rather as beings who either lived underground or close by us in 'other worlds'. These beings were usually described as 'fairies' [qv]. Thomas the Rhymer [qv] and the Reverend Robert Kirk [qv] provide the best known examples of historic abductees, both claiming to have been carried away to the lands where fairies lived.

Although witnesses still encounter fairies their existence is not taken seriously, but the abduction phenomenon is still with us. In the last thirty years it has taken new life with the culprits now seen as alien entities from distant worlds—extraterrestrials.

In some cases it is clear that the beings involved are distinctly non-human although that is not always the case. And by comparison we should note that fairies, although smaller than humans, were definitely like us in appearance. In some recent Scottish abduction incidents, however, the alien and fairy elements seem in some way to be combined. That can be seen in an encounter from 1976 near the village of Meigle, when a ten-year-old girl who was walking in a wood came across several small entities. They looked just like tiny humans, but at the sight of them she was unable to move, instead being 'frozen to the spot'.

The entities started to come towards her and as they did so she could see that not only their eyes but, more remarkably, their skin was coloured blue. She felt hands touching her, cold and slimy. An enormous light appeared from nowhere and she found herself lying on a big circular table. Entities surrounded her, somehow reassuring her telepathically that everything was all right. These beings looked human, but she also caught sight of taller entities whose bodies were incredibly thin, like stick insects.

The place she was in was dark, but a light shone from somewhere. Drops were put into her eyes which paralysed them for a while, and some form of examination was carried out by a contraption which covered her whole body. Eventually, dazed and shaken, she was returned to the spot where her abduction had begun. On arriving home she discovered that it had been over eight hours since she had set off for the wood.

Key alien abduction encounters in Scotland include the A70 case [see Wood, Gary], the Meigle Wood Encounter mentioned above, and the Fife Incident. The last named has aroused serious differences of opinion among Scottish ufologists and some now consider it a hoax. The event, which occurred over several hours one evening in 1996 near Leven, involved a family who had a series of bizarre encounters. The first was a bright oval-shaped light low down in the sky, which turned out to be a triangular craft. This UFO then moved away swiftly, rotating slowly to display small red dots of light. Later, in a wood near to the spot where the UFO had flown over them, they saw moving among the trees several small entities, definitely not human. Above the creatures towered a tall individual, its height estimated at around seven feet, which seemed to be in charge of its smaller companions.

Using binoculars it was possible to get a much better view, and they could see a shimmering ball which appeared to be emitting energy of some kind. It looked amber in colour, with an irregular surface and dark patches. One of these darker patches, situated near the base, could be identified as an opening. The ball did not appear to be resting on the ground, but was hovering or possibly held up by thin supports. It appeared to be rotating and tilting rhythmically.

To the right of the object, but definitely on the ground, lay a circular disc, coloured dark red but possibly reflecting the amber colour of the ball-shaped craft. Groups of the small creatures were transporting boxes and tube-shaped objects from the wood towards the craft. One of the witnesses described these beings as having 'very big, dark eyes and with heads too big for their bodies. They didn't appear to have mouths'. The taller 'supervisor' was still visible and, say the witnesses, they could make out his brown skin and narrow eyes.

Later, weeks after the incident was over, one witness began to have dreams about being taken into the craft, and in this way the question of an abduction experience emerged.

It is noticeable that all these key incidents took place out of doors and therefore, in theory, could have been witnessed by the public. On the other hand there have been several encounters which have occurred inside the abductee's own home. Often the people involved have revealed a definite wish to be involved with extraterrestrial contact—for them it is certainly not an encounter to be feared.

Alien abduction incidents were not reported in Scotland till nearly thirty years after the first cases surfaced in the United States (these occurred in the 1960s). In England the first incident to emerge into the open was the Aveley encounter of 1976. But it was not until the 1990s that the abduction phenomenon came to the surface in Scotland when several bizarre and puzzling cases came in quick succession to public attention. What was curious was that a number of these related to events that had taken place as far back as the 1970s, but were not reported at the time. Compared to the USA, there has not been anything like the same volume of reported abductions. In this respect Scotland is in line with England where there have been relatively few incidents.

Reactions of abductees to their experiences have varied. For a time A70 abductee Gary Wood 'was scared to sleep at night' and admitted that 'the incident has changed my life'. Others take a more relaxed view. One female abductee stated: 'I felt elated by my experience. It confirmed what I had felt for years about our relationship to the stars.'

ARDVRECK CASTLE DEVIL

Ardvreck Castle still stands today, a lonely ruin on the shores of a loch in the wilds of Assynt. It has a long and melancholy history, and became infamous as the place where James Graham, Marquis of Montrose, was betrayed by Neil Macleod, Laird of Assynt, on 30th April 1650. Montrose had sought refuge at Ardvreck, but Macleod had him flung into the castle's dungeons and soon afterwards sold him to his enemies for 25,000 pounds Scots. Apparently, the money was never paid and Macleod was consigned to history as a man without honour.

The following account, from Hugh Miller's *Scenes and Legends* (1835), shows how the castle's evil reputation still endured almost two hundred years later:

'Somewhat less than a century ago (I am wretchedly uncertain in my dates), the ancient castle of Ardvrock [sic] in Assynt was tenanted by a dowager lady—a wicked old woman, who had a singular knack of setting the people in her neighbourhood together by the ears.

'A gentleman who lived with his wife at a little distance from the castle, was lucky enough to escape for the first few years; but on the birth of a child his jealousy was awakened by some insinuations dropped by the old lady, and he taxed his wife with infidelity, and even threatened to destroy the infant. The poor woman in her distress wrote to two of her brothers, who resided in a distant part of the country; and in a few days after they both alighted at her gate. They remonstrated with her husband, but to no effect. "We have but one resource," said the younger brother, who had been a traveller, and had spent some years in Italy; "let us pass this evening in the manner we have passed so many happy ones before, and visit to-morrow the old lady of Ardvrock. I will confront her with perhaps as clever a person as herself; and whatever else may come of our visit, we shall at least arrive at the truth."

'On the morrow they accordingly set out for the castle—a grey, whinstone building, standing partly on a low moory promontory, and partly out of a narrow strip of lake which occupies a deep hollow between two hills. The lady received them with much seeming kindness, and replied to their inquiries on the point which mainly interested them with much apparent candour. "You can have no objection," said the younger brother to her, "that we put the matter to the proof, by calling in a mutual acquaintance?" She replied in the negative.

'The party were seated in the low-browed hall of the castle, a large, rude chamber, roofed and floored with stone, and furnished with a row of narrow, unglazed windows, which opened to the lake. The day was calm, and the sun riding overhead in a deep blue sky, unspecked by a cloud. The younger brother rose from his seat on the reply of the lady, and bending towards the floor, began to write upon it with his finger, and to mutter in a strange language; and as he wrote and muttered, the waters of the lake began to heave and swell, and a deep fleece of vapour, that rose from the surface like an exhalation, to spread over the face of the heavens. At length a tall black figure, as indistinct as the shadow of a man by moonlight, was seen standing beside the wall.

' "Now," said the brother to the husband, "put your

questions to *that*, but make haste;" and the latter, as bidden, inquired of the spectre, in a brief tremulous whisper, whether his wife had been faithful to him. The figure replied in the affirmative: as it spoke, a huge wave from the lake came dashing against the wall of the castle, breaking in at the hall windows; a tremendous storm of wind and hail burst upon the roof and the turrets, and the floor seemed to sink and rise beneath their feet like the deck of a ship in a tempest. "He will not away from us without his *bountith*," said the brother to the lady, "whom can you best spare?" She tottered to the door, and as she opened it, a little orphan girl, one of the household, came rushing into the hall, as if scared by the tempest. The lady pointed to the girl. "No, not the orphan!" exclaimed the appearance; "I dare not take her." Another immense wave from the lake came rushing in at the windows, half filling the apartment, and the whole building seemed toppling over. "Then take the old witch herself!" shouted out the elder brother, pointing to the lady—"take her."

'"She is mine already," said the shadow, "but her term is hardly out yet; I take with me, however, one whom your sister will miss more." It disappeared as it spoke, without, as it seemed, accomplishing its threat; but the party, on their return home, found that the infant, whose birth had been rendered the occasion of so much disquiet, had died at the very time the spectre vanished. It is said, too, that for five years after the grain produced in Assynt was black and shrivelled, and that the herrings forsook the lochs. At the end of that period the castle of Ardvrock was consumed by fire, kindled no one knew how; and luckily, as it would seem, for the country, the wicked lady perished in the flames; for after her death things

7

went on in their natural course—the corn ripened as before, and the herrings returned to the lochs.'

AULDEARN

The village of Auldearn, some eighteen miles from Inverness, has one major claim to paranormal fame. It was the spot where in the 1660s Isobel Gowdie [qv] allegedly became a servant of the Devil.

So detailed was her confession that it convinced 20th-century writers such as Margaret Murray and Montagu Summers of the reality of an ancient witchcraft [qv] religion. Their books inspired the revival of the modern cult of Wicca, which continues to grow today. Isobel Gowdie's activities in promoting her new 'religion' are dealt with separately, but it should be noted that there appears no special reason why Auldearn was targeted by the Devil (just as there is no explanation as to why particular areas became UFO 'hot spots'). The church at Auldearn was allegedly used as a meeting-place by Satan with those he had recruited to his cause, although Isobel herself was 'picked up' and persuaded to join the coven as she was walking between two local farms. In traditional accounts, the Devil often appears to have recruited people in this way in lonely spots when there was no one else around.

Having agreed to become a coven member, Isobel visited various sites around the area, including Downie Hill—where she was taken inside to meet the fairies who lived under the ground. The coven's less savoury activities included an attempt to kill Harry Forbes, the minister at Auldearn. Another witch, Margaret Forbes, threw a magic dart at him 'at the standing stones'. The location of this attempted murder is surely of significance in its connection with the old pagan religion. It seems that the witches met Satan at the stone circle on a number of occasions, if the confessions they made are to be believed.

After the arrest of Isobel and her accomplices, Auldearn drifted back into the obscurity from which it had so briefly though notoriously emerged. There are no records of any further outbreaks of witchcraft, nor of any other type of paranormal activity in the area. For a brief period in 1662 Auldearn apparently became a focus of the Devil's interest, but the reason for this remains a mystery. Nevertheless, Auldearn is a key site in the history of Scottish witchcraft and has become a place of pilgrimage for modern practitioners of the witches' craft.

B

BALL LIGHTNING

Ball lightning has gained respectability in recent years. It is accepted by some though not all scientists as a phenomenon which seems to exist even if it can not be explained. But to those interested in the paranormal it raises a number of questions. Could ball lightning explain UFO sightings, for example? And how can we account for movement that at times seems to be under intelligent control—it often appears as if the glowing balls of light are acting under some kind of guidance. And does the phenomenon extend to every small light which is seen moving around? There may be disagreement as to what exactly comes under the description of 'ball lightning', but the following incidents which have taken place in Scotland may all fall within the range of this strange phenomenon.

In the 1950s Brian Allan, in one of the earliest known cases, reported seeing a ball of blue light hovering at the top of a hill as he and a friend were out walking. The light suddenly shot in their direction and actually passed between them leaving behind a strong smell like that of an electrical discharge. It is noticeable that this occurred within what was to be later known as the 'Bonnybridge Triangle' so there may be a link here with the UFO phenomenon even if it does not appear especially strong.

One of the most memorable incidents took place in Crail on the Fife coast. In this case the glowing ball moved across the foreshore forcing everyone to jump out of its path. It seemed to witnesses to be searching for someone or something, and eventually wandered into a beach cafe. From there it returned to the sea and disappeared beneath the waves with a hissing sound. But the phenomenon has even occurred in the heart of Glasgow. In November 1979 a man walking in George Square was almost hit by a football-sized object. It let out a high-pitched hissing sound and left behind a strong smell of sulphur. The object was round and coloured grey. The witness felt that the ball was moving as if it was under some sort of intelligent control.

An incident at High Camilty in West Lothian is of particular interest because of its proximity to the 1979 Bob Taylor encounter [see Livingston UFO]. In autumn 1989 a white light was seen hovering in a field by a witness looking from an upper bedroom window of a large detached house situated in an isolated stretch of countryside. The ball had appeared to travel down from the Pentland Hills and moved towards the house at about tree-top height. It approached to within a couple of hundred yards then sped away towards a nearby stream.

Interestingly, in the same area a few years earlier a man had been followed by a bright light as he walked towards his farm cottage. It has to be asked whether it is just coincidence that these odd balls of light are appearing in an area which has produced so many UFO reports. This last incident has an uncanny similarity to a report from three hundred years ago, the Rerrick Poltergeist case [qv], where one of those involved was followed by a bright light as he returned from work in the fields.

Alan Cameron described an interesting experience he had as a young boy while staying at a house near Inverinate beside Loch Duich. There had been a tremendous thunderstorm when suddenly he saw 'travelling towards the house a small ball, blue/white in colour with smoke or gas around it. It was moving as though looking for something. My auntie said something in Gaelic which she translated roughly as "It's a sprite from the loch. We see them sometimes". I was interested in this apparent supernatural cause, but was shocked and scared as the object came right into the house and floated by, popping and fizzing, causing hair to stand on end. It was about three inches across, like a tennis ball. It went towards my mother and floated down towards the metal based caliper on her leg, and popped like a soap bubble on the heel of her adapted shoe. She felt no shock, just a tingling'.

The theory that intelligence may be behind ball lightning is a key element in an incident which occurred in November or December 1981 (the witnesses could not recall the exact month). Mr and Mrs Buckley were walking along the pavement close to their Musselburgh home when they spotted an object which appeared like a brilliant white tennis ball. It was hovering beside a lamp-post and the couple at first thought it was just the light from the lamp, but then it started to move. As it did so they saw that there were, in fact, two balls close together. They were very white and gave the appearance of 'metal boiling hot'. The objects descended from twenty feet to a couple of inches from the pavement, then moved in front of the couple as if they were 'playing a game'. The couple felt that the balls had 'a mind of their own' and that one ball 'seemed more dominant than the other'.

The UFO sceptic and author Steuart Campbell at one time argued that the phenomenon could explain incidents such as the 1979 Livingston encounter, although this view has not been widely accepted. It is possible that the earthlights [qv] and ball lightning phenomena are connected although it is hard to believe that even together they would account for the many thousands of UFO reports or explain, for example, encounters with alien entities.

BALLECHIN HOUSE

Ballechin House stands two miles west of the village of Logierait in Perthshire. The incidents related here took place a hundred years ago, and bear no relation to the house as it stands today. But at the end of the 19th century Ballechin had, briefly, the reputation of being the most haunted house in Scotland.

The house was originally built in 1806, but by 1884 all but one still fairly substantial wing had been demolished. It was owned, until his death in 1877, by Major Robert Steuart, who by all accounts was an eccentric man, some said irascible and difficult. He seemed to take as much pleasure in the company of his dogs, of which he had many, as in that of humans. He believed in the idea of spirit return, and indeed often said that he would come back after death and enter the body of a particular black spaniel of which he was especially fond. So well-known were his statements on this matter that, after his death, all of his 14 dogs, including the spaniel in question, were shot, 'apparently in order to render impossible any such action on his part'. But in spite of this, the house soon acquired a local reputation for being haunted. People in the neighbourhood avoided its avenue after dark, and stories of strange apparitions and noises abounded.

The house had been inherited by a nephew of Major Steuart, but was generally rented out and looked after by a factor. In 1892 a Catholic priest named Father Hayden took a party of nuns on retreat there. He had been subjected, it was subsequently disclosed, to 'noises between his bed and the ceiling, like continuous explosions of petards, so that he could not hear himself speak . . .', and to other unusual experiences. In August 1896 the house was leased for a year to a wealthy family who intended to use it for shooting. They left after seven weeks. When, in an article in *The Times* the following year (which was written after visiting the house during an investigation into the haunting, as explained below) it was suggested that the disturbances which had caused the family to give up the lease were the result of mischief on the part of the tenant's children, the family's butler, one Harold Sanders, wrote to the paper to protest.

He had always been a sceptic as far as ghosts were concerned, he said, and even now remained one, but things that had happened at Ballechin had made him certain 'that there is something supernatural in the noises and things I heard and experienced. . . .' He described loud knockings which he at first thought came from the hot water pipes, but which could not be traced to that or any other 'mundane force'. Others had heard the same noises, and one man had had the feeling that someone was pulling the bedclothes off him at night. Sanders often sat up at night, to discover what was going on. 'When watching,' he wrote, 'I always experienced a peculiar sensation a few minutes before hearing any noise. I can only describe it as like suddenly entering an ice-house, and a feeling that someone was present and about to speak to me. On three different occasions I was awakened by my bedclothes being pulled off my feet.' Another night he heard groans and what sounded like 'someone being stabbed and then falling to the floor.' These noises almost always occurred at night, between about 2 and 4 a.m.

Later investigations of paranormal activity at Ballechin, particularly the one undertaken by members of the Society for Psychical Research and others during the course of a bizarre house-party in 1897, produced reports of all manner of ghostly incidents. But this simply added to the mystery of what was really going on there. Although more than 100 incidents were catalogued, the reliability of the witnesses was questioned, and the true nature of the phenomena was lost amid a mass of adverse publicity.

BARGARRAN IMPOSTER

One of Scotland's most notorious paranormal encounters. As with many classic poltergeist incidents, events at the home of John Shaw, Laird of Bargarran in the county of Renfrewshire, centred around a young girl—in this case John Shaw's eleven-year-old daughter Christine. On 21st August 1697, and for no obvious reason, Christine began to exhibit the most bizarre phenomena. She woke from a deep sleep, cried out for help, tried to stand up then suddenly rose into the air and literally flew like a bullet across the room. When her father reached her she was lying stiff as a board as if she was dead. When she recovered she complained of being in constant pain. Over the next few days her body contorted and twisted into strange shapes. At one point she 'jack-knifed', with her head and feet touching the floor at the same time.

However, the source of the problem was soon revealed. Christine claimed that two local women—Katherine Campbell and Agnes Naismith—were coming to her bedside and repeatedly stabbing her. The women were invisible to everyone else but Christine claimed she could clearly see both women standing at the foot of her bed. She even engaged in long conversations with her invisible assailants, trying to find out why they were so determined to torment her. At one point, according to Christine, the Devil himself turned up to argue with her, and Christine could be heard quoting extracts from the Bible as their discussions continued for hours on end.

In spite of all this mayhem John Shaw was not convinced that the supernatural was involved, and preferred to have his daughter treated by the medical profession. But it became increasingly hard to view the case as straightforward, especially as it went on without interruption for nearly three months. As a last resort he had Christine taken to a doctor in Glasgow on 12th November. On the boat travelling up the Clyde, Christine astonished her fellow travellers by spewing up clumps of hair of different colours. But that was only a prelude to more bizarre events. When they met the doctor, Andrew Brisbane, cinders the size of chestnuts sprang from Christine's mouth to land with a distinct hiss on the floor. Brisbane found the cinders so hot he could hardly hold them. Over the next few days Christine vomited straw, chicken bones, candle grease, eggshells and duck bones.

John Shaw now began to wonder if strange powers really were involved in his daughter's problem. By January 1698 a search for witches who may have been involved in cursing Christine was under way, and several local men and women were arrested for engaging in witchcraft. Following interrogation a number confessed to having made a pact with the Devil and to have deliberately set out to torture Christine. Others of the accused, however, steadfastly denied their guilt. It did them no good, and in June 1698 three men and four women were found guilty of the crime of witchcraft. On 10th June 1698 all seven were hanged and the bodies burnt. One, James Lindsay, was only 14 years old.

Christine Shaw never gave any indication in later life that the events which started in 1697 were anything but genuine. In her 30s she married a lay preacher, John Miller, and helped to develop a fine sewing thread known as 'Bargarran thread' after the family. Christine never talked of those bizarre days when poltergeists and demons apparently tormented her for months on end as she approached her teenage years. So we may never know to what extent they were all the fantasy of her troubled mind. Or a genuine paranormal event.

BLACK LADY OF LARKHALL

Visions of female ghosts seem to come in many different colours. The best known 'Black Lady' is that seen on numerous occasions in Larkhall. The ghost is said to be of a known person, Sita Phuradeen, a black servant who worked for a local aristocratic family at the end of the 19th century, but who disappeared in mysterious circumstances.

Much of our knowledge of this haunting comes from the research of local investigator Helen Moir. Helen has a strong link with the site. Her grandmother worked for 70 years as a domestic at Broomhill Mansion, home of the Hamilton family. She met and knew Sita Phuradeen, and Helen Moir feels that she may have been contacted by the spirit of Sita because of her family link with the estate. In a dream Helen saw 'a room with a bay window, a piano and ornate fireplace. A distinguished-looking man stands on one side and a beautiful coloured woman on the other. They are having a heated discussion. She walks towards him, but he strikes her with a candlestick and she falls to the floor. He then drags her out of the room across a marble floor and down to the cellar.' Helen also believes that she caught a glimpse of Sita's ghost one morning. She described it as like 'a shadow on a dark night which was caught in the light of a torch'. Helen still makes regular visits to the site although the house is now a ruin. On one occasion she brought psychics to the estate. They sensed that witchcraft activities had taken place there, but as the site has been occupied for centuries we cannot be sure that this is linked to Sita's disappearance.

In fact, there is no evidence that Sita was murdered by her employer Henry Hamilton, or anyone else. The police were never called to investigate. The story of her sudden disappearance from the area does, however, seem to be based on fact. The rumour at the time was that her relationship with her employer was more than that of a servant. It is possible that Sita, a high caste woman from Ceylon, did have an affair with her employer, and this could explain her disappearance. If she did meet a tragic end in the cellar of Broomhill, it might explain why her ghost still haunts the area.

Her phantom has probably been witnessed more times than any other in Scotland. One ex-miner who confronted the spectre described seeing an 'exotic figure, quite tall, but sad-looking. We stood and stared at each other till she vanished.' On another occasion a local postman saw her walking towards his van. A woman who broke her leg on the estate, and was lying for hours unable to move, told of being comforted through the night by a mysterious lady who disappeared at dawn.

BLACK TRIANGLES

When we think of an unidentified flying object we tend to think of a disc shape, the traditional 'flying saucer'. But in the 1990s the world of ufology was puzzled by the appearance of black triangular UFOs. A number of areas established themselves as 'hot spots' where the mysterious black triangles seemed to be regular visitors, but the key location in Scotland appeared to be around the county of Ayrshire. In September 1996, from her home in St Leonards Road, Ayr, Margaret Barrie watched a triangular craft hovering in daylight over Prestwick Airport. She described it as a large dark object 'a bit like a delta-wing type plane, but not at all like a plane as the wings were slowly opening and closing'. Black triangles were also seen twice in a matter of days near New Cumnock in February 1997. In June of the same year one was reported over the village of Galston, and in July over Kilmarnock.

Activity in Scotland was matched elsewhere, with identical reports from England, for example over Lancashire in early 1996, and a 'wave' of incidents in the Low Countries which attracted worldwide attention because Belgian military aircraft were scrambled to investigate. It certainly seemed as if we were dealing with a global phenomenon, but why was the area on the Kilmarnock/Ayr axis being especially targeted?

Some argued that what witnesses were seeing was the secret testing of a stealth bomber, as the military were trying to judge the ability of stealth aircraft to operate undetected over urban centres—an idea which does not seem unreasonable. However, some who saw the triangles reported that they carried out strange manoeuvres. Sharp right-angled turns, stopping and starting abruptly, or simply travelling at impossible speeds. In other words, performing manoeuvres that we associate with UFOs rather than terrestrial craft, no matter how advanced. Nothing Western technology has come up with could match the movement of these objects. As UFO investigator John Morrison wrote, after comparing known stealth capabilities against manoeuvres performed by UFOs as reported by witnesses, '[stealth] is a relatively conventional aircraft with an unusual shape which fires people's imagination. Whatever the public are reporting in the world's skies performing impossible feats, it is not stealth'.

Perhaps the most convincing argument against stealth as an explanation for Scotland's black triangles lies in the fact that sightings pre-date the invention of stealth. As early as 1976, a black triangular-shaped UFO was reported over Carluke in Lanarkshire—which is, in fact, only a few miles from the Ayr/Kilmarnock hot spot. And even blue-coloured triangles have been seen.

It has to be accepted, however, that the military would never admit that tests of advanced technology craft were being carried out, so we can never be sure of what is 'at the edge of known technology' and what truly is 'out of this world'.

BLAIRGOWRIE

Blairgowrie gained notoriety in the early 1990s as Scotland's premier UFO hot spot. Oddly, the event which first attracted press interest to this Perthshire town, a famous fruit growing area, was not the UFO phenomenon, but the appearance of Scotland's first crop circles [qv]. In June 1990 two appeared on the slopes of a field lying just on the edge of the town. Paranormal investigators Ron Halliday and Ken Higgins revealed that strange balls of light had been seen frequently in the area not far from the field where the circles had appeared. The circles themselves were simple in shape, circular rather than the exotic varieties that had appeared down south, and lying one above the other. They were about 70 feet across. The combination of UFO sightings and crop circles together proved irresistible to the media and other paranormal investigators. Soon a whole series of other incidents were being reported.

It emerged that UFOs had been reported in and around Blairgowrie as far back as the 1950s, and as long ago as the 18th century a huge ball of flame had apparently travelled several miles along the River Ericht and flattened houses in the village. The key UFO encounter in recent times was that of April 1984 involving the Freeman family from Riverside Road. Not publicised at the time, the event did not become widely known till the 1990s.

On April 25th 1984, at around 5.30 p.m., Mrs Gwen Freeman was sitting in the back garden of their bungalow, weaving a tapestry. Her son Sid, meanwhile, was at the front, working to clear a flowerbed of weeds. Suddenly, Gwen noticed the family dog cowering and watched as it ran into the kitchen, its tail tucked between its legs.

Seconds later her attention was caught by what she later described as a strange cloud of light which enveloped her and then, for a split second, actually blinded her. Then, directly in front of her, less than five feet away, a forsythia bush began to shimmer with sparkling lights.

Her attention was caught next by a beam of light which flowed upwards from the bush, travelled between two fir trees and passed over the roof of the garden shed. Gwen followed the beam skywards where it led to a silvery shape, hovering over her house. Stepping to the side she was able to get a better view of the object, realising as she did so that she was confronting a truly awesome phenomenon. It looked like a some sort of 'spaceship'. Gwen later described it as a large, bulbous-shaped object with a long tail. Beneath the tail section, a light illuminated five V-shaped projections. As she observed this, the front of the 'spaceship' lit up and she noticed that a lip or flange surrounded the circular area. Suddenly the light was extinguished and the whole object began to rock from front to back.

Gwen then shouted to Sid: 'You'll never guess what I'm looking at! Come quickly before it goes.'

Anxious to find out what had caused so much excitement, Sid hurried to the fence that separated the front and back gardens. Unfortunately, he paused for a split second before following Gwen's finger, pointing skywards. The object was now rapidly diminishing in size and intensity. A bright flash followed, and the UFO was gone.

At this point Gwen's husband, Sid senior, arrived on the scene. He had not witnessed the encounter, as he had been gardening directly in front of the bungalow out of sight of both Gwen and the hovering object. From where he knelt the 'spaceship' was hidden from view by a cluster of trees. Sid, however, was intrigued by the incident and together the family attempted to estimate the size of the object Gwen and her son had seen. They judged it to be around one hundred and fifty feet in length, floating about eighty feet above the ground. Gwen said that in shape it reminded her of a Yale key.

The family decided to call in the local police, and two officers soon arrived. One remarked to his colleague, perhaps not intending Sid to hear, that the 'Yale key' sounded just like an object that had already been reported over Blairgowrie. The officers then moved outside and searched the garden, taking soil samples from the area where Mrs Freeman had been sitting, and collecting leaves from the forsythia bush. After about two hours, the policemen left, telling the family that they would keep them informed of the outcome of the investigation. In fact, from that day to this the Freemans have not heard one more word from the police. Why, it may be asked, the secrecy? Attempts in the early 1990s by UFO investigator Ken Higgins to locate police reports of the incident met with no success. No one at the police station remembered the incident, and Ken was informed that any documents relating to it would have been transferred and probably destroyed.

But the family's strange encounter was to be only the start of a sequence of unexplained events. One morning Sid and Gwen heard an unusual rumbling above the house. The noise grew louder until it became deafening, and the whole bungalow seemed to vibrate. Looking from the back door, they were shocked to see a large military helicopter hovering some forty feet above the house. Underneath it were slung two box-like devices, one black and the other orange. They were hanging so close to the roof that Gwen could see a small red light on one of the boxes. It seemed that the crew were filming the area around the Freeman home. From the way the helicopter was moving they got the distinct impression that it was also testing the air. In the light of the family's recent encounter, if it was a coincidence, it seemed a remarkable one indeed.

Sid phoned the nearest RAF station, Leuchars, to find out just what was going on. After some initial difficulty, he was informed that the helicopter was simply 'on manoeuvres', and that there was nothing for the family to worry about. Two days later, however, they were startled by the reappearance of the helicopter and were struck by the fact that it repeated the earlier tests. Significantly, the RAF had not chosen Blairgowrie previously to carry out exercises, nor have they found it a suitable spot since.

When Ron Halliday visited Sid in the summer of 1991, shocking new details of the events of 25th April 1984 began to emerge. Some time before midday, Mrs Freeman had called her son to the window, and they both watched in silence as a group of strangely dressed men walked quietly up the deserted street. The sight was remarkable: some twelve men, all dressed in black, wearing hats of the same colour and several with pigtails stretching down their backs.

Sid's curiosity, however, turned to anxiety when the group of strangers walked up the path of a neighbour's house, then disappeared inside without even bothering to ring the doorbell. Gwen was struck by one other odd fact. The twelve had kept moving in single file, a regular space between each one, from the moment they had caught her attention to the time they entered the next-door bungalow.

Gwen and Sid had no wish to be nosey, but as good friends of the woman next door they were concerned for her safety. Just as they had made up their minds to go and investigate, the same twelve came out of the front door, still in single file, and walked back the way they had come. Convinced that something odd had taken place, Sid and Gwen decided to make sure that nothing had happened to their friend.

They rang the doorbell, then waited anxiously. The door was soon opened by their friend who, seeing their worried faces, asked what the matter was. Taken aback, Sid explained why he and Gwen had called round, describing the strange figures they had seen on her garden path. It soon became clear that, as far as she was concerned, no one, and certainly not any mysterious men in black, had entered her house either that or any other day. On hearing this, the Freemans were staggered, embarrassed and worried. Muttering apologies, Sid and Gwen hurried home.

Accounts of mysterious 'men in black', or MIBs as they are known, are by no means uncommon in UFO-related cases. In *Fact or Fantasy*, Hilary Evans discussed several such cases. Typical is one that occurred in September 1976, involving Dr Herbert Hopkins of Maine, USA, who was acting as a consultant in an alleged UFO case. He was telephoned by a man claiming to be a UFO investigator, who shortly afterwards arrived at his door dressed completely in black. The visitor behaved in such a strange way that Hopkins 'was very much shaken' by the incident. The Freeman case has similarities to Dr Hopkins' tale—a UFO event associated with the appearance of odd individuals in black—but it is interesting to note that the Blairgowrie men in black were seen *before* the UFO incident, rather than after it. Whoever they were, and whatever the purpose of their visit, the appearance of MIBs in Blairgowrie on the same day as the UFO encounter is, at the very least, an extraordinary coincidence.

BOLESKINE HOUSE

It was the search for a secluded place for meditation, prayer and esoteric ritual which, as the 20th century dawned, led a young man northwards, to a large house surrounded by two acres of land in the Highlands of Scotland.

Boleskine House, built in the 18th century by Archibald Fraser, a relative of Lord Lovat, lies on a wooded hillside on the eastern side of Loch Ness, close by the village of Foyers. The new occupant was Aleister Crowley, who had already, at the age of 25, begun to carve a name for himself as a master of the occult.

Both his parents were devout members of the Plymouth Brethren, and from an early age Crowley had been taught of the terrible power of unearthly forces. Passages from the Bible, in particular images from the Book of Revelation, haunted him, so that in later life he would call himself 'The Beast', a name which he claimed had been cast upon him by his mother. Indeed, he went out of his way to defy all conventions of morality—hence his description of himself as 'the wickedest man in the world'.

Crowley had rebelled against his strict Christian background while an undergraduate at Cambridge, where he read moral science. Though he left the university without gaining his degree, he did manage to have two books of poetry published—one satanic, and the other pornographic, the latter work having to be printed abroad.

A keen and courageous mountaineer—he was said to thrive on the thrill of danger—Crowley was in Switzerland during the summer after leaving Cambridge when he encountered an English chemist, J L Baker, with whom he attempted to discuss alchemy. Baker knew little about the ancient mysteries of the alchemists, but was able to put Crowley in touch with a friend who was a member of a covert magical sect called the Hermetic Order of the Golden Dawn. It was a turning point in Crowley's life, and he was not slow to immerse himself in the secrets of the Golden Dawn.

Within two years Crowley had become a leading member of the sect, and wanted solitude in order to further his training. He had scoured the Lake District, but settled upon Boleskine House as the most suitable site for his dark purposes. A north-facing room was called for, with a door opening on to a terrace strewn with sand—he was able to obtain all the sand he needed from the loch-side—and at the end of the terrace a lodge, within which evil spirits could gather.

And gather, it seemed, they did. Crowley wrote of his experiments in raising spirits, declaring that his success was so great that things got out of hand, and destructive forces were unleashed whose influence spread into both the house and the surrounding countryside. He claimed that one of the workmen on his land became deranged and attempted to kill him; that his coachman, a non-drinker, began to suffer from *delirium tremens*; and that his housekeeper disappeared, too terrified to remain in the house. The wider influence was revealed when Crowley carelessly wrote down the names of two demons on a bill from the local butcher. Soon after, while cutting meat for a customer, the butcher severed an artery and bled to death.

But this was only the beginning of Crowley's activities at Boleskine House. He reputedly held black masses there, indulged in orgies and obscene rituals, and many are the tales of weird happenings involving sex, magic rituals, alcohol, drugs and madness. 'Chaos magic'—the opening of one's mind to all influences, regardless of the consequences, in an effort to confront, control and manipulate the powers of darkness—was practised in extremis by Crowley.

Some of his less unusual activities also provoked a response from local people. Shortly after his arrival, Crowley recalled in his autobiographical *Confessions*, 'I innocently frightened some excellent people by my habit of taking long walks over the moors. One morning I found a large stone jar at my front door. It was not an infernal machine; it was illicit whisky—a mute, yet eloquent appeal not to give away illicit stills that I might happen to stumble across in my rambles. I needed no bribe. I am a free trader in every sense of the word.'

The house itself is reputed to be haunted, although this may be due as much to Crowley's reputation as anything. A poltergeist, which removes and later replaces items, is one of its supposed spirits. According to legend, an underground tunnel connects the house with Boleskine burial ground, across the road on the shores of the loch, which contains the ruins of the old kirk and many ancient gravestones. Witches are said to haunt the burial ground.

However, the subsequent owners of Boleskine House, Ronald and Annette MacGillivary, dismissed any notion that the house is haunted. In an article in the *Daily Record*, Mrs MacGillivary described the stories as 'a load of bunkum'. They had never had a disturbed night in the five years since they had bought it. She explained that the house's reputation was more of an irritation than anything else, as Crowley's admirers still regard it as a kind of mecca.

Jimmy Page, lead guitarist of Led Zeppelin, who owned Boleskine for twenty years from the 1970s, never lived there himself, but rented it to a friend, Malcolm Dent. Dent retains a healthy respect for the house's ill-repute, claiming that he had had a few scary moments there himself, and that nothing about the place would surprise him.

BONNYBRIDGE

Bonnybridge has been labelled the 'UFO capital of Scotland', and is now widely regarded as a UFO 'hot spot'. Situated within the so-called 'Falkirk Triangle', the surrounding area has also witnessed intense UFO activity, with numerous sightings reported from Stirling in the west to Fife and the fringes of Edinburgh in the east, while West Lothian has experienced a frequency of incidents out of all proportion to its size and population density.

If, as local councillor Billy Buchanan claimed, Bonnybridge (population 5,500) does indeed have over 2,000 witnesses to

UFO sightings then it truly is a world hot spot. A similar proportion of witnesses to population in Edinburgh would mean around 200,000 people had seen a UFO in Scotland's capital.

The recent spate of sightings in the area started quietly enough with a number of interesting, albeit typical, UFO reports. These incidents began in January 1992 when Mr James Walker witnessed a cross-shaped formation of stars hovering above the road as he was driving along. He stopped his car and looked back, noting that the lights had now assumed a triangular shape. Mr Walker was understandably mystified by the incident which he felt could not be put down to any obvious source, such as an aircraft.

Perhaps the best known incident took place in March of that year. At around 7 p.m. the Slogett family were walking towards Bonnybridge when Steven Slogett caught sight of a circle of light. He drew the attention of the rest of the family to the strange light, before it appeared to land in a nearby field. As the family walked on, they were halted in their tracks by a football-sized blue light hovering above the road ahead. Isabella Slogett later reported: 'My daughter Carole and I saw a UFO land right in front of us. A door opened and there was a howling sound. I screamed and ran off terrified.' According to Carole, 'There was a flash of light as if we were being photographed'. When they reached their home in Bonnybridge, the mysterious object was still visible and was seen by several other witnesses.

Reports continued throughout 1992. In November, for example, a Mr Anderson reporting a 'bluish-white light, very bright, which disappeared behind clouds', and a father and daughter witnessed an unidentified triangular-shaped object.

It was not the nature of the incidents, however, which attracted media interest in the area, but rather the sheer volume of sightings which were relayed to the media by local councillor, Billy Buchanan. He explained that his constituents were coming forward with reports of UFO encounters and that it was his duty, therefore, to seek an explanation of the incidents.

By the end of December 1992 over 200 witnesses to unexplained events were being cited by Councillor Buchanan and a public 'skywatch' was announced on TV. As a result, a considerable amount of publicity was generated, although to the disappointment of those who turned up, including the TV cameras, no UFO activity was observed. All this publicity simply led to even more reports of UFO sightings and some ufologists began to question whether it was now possible to disentangle the original reports from the many new sightings inevitably created by media interest. It is well known that individual reports of UFO incidents increase after existing incidents are highlighted: what previously was simply a light in the sky becomes a UFO.

In order to calm the situation, a public meeting was arranged at the Norwood Hotel in Bonnybridge by Billy Buchanan for Sunday 31st January 1993 at 7 p.m. The *Sunday Post* newspaper reported that: 'A town plagued by UFOs has called in the experts as concern grows among residents'. Councillor Buchanan was amongst those claiming to have seen a UFO and added: 'I've had around 400 calls in the past few months'. The article revealed that some of the town's residents were to be 'hypnotised in a bid to find any sub-conscious memories of being taken aboard an alien spacecraft'. In the event the hypnotist did not turn up—although an audience of almost 300 did, to hear Malcolm Robinson lecture on worldwide UFO incidents, including alleged abduction cases.

At this point Scottish Earth Mysteries Research, in a radio broadcast, urged caution over the Bonnybridge sightings until a proper investigation had been carried out and the number and nature of the sightings could be accurately assessed. As events moved rapidly along, however, it was clear that media interest was not going to subside.

In the *Stirling Observer* Malcolm Robinson was quoted as being convinced that Bonnybridge is one of the world's few 'windows' to another dimension. Meanwhile, according to the reporter, Councillor Buchanan had more than UFOs on his mind—the suggestion being that it had been his intention from the start to generate favourable publicity for Bonnybridge.

Some aspects of the Bonnybridge experience quickly degenerated into farce, as writer Edward Talisman noted in *Phenomenal News*. Describing the controversy over a supposed alien called 'Zal-us' [qv], Mr Talisman wrote:

> Sceptics of the Bonnybridge 'hot spot' were given added fuel by the unfortunate antics involving 'Zal-us' and the 'Council of Nine'. Zal-us, according to some newspaper reports, was an alien who had an important message to give to the world. The message was going to be revealed at a meeting in Falkirk Town Hall, one evening in October. The hall had been booked for the affair, by Councillor Billy Buchanan, no less.

While all this was going on, genuinely odd incidents were taking place in the area. In October 1994 three cleaners, while on their way to work at the Union Chemical Factory at Carronshire, saw five UFOs. Beatrice Campbell reported that she had first noticed the UFOs at around 5.40 a.m. She described one large object which had an orange glow and four smaller ones sparkling on and off. The larger object appeared to be sending out beams of light to the smaller sparkling objects. Beatrice reported the sighting to her manager, Bill Downie. Soon other employees were coming forward to give their accounts, which seemed to indicate that strange objects had been appearing in the area for some days. The previous Wednesday at 7 p.m., Diane Keating from Camelon had witnessed a reddish-coloured ball which disappeared and then reappeared. She was sure it could not have been an aircraft because she saw one fly under it. At the same time Steve Lewisham saw a 'bright white' object which moved away, then 'came back and began to glow red and orange. It was going really fast. We saw a passenger plane with its landing lights on underneath it. The object was very much faster than the plane.'

Incredible claims were made about the number of reported sightings, culminating in author Nick Pope's statement that there had been over 8,000 which could not be explained—a number larger than the entire population of Bonnybridge village. Such outlandish statements naturally generated controversy, with demands that details of the incidents be released as proof. Some ufologists questioned whether there were anything like that number of documented sightings. Buchanan himself never claimed that there had been more than 2,000, but given the size of the area and population it was still a phenomenal number. Malcolm Robinson appeared concerned about the number of alleged reports that were being bandied around and blamed the TV programme *Strange But True* for having made the 2,000 sightings claim. He expressed the view in an interview with *Phenomenal News*, the magazine of SEMR, that the real figure was 200 unexplained sightings. A substantial number, but a world apart from Nick Pope's 8,000.

The 'Bonnybridge phenomenon' has its sceptics, and if the village alone is considered, then there is much to doubt. However, it is undeniable that a wider area which includes the village produced a large volume of UFO reports between 1992 and 1996. But the witnesses were spread over a much larger area which took in substantial towns like Falkirk and Grangemouth, and smaller communities like Stenhousemuir and Larbert. It was this wider area which produced the highest concentration of UFO reports in Scotland and even the UK. It also included some of the best video evidence [qv] to come out of Scotland—including footage taken by Margaret Ross, Brian Curran, John and Craig Malcolm and Barry McDonald. The claims of those involved may have been exaggerated, but clearly something strange was happening in this area of Scotland.

BOTHWELL, EARL OF

The involvement of the Scottish aristocracy in witchcraft [qv] and magic can be illustrated through the activities of the Earl of Bothwell. At one time a close associate of King James VI, he was even entrusted with Scotland's security when, in 1590, James sailed to Scandinavia to bring back his bride Anne of Denmark. However, he rapidly fell out of favour on James' return. James suspected, or was encouraged to suspect, Bothwell of having plotted against him with the aim of taking over the kingdom for himself. At this period in history Europe was in the grip of a widespread 'witch craze'. It was generally believed that there were hundreds of thousands of witches, all of whom were in direct league with the Devil. Although he later changed his mind, at this point in his life James was a believer in an organised conspiracy of witchcraft. Those who were trying to bring about Bothwell's downfall seized upon the opportunity to link him to the satanic crew.

This 'high politician' became intertwined with witchcraft through a long twisting trail which started when Agnes Sampson, a 'white witch', confessed to having attempted to kill James by magic. She also implicated Dr John Fian [qv], who acted as Bothwell's secretary, in her murderous plot. Agnes then tied Bothwell into events by admitting that he had consulted her about the future—in particular how long the King was likely to live. Fian was burnt as a practising witch and the finger of suspicion now seemed to be pointing to the Earl himself.

The extent to which Bothwell was involved in black magic remains unclear. He almost certainly consulted astrologers and fortune tellers and was openly alleged to practice necromancy, the raising of the spirits of the dead by magical rites. But claims that he took on the guise of the Devil at a coven meeting in North Berwick Kirk and led an organisation of witches rest solely on Fian's highly unreliable confession, which was extracted under extreme torture. Involvement in 'white magic' was widespread at the time, especially to deal with illness and pain. Bothwell probably went beyond that, although how far it is not possible to be sure. His political and social standing, whilst providing protection, also meant that he could not hide his activities. And anyway he does not seem to have been inclined to, his privileged position probably creating a false sense of security. Across Europe many high-ranking individuals found themselves brought down through being connected to witchcraft, which was a convenient way of attacking people. Whether or not Bothwell himself was a 'servant of the Devil', or involved himself in any serious way in the world of magic, the manner in which his downfall was brought about shows how easily the accusation of involvement, however insubstantial, could be put to good use by determined enemies.

Bothwell's role in the 'North Berwick Witch Trial' (as it is now called) is significant in demonstrating the extent to which interest in the practice of magic involved all classes. Scotland and Europe may have been Christian societies, but there was still room for belief in the paranormal. Witchcraft may (or may not) have been a mass illusion, but belief in the power of magic had deep roots as Bothwell's activities show. But while John Fian and Agnes Sampson were executed Bothwell escaped punishment, though not fate. After being imprisoned, tortured, and driven insane, he ended his days in the dungeons of Dragsholm Castle in Denmark in 1578.

BRAHAN SEER

The Brahan Seer is a title, not a name. However, over the years it has become inextricably linked to one 'seer' or medium as we might call it today. That person was Kenneth Or. He is the 'Brahan Seer' in most people's eyes to such an extent that it is often considered to be his name.

Few actually know anything about the man behind the title. Often compared to Nostradamus, the Brahan Seer's fame similarly rests on predictions he made. Those of Nostradamus have become very well known. Not only did he write down his own account of the future (in verse) but he covered wide-ranging events which could have been seen as having an impact across the world. Nostradamus also wrote several hundred years before Kenneth Or, so his long-term prophecies seem impressive in retrospect. By comparison Or's predictions are concerned almost entirely with Scotland and more specifically with the Highlands, the area in which he lived and was active. The scope of his comments about the future, therefore, is limited. But on the other hand, the less wide-ranging nature of his predictions provides a better opportunity to assess the accuracy of his forecasts.

His most famous prophecy is seen as the one relating to 'black rain'. This runs:

> Sheep shall eat men, men will eat sheep, the black rain will eat all things. In the end old men shall return from new lands.

With the discovery of oil in the North Sea and the development of the industry in the Highlands, it seems that the prophecy has been fulfilled. It would be unreasonable to accuse Or of lacking accuracy just because he didn't call the 'black rain' oil or report seeing an Esso petroleum platform in the North Sea. But it is clear that this vision of the future can be interpreted in various ways. 'Black rain' might be oil. It might also refer to acid rain or even nuclear fallout. And if the reference to sheep covers the Highland clearances then Or left a mixed prophecy which spans two hundred years of history.

But how much accuracy have we a right to expect? A 'seer' is only catching a glimpse of the future and, as a prisoner of their own time can only interpret it in a way they can understand themselves.

The same would apply to Nostradamus, although his writings were so extensive that their interpretation has become an industry. It is probably true (but by no means certain) that Nostradamus knew what he meant when he wrote his prophecies down. But as subsequent generations have applied his predictions to many minor and major events it is no longer possible, even in a broad sense, to be sure what Nostradamus' visions were intended to relate to.

This is certainly true of Or and must inevitably be the fate of all who try to predict what is going to happen in the future. In Or's case, one particular difficulty has been the extent to which his original prophecies have been added to over the years. This is also a real problem with Nostradamus. The answer is that we cannot be sure. Or himself wrote nothing down. The story of Or's life and his prophetic visions were compiled by folklore enthusiast Alexander Mackenzie in 1877, although his story was well known in the Highlands, and a seer called Or (or Coinneach Odhar in Gaelic) was certainly active in the 16th century. Some, however, doubt that the present collection of 'visions' can be linked to Or and point out that one of the supposed prophecies has also been attributed to the Scottish wizard Michael Scott [qv], who lived in the 13th century. However, the survival of Or's name does suggest that not only was he a real figure, but that he was widely believed to have special powers of prediction. It is hard to account otherwise for the survival of his memory in the highlands and his continuing reputation.

Even into the 20th century Highlanders were seen as possessing a special ability to see into the future. That tradition has carried on to the present with the current Brahan Seer, Swein Macdonald, who lives on a hill near Dornoch. But what the 'Brahan Seer' does is in a sense no different from the activities of a psychic. However, inheriting the title implies that, as a medium, the 'Brahan Seer' stands well above the average in psychic ability.

Another of Or's prophecies is quite specific, but has not yet come to pass: 'When the Ullapool ferry crosses to Stornoway it will sink with all lives lost'. If such a tragedy occurs, will it be proof that Or had a vision of the future or simply unfortunate chance dealt out by the hand of Fate?

BYERS, JOYCE

One of Scotland's least known, but most prolific UFO witnesses.

Almost single-handedly Mrs Byers, a Moffat housewife, produced a 'wave' of UFO reports in the Dumfriesshire area in the late 1970s. She claimed a large number of sightings, one hundred of which she had recorded in a diary she kept of the incidents. Unfortunately, the diary, once in the possession of a UFO investigator, is now lost. One of the UFOs seen by Mrs Byers was in the shape of an egg timer. Another regularly seen was nicknamed 'Big Bertha' because it made a rumbling noise whenever it appeared.

According to Mrs Byers the UFOs may have had sinister intentions and been responsible for downing conventional aircraft. There were certainly a number of unexplained aircraft crashes in the area during this period but there is no evidence to link them to any UFO incidents. However, Mrs Byers claimed that on one occasion (13th April 1978) she witnessed a plane apparently taking photographs of 'Big Bertha'. The UFO responded by flying directly towards the 'spy' and chasing it away.

Joyce Byers was by no means the only witness to UFO incidents in this area. Mary Watson, an eighty-year-old neighbour of Joyce's, also claimed to have seen 'Big Bertha' and several other UFOs. There were numerous other individual reports including sightings by the police. Mrs Byers clearly came across as a credible witness and when this was coupled to repeated incidents in a geographically confined area a UFO 'hot spot' was in the making. There were even claims of a 'Scottish Triangle' stretching from Dumfriesshire to Edinburgh. An early echo of the later 'Bonnybridge UFO triangle' [see Bonnybridge].

For personal reasons it seems that Mrs Byers stopped

reporting her sightings. Whether by chance or not, at around the same time the area started to 'close down'. After 1980 the reports simply petered out. Dumfriesshire's period as a UFO 'hot spot' is now largely forgotten—in fact, it has become something of a 'cold spot' for UFO sightings. Should we believe that UFOs are now avoiding the area? If so why? Perhaps the sharp decline in UFO reports provides a clue to the nature of the UFO phenomenon if we could only solve the puzzle. Or is it simply that there is no one prepared, as Mrs Byers was, to speak out about his or her experiences?

C

CALLANISH

The standing stone circle at Callanish cannot match Stonehenge in size and grandeur, but with its forty-eight monoliths laid out in a labyrinthine pattern it is certainly more complex. In fact it is Scotland's—and the UK's—most intricate prehistoric monument.

Its location too appears a puzzle. Situated on the western edge of the island of Lewis it seems far removed from the centres of population. Its isolation at a spot remote from urban living adds a great deal of romance and mystery to the enigmatic arrangement of carefully placed stones.

But 5,000 years ago when this complex was started our ancestors clearly had no idea that they would be creating a puzzle for their descendants. They had a purpose in mind. So what was the intention behind their planning? At that time, far from being a distant outpost, the western Isles were a centre of population. The climate was milder, cultivation easier and the island communities may well have formed the heartland for a tribal society stretching across northern Scotland. Callanish was created by a dynamic people with a substantial population base to draw on. Not by a society of stone age 'New Agers', but by a large group of people who created the site for a definite purpose.

That purpose goes to the heart of the debate on the paranormal. Was it meant for religious ceremonial? Perhaps it was an open-air temple to celebrate religious rites. Or a meeting place, or debating chamber. Did it have a practical purpose as an early astronomical observatory to chart the movement of stars and planets? It is known that the ancient Egyptians used observation of the stars to predict events on Earth. And if that was also the case at Callanish then we have the operation of 'magic'—the belief that change in the universe can have an impact on the life of an individual and society and that those with the knowledge can predict that effect.

It certainly seems to be the case that astronomy played a part in Callanish's layout. It was laid out in a symmetrical pattern running east to west, with the axis running through a large stone at the centre of the monument. The eastern part of the ring is flattened from a true semicircle, perhaps to take account of an alignment with the spring sunrise. The southern row, consisting of five stones, points directly south to an outcrop known as Cnoc an Tursa. Every 18.6 years, when viewed from the avenue of stones, the moon appears low down over the hills to the south and passes through a notch in the outline of the stones against the horizon. But there are hundreds (if not thousands) of possible lines of sight to land and sky objects. Professor Alexander Thom investigated Callanish's alignments at considerable length in his determination to prove that stone circles in Scotland were ancient observatories.

He came to the conclusion that the stones had been deliberately aligned to mark certain key 'sights' in the heavens. He also concluded that the builders of Callanish—indeed builders of stone circles across Europe—had used a common measurement: the 'megalithic yard' of 2.72 feet.

The extent to which they were created for that purpose remains controversial—at least among professional archaeologists. They argue that many of the supposed alignments, could be simply accidental, and point to examples—the western row of stones at Callanish runs almost exactly along the current Ordnance Survey gridlines found on modern maps. To archaeologists this is proof that lines of sight are equally likely to be the result of pure chance. The 20th-century mind is creating links which did not exist as far as our ancestors were concerned. But can we so easily dismiss the connection between a 5,000-year-old stone circle and modern mapping? Maybe our ancestors were equally adept at marking out the world according to a system. The more we have learned about 'prehistory' (as we call it) the more we have discovered how sophisticated our ancestors in fact were. So we should not dismiss the idea that Callanish was created for a purpose that was more in tune with 20th-century ideas than we imagine.

But how far did the builders of Callanish go? Did they use the power of the stones to communicate with other peoples? Or with other worlds? Was there a form of energy that the Callanish stones drew on which allowed their people to penetrate into new dimensions? We know that dowsers have been able to detect powerful currents of ley energy running through stone circles. It seems highly likely that circles were set up at key spots where this energy was particularly strong. In some unexplained way the stones appear to enhance and redirect leys as they pass through the monument. A relevant factor may be Callanish's link to eleven other stone circles which are seen as satellite sites. Could it be that a massive amount of earth energy would, under the right circumstances, be focused on Callanish? If that is the case, then we would have to move away from the mundane and down-to-earth explanations so favoured by archaeologists.

The secret of Callanish died with the people who built and serviced it. Perhaps the earth energy they drew on moved away. The arrival of Christianity certainly undermined the faith of those who saw in Callanish a focus for their spiritual needs. Maybe one day we will learn the secret of the stones there, but for the time being the meaning of the site remains an unsolved mystery. [See also Standing Stone Circles]

CASTLE GHOSTS

Almost every castle in Scotland seems to have a ghost connected with it. Many have several. In fact it might be more sensible to speculate why some castles do not have a ghost.

Anyone interested in following up castle hauntings will find a considerable body of information on individual castles.

It has to be said, however, that from the paranormal investigator's point of view there seems little to link castle ghosts. There are so many castles and such a variety of incidents that it would be wrong to suggest a generalised ghost or ghosts. However, it does seem to be the case that castle ghosts can be split into a limited number of different categories.

The most obvious is that of a famous historical figure, although the person may not necessarily be connected with the castle. Craignethan Castle near Crossford, Clydesdale, has a headless ghost often thought to be the beheaded Mary, Queen of Scots, even though her link to the castle is slight. There is no evidence that she ever spent a night there, although she may have passed through the village. More understandable is the phantom of Bishop Cameron sometimes seen at Bedley Castle near Moodiesburn. Cameron has been haunting the place since 1350 when his dead body was discovered in mysterious circumstances beside a local loch. Cardinal Beaton's spirit haunts Ethie Castle in Angus although he was actually murdered in St Andrews Castle (in 1546). However, Ethie was his home for a while.

There are numerous castles with haunted rooms where murders are alleged to have taken place. Culdreuch Castle near Fintry has one known as the 'Chinese Bird Room' because of its three-hundred-year-old style of wallpaper. Details of the murder which allegedly took place in the room are vague, but as in all such instances there may well be truth behind the tradition.

Ghosts appearing as a warning or portent are another well known phenomenon. At Taymouth Castle beside Loch Tay a ghost is reputed to appear just before some tragedy is about to befall a member of the Campbell family.

The biggest single number of castle ghosts, however, arises from incidents involving women and blighted love—ladies who have died in unfortunate circumstances usually connected with a love affair of some kind. Cawdor Castle, close to the town of Nairn, may have the most gruesome—the ghost of a woman who has no hands. The tradition runs that the spectre is that of a daughter of Lord Cawdor who defied her father by embracing a forbidden lover. He cut off her hands to prevent her putting her arms around the man again. A common variation of the 'tragic woman' theme occurs in Castle Grant, Grantown on Spey. In this case it was a daughter called Barbara Grant who suffered at her father's hands. It is said that he locked her in a room because she refused to marry a husband he had chosen for her. Here Barbara died through grief.

Animal ghosts are well represented in castle hauntings. One of the most unusual is to be found at Drumlanrig Castle, Nithsdale. The spirit of a monkey has been appearing since 1700 in a chamber now called the 'Yellow Monkey Room'. It should be said that the creature cannot be definitely identified as a monkey although its furry appearance suggests that it may be. There are several castles visited by ghostly dogs. Barnbougle Castle on the shores of the Firth of Forth has the spectral 'Hound of Barnbougle', which reputedly howls all through the night each time a laird of the castle moves to the next world.

Not surprisingly the spirits of dead musicians frequently seem to remain attached to castle buildings. Cortachy Castle by Kirriemuir is haunted by a ghostly drummer who is heard beating his drum when a member of the Airlie family is about to die. Culzean Castle in Ayrshire, although of relatively recent origin as castles go, has a phantom piper who in this case plays his pipes when one of the Kennedy family (one-time owners) is about to get married.

Scotland's castles have experienced many strange incidents stretching back through the centuries. Their sheer age, durability and their continuing links with one family mean a paranormal visitation in a castle is far more likely to be remembered and passed down through the generations. By which time most ordinary houses have either been demolished or have come under completely different ownership. [See also Glamis]

CHILD GHOSTS

The ghosts of children and even babies are a reminder that spirits of all ages can be trapped between this world and the next. In the Trinity district of Edinburgh an old house is said to be haunted by the ghost of a little girl. Not only has her apparition been glimpsed, but on several occasions the occupants have heard the sound of a ball bouncing. Even in the spirit world it seems the wee lass is still playing her favourite childhood games.

But sometimes even child ghosts can be unnerving. In October 1993 a young woman who moved into a flat in Tillicoultry was plagued by the activities of a mischievous spirit. Articles were moved around the house and toothpaste was smeared on the bathroom wall. Psychics believe that the cause of the disturbance was the spirit of a toddler who had been drowned in a nearby pond.

By way of contrast, top Scottish medium Gary Gray has a young spirit friend called 'George' who visits him after 9 p.m. every night. According to Gary, George looks like a street urchin and visitors to his house have seen the ghost of a little boy with bare feet and ragged clothes running past the sitting room door.

Child ghosts often appear to be attracted to a place they once lived in. Music teacher Mike Johnson, who lives in an old cottage near Clackmannan, found a child's lace-up boot in his back garden. Experts dated it to the 1880s. Around this time Mike experienced strange footsteps and other odd incidents in the cottage. A photograph taken of the house shows a young girl looking out of a ground floor window. No one knows who she is or how she got there. But the suspicion is that she is the ghost of the little girl whose lost boot turned up in the cottage grounds.

In a former church building in Stirling, once used as a school, but now as offices for small businesses, tiny foot-steps have been heard. According to Val Hunter, one of the occupants, 'It sounds just like a little girl skipping. Perhaps a lass aged eight to ten years. The sounds are coming from the corridor where the classroom used to be'.

Minette Angus from Irvine never sees her ghostly visitor. All that marks the spirit's presence are tiny footprints left in the snow in Minette's back garden. Minette explained: 'The footprints start a good distance from the gate and head in the direction of the surrounding fence. There are no marks before or after. They start in the middle of nowhere and always appear in the same place—a dark area of grass in the garden.'

But the footprints only appear at a certain time of year and under certain conditions. According to Minette: 'It only happens when it snows. But it has to snow between twelve at night and five in the morning. If it snows after five, no footprints appear. And they never appear during daylight. They're deep footprints, but tiny. Bigger than a toddler's. I would guess a child of about three years of age. There are always eight of them, but I've no idea why.'

COFFINS

Why would someone go to the trouble of making 17 miniature coffins, and then hiding them? This puzzle lies at the heart of one of Scotland's most enduring mysteries.

The strange discovery on Arthur's Seat was made in 1836 by a group of schoolboys out playing. Behind three pieces of upright slate they uncovered a small space dug into the hillside. It had clearly been meant to be hidden from the public eye. Packed into this area were 17 tiny coffins arranged in three layers. Eight coffins could be counted on the bottom row and the same number resting above. A single coffin lay on the top, suggesting that there were more to be added. When the coffins were opened, inside each one lay a tiny doll, fully dressed. They had clearly been intended for their resting place as the dolls were wearing funeral clothes with boots painted black. Several coffins had been carefully lined with cloth. Someone had clearly gone to a lot of trouble to create a realistic funeral scene. According to a report in *The Scotsman*, 'The coffins are about three or four inches in length, and cut out from a single piece of wood, with the exception of the lids, which are nailed down with wire sprigs or common brass pins. The lid and sides of each are profusely studded with ornaments formed of small pieces of tin, and inserted in the wood with great care and regularity.' From the condition of the lower layer of coffins it was clear that they had been put in place over a number of years, possibly even decades. Some suggested centuries.

Since the discovery, various suggestions have been made to account for these macabre boxes. It was argued that they were merely a child's toy. But why would a child want a collection of coffins to play with? It seems unlikely. And then why hide them all? The fact that they had been put there over a number of years seemed to suggest that it had been a long-term event, not just a one-off entombment.

But if they were not a child's toy, why had they been hidden on the hillside? Mystic solutions were put forward, although these were ridiculed at the time. Could they have been put there as some sort of witch's curse? It was common practice to make a model of a person to whom harm was intended. But usually these figures would be of a material that could be quickly destroyed—melting a wax effigy over a fire was the traditional 'spell'. This was not the case with these figures, which were made of more long-lasting material and, what is more, were enclosed inside a wooden box providing protection against the elements.

When the coffins were put on display in the National Museum in Edinburgh in the early 1990s, another possible answer to the enigma emerged. Dr Sam Menefee, an American lawyer and anthropologist based at the University of Virginia, suggested that the coffins might in some bizarre way be linked to the crimes of Burke and Hare, the infamous bodysnatchers who were operating in Edinburgh only a few years before the coffins were discovered. One factor which tends to support this theory is the fact that there were a total of 17 coffins—exactly the number of bodies Burke and Hare were said to have sold to the anatomists.

The Scotsman, however, could not find any satisfactory explanation for what it called this 'singular fantasy of the human mind', a phenomenon which seemed 'rather above insanity, and yet much beneath rationality'. The newspaper's own opinion would be, it concluded, 'had we not some years ago abjured witchcraft and demonology', that there were still a few witches who gathered on the hill, who retained 'their ancient power to work these spells of death by entombing the likenesses of those they wish to destroy'.

COMPTON, CAROLE

Carole Compton hit the headlines in November 1983 when she was suspected of being a witch. Or at least that is how the case was portrayed by the tabloid press. Carole, a twenty-one-year-old from Aberdeen, had been working as a nanny with the Ricci family at their holiday home near Bolzano in the north of Italy. Events at Bolzano were to contribute to her later arrest and trial—for example, several fires had mysteriously started at the house during the time she was employed there in July 1982, although no one was injured. However, when she took up a new post at Mario Cecchini's home on the island of Elba, fires erupted the day after she arrived in August 1982.

Suspicion fell on Carole for several reasons. The fires coincided with her arrival, it was claimed. There seemed to be no other likely suspect and it was felt that the fires had been started deliberately. Furthermore, one blaze had occurred beside the cot of three-year-old Agnese Cecchini, who Carole had been taken on to look after. Carole was accused of the attempted murder of Agnese, a charge she strenuously denied.

It was at this point that the paranormal entered the debate. It was claimed other odd incidents had happened when Carole appeared on the scene. As *The Scotsman* newspaper reported: 'in the Elba home . . . a statue fell to the ground soon after her arrival, then a glass bowl crashed to the floor without anyone being near it and a cake-stand fell from a table.' Even the fire which threatened Agnese had not behaved as normal. As a fire investigator explained: 'Normally fires start at the bottom and work upwards, but in this case the flames had travelled downwards. It was very strange.' Professor Antonio Vitolo, a chemical expert, added: 'In the 45 years of my career I have never seen such an atypical fire.'

There were certainly puzzling factors. The two mattresses beside Agnese's cot were burned only on the outside. And each was burned to the same extent although one was made of wool and the other of horsehair, which burns more easily than wool. Even weirder was the fact that it turned out to be the material woven into the horsehair that burned, and not the horsehair itself.

But these strange aspects hardly justified accusations of 'witchcraft'. So what was the connection? It was alleged that her employer suspected her of having started fires by pyrokinesis, i.e. by psychic means through the power of thought. How much of this was a concoction by the media is unclear. Undoubtedly the 'paranormal' acted as an undercurrent to the trial—that was confirmed when Ciara Lobina, a local faith healer, turned up at the court carrying a large wooden crucifix and a small bottle of Holy Water, stating that Carole and her mother were possessed by an 18th-century witch. Ciara claimed: 'I want to touch them and cleanse their spirits.'

However, contrary to banner headlines, Carole Compton was not put on trial for witchcraft or being a psychic arsonist. This was the invention of the popular press. There were paranormal aspects to the case, or incidents that could be interpreted this way, but the Italian court was not sitting in judgement on whether or not Carole Compton was possessed of supernatural ability. Carole was eventually acquitted of attempted murder but sentenced to two and a half years' imprisonment for fire-raising, then immediately released to return to Aberdeen. The court's written judgement touched on Carole's alleged psychic ability and commented that if she did in fact have such power, why had she apparently caused no fires before her arrival in Italy or after her departure.

Even though the judges rejected the paranormal as a component, the fact that they felt obliged to mention it reveals the extent to which the psychic aspect had grabbed the attention of the world. Carole Compton produced her own version of her arrest and trial in *Superstitions,* published in 1990, several years after the events which drew huge media attention to a remote part of Italy.

CORPSE TOUCHING

Before we had police forces and the introduction of forensic science there was no obvious way of proving a link between the killer and his or her victim. People may have had their suspicions about the person responsible for an unexplained death, but how could they be sure? One method was to resort to the paranormal. Corpse touching, also know as the ordeal of the bier or 'bier right', was often used where there was a suspect but no evidence of involvement in the crime. It was based on the belief that the wounds of a corpse would bleed in the presence of the murderer. It was used as a test, recognised even by the courts, to determine the innocence or guilt of the accused person.

King James VI described how the procedure worked in his book of the 1590s called *Demonology.* He wrote: 'In a secret murder, if a dead carcass be at any time thereafter handled by the murderer, it will gush out blood, as if the blood were crying to Heaven for revenge of the murder.' We know today that fresh blood flowing from a corpse is not medically possible so that any instances of such an event happening would suggest the supernatural at work. And there are accounts of just such extraordinary incidents taking place.

In 1661 Christine Wilson from Dalkeith was accused of murdering her brother, Alexander Wilson. Christine came under suspicion because it was well known that she and her brother had fallen out. She did not help her case by being noticeably absent when Alexander's body was discovered, or unmoved when told of his suspicious death. Christine was ordered to come to the murder scene by both the baillie (an early Justice of the Peace) and the church minister. As a contemporary writer described events, Christine 'refused to come to the corpse, saying that she had never touched a dead body in her life. But being earnestly desired by the minister and bailiffs to touch the corpse gently she agreed to do it . . . so touching the wound of the dead man very softly, it being white and clean without any spot of blood, yet as soon as her finger was on it blood rushed out to the great astonishment of all who saw it, who took it as confirmation of the murder.' [*Author's note: some expressions used in this account have been modernised.*] Strangely, Christine was never brought to a formal trial even though she was also suspected of being a witch. So it is not certain that corpse touching was always regarded as a foolproof way of detecting the killer.

In Dumfriesshire in the 1690s, corpse touching was still being used in even more bizarre circumstances. The case of the Rerrick Poltergeist [qv] sheds light on the reliance on paranormal methods of criminal detection even as late as the 17th century. In this incident there was not even a corpse for suspects to touch. All that had been discovered was a part carcass of meat and bones which might not in any case have been human, but had been secreted as part of a witch's curse— or so it was believed. In this instance the test was a failure, as there was no reaction after several suspects laid their hands on the grisly bundle.

Corpse touching was not confined to Scotland and was widely practised elsewhere. There was a surprisingly late case from Lincolnshire, described in the *Boston Herald* of 17th July 1832. 'When the body was taken from out of the water a number of persons were decreed to touch the face.... Among these was a young fellow by name of Taylor. It was stated that when he laid his hand on the dead boy's cheek blood issued from the nostrils, which caused great suspicion in the minds of the superstitious.'

CROMBIE, R O

By all accounts a retiring, quiet-mannered person—an appearance which masked an extraordinary personality. Not a great deal is known of his activities before the 1960s when his involvement with the foundation of the Findhorn [qv] community brought him to a wider audience.

Crombie could be called a 'psychic', although his ability to see things invisible to most of us seems to have been confined to those entities called 'nature spirits'. An encounter in 1965 which took place in Edinburgh's Royal Botanic Gardens appears to have been a turning point which gave his life a new direction. This was Crombie's encounter with a centaur called Kurmos. As Crombie describes it: 'I could see shaggy legs and cloven hooves, pointed chin and ears, and the two little horns on his forehead'. Following this first meeting Kurmos came to Roc's (as Crombie was nicknamed) home where they discussed various occult matters. But this initial encounter was only an introduction to Crombie's meeting with the god Pan himself—and this, as Crombie told it, took place in a very public thoroughfare—Edinburgh's Princes Street. According to Crombie: 'He is a great being. The god of the whole elemental kingdom as well as of the animal, vegetable and mineral kingdoms. People may feel uneasy in his presence because of the awe he inspires, but there ought to be no fear.'

Through these meetings Crombie came to know and learn of the nature spirits. A more concrete result was his involvement with Eileen and Peter Caddy in the foundation of the Findhorn Community. It has been suggested that it was Crombie's communication with the Elf King and the local nature spirits which convinced Eileen and Peter Caddy that they had chosen the correct site to start their social experiment. His contact with these entities apparently also secured their help in growing outsize vegetables which, in an unexpected way, brought the community world attention. Findhorn became a beacon for the 'New Age' and the Green movement, and Crombie played an important part in that development.

However, his role has largely been forgotten and the part he played in founding Findhorn written out of its history. And though Crombie apparently produced an extensive body of writing, now in the possession of a friend following Crombie's death, none of it has been published. If it does ever see the light of day, further insight might be gained into the existence of the world of nature spirits. And, of course, Crombie's contact with them.

CROP CIRCLES

Crop circles were one of the most publicised phenomena of the late 1980s and early 1990s. But if they were a genuine paranormal event why was there a marked difference between the number of circles reported in England compared with Scotland? For every hundred circles that appeared down south, only one was seen north of the border.

One solution may be that the number of circles reported in Scotland did not accurately reflect the real total. The type of land on which the circles occurred could also be a factor—all of the circles which appeared in southern England occurred in standing crops, i.e. farmers' fields. In Scotland, as the appearance of a circle in reeds and grass at Corpach near Fort William shows, circles may have been created in uncultivated areas where there was no one to see or report them. Even so, it seems hard to come to a conclusion other than that far more circles occurred in England than in Scotland. In this it is England that is out of line compared with Europe or indeed the rest of the world. For although crop circles have been reported in many countries, nowhere else have they appeared with such frequency.

All the circles that emerged in Scotland seem to have been a 'straightforward' round shape (although strictly speaking elliptical is the correct description). Unexplained incidents include Blairgowrie [qv] (1990), the first publicised appearance of the phenomenon in Scotland, Limekilns (1991), Linlithgow Loch (1992), Strathmiglo (1995) and Corpach (1996). There seem to have been a number of others reported from Aberdeenshire, and around Dundee and the Borders, but it is clear the overall total is in the dozens rather than hundreds. The circles varied in size from six feet in diameter (Linlithgow) to several hundred feet (Limekilns).

Although Scotland did not produce strange shaped 'circles' the phenomenon seemed to be edging towards greater complexity. At Blairgowrie two circles had appeared next to each other, and the Limekilns circle had an inner and outer ring with untouched standing crops in between. The only non-circular 'circle', which was reported near Prestwick in Ayrshire, turned out to be a hoax. It was shaped as a fertility symbol and had appeared in a field of rape. The individuals who claimed to have carried out the hoax simply used a rope and ladders. They left virtually no trace of their activities, and were able to fool scientists from the nearby College of Agriculture.

The relative lack of circles in Scotland has made it difficult to assess whether there has been any distinctive Scottish aspect. Although there is evidence to suggest that there is a genuine phenomenon occurring, the difference in frequency between Scotland and England—a difference not found when considering other strange phenomena (ghosts, poltergeists, UFOs, etc.)—remains puzzling. It may be that the real divide is between the south of England and the rest of the UK—in the north of England there have been comparatively few incidents. Investigation by Anthony Horn from Scarborough certainly unearthed more occurrences in remote spots, but even so the discrepancy is marked.

Crop circles were discredited in the 1990s by widespread hoaxing. It was clear that even experienced investigators could not tell a genuine incident from a man-made affair. Hoaxing was not a significant problem in Scotland as the phenomenon was generally low key. But there was, as elsewhere, a general difficulty in explaining the origin of circles if they were not simply caused by an unknown weather phenomenon. Scottish investigators, such as Professor Archie Roy and the Earl of Haddington, tended to be linked to UK organisations and there was no distinctive Scottish approach or solution to the phenomenon.

As is true elsewhere, it has not been possible to establish a definite link between crop circle formation and UFO reports. It is true that the first circles to be reported in Scotland, those at Blairgowrie, did appear in an area where UFO incidents have occurred. But the same connection cannot be made so clearly in other cases. The Linlithgow Loch circle did appear within the 'Bonnybridge Triangle' and there have been many UFO reports in Fife where we have the Strathmiglo and Limekilns circles. However, this may be simply coincidence. And it cannot be claimed that the occasional appearance of circles is adequate evidence to prove a connection with other phenomena. Unfortunately we may now never get the chance to prove such a connection—in the late 1990s crop circles, or at least reports of them, virtually ceased in Scotland, although they continued to appear in England.

D

DEVIL

Hugh Miller [qv] told this chilling story of an early 19th-century encounter with the Devil in the Highlands:

'Not much more than thirty years ago [c. 1805], a Cromarty fisherman of staid, serious character, who had been visiting a friend in the upper part of the parish, was returning home after nightfall by the Inverness road. The night was still and calm, and a thick mantle of dull yellowish clouds, which descended on every side from the centre to the horizon, so obscured the light of the moon, though at full, that beyond the hedges which bounded the road all objects seemed blended together without colour or outline.

'The fisherman was pacing along in one of his happiest moods; his mind occupied by serious thoughts, tempered by the feelings of a genial devotion, when the stillness was suddenly broken by a combination of the most discordant sounds he had ever heard. At first he supposed that a pack of hounds had opened in full cry in the field beside him; and then, for the sounds sunk as suddenly as they had risen, that they were ranging the moors on the opposite side of the hill. Anon there was a fresh burst, as if the whole pack were baying at him through the hedge. He thrust his hand into his pocket, and drew out a handful of crumbs, the residue of his last sea stock; but as he held them out to the supposed dogs, instead of open throats and glaring eyes, he saw only the appearance of a man, and the sounds ceased.

' "Ah!" thought he, "here is the keeper of the pack;—I am safe." He resumed his walk homewards, the figure keeping pace with him as he went, until, reaching a gap in the hedge, he saw it turning towards the road. He paused to await its coming up; but what was his astonishment and horror to see it growing taller and taller as it neared the gap, and then, dropping on all fours, assume the form of a horse. He hurried onwards; the horse hurried too. He stood still; the horse likewise stood. He walked at his ordinary pace; the horse walked also, taking step for step with him, without either outstripping him or falling behind. It seemed an ugly mis-shapen animal, bristling all over with black shaggy hair, and lame of a foot.

'It accompanied him until he reached the gate of a burying-ground, which lies about two hundred yards outside the town; where he was blinded for a moment by what seemed an intensely bright flash of lightning; and, on recovering his sight, he found that he was alone.'

DISCO HAUNTING

A dance floor seems an unlikely place to meet a ghost, far less a poltergeist. But if houses and castles can be haunted why not a disco? 'Coaster's' disco in the Tollcross area of Edinburgh was plagued by strange incidents which stretched back over several years, but which came to a head during the months of January and February 1989.

The disco was on two floors—a general dance hall on the lower section called the 'Bermuda Triangle' and another with a bar on the upper floor which was known as the 'Barbados Suite'. The two halls were connected by a staircase and it was possible to move quite freely between them. A second staircase, made of wood, ran from the bar to the lower hall, but this was for use only by staff.

Events came to public attention when the three women employed as early morning cleaners refused to work in the halls on their own. They had been rattled by several unnerving incidents. On one occasion the vacuum cleaner they used every day suddenly started moving around the floor of the Barbados suite all on its own. What was even more puzzling was that the machine had not been switched on at the time and was thought not even to have been plugged in. At the same time, gantry lights suspended from the ceiling flashed on and off as if they had been activated. But the cleaners were adamant that no one could have got in to play tricks on them.

Bar staff also experienced odd incidents. Glasses stacked on shelves at night would be found smashed on the floor the following morning. Anything from whisky bottles to dish cloths would be moved around as if someone was trying to make a nuisance of themselves. Doors were heard opening and closing. Pools of water appeared on the floors from nowhere. There was a constant smell of burning wood hanging in the air at the top of the stairs leading to the lower dance hall. One cleaner, Hettie Graham, claimed that she felt an invisible hand touch her as she passed this spot, and there is no doubt that this area seemed to be a focus of activity. All of which pointed to a poltergeist presence.

But the events seemed to go beyond that. Female screams and scratching noises had been heard when the building was empty. Most frightening for staff was the possibility that a phantom spirit was prowling the building. Cleaners who had gathered for a chat and cigarette in the 'Bermuda Triangle' hall spotted a strange figure. It had appeared where the staff staircase ran from the lower hall to the bar. The door, normally shut, had been seen opening, and a dark figure had appeared and then vanished. The reflection of the apparition had been caught in the mirrors opposite the doorway, so there can be no doubt that something was seen. The staff were adamant that they were not involved in a publicity stunt and that the incidents they had witnessed had definitely taken place.

Medium Joan Davidson used her psychic powers to try and establish what was going on. Her view, through contact with the 'other side', was that the manifestations were being caused by the spirit of a fair-haired young man, 20 years old, who had been killed in a fire on the site where the disco now stood. But when this had happened, and why he should suddenly start to cause havoc in the disco, was not made clear.

However, one member of staff, Margaret, who worked as a

toilet attendant, claimed to have sensed the cause of the problem through her own psychic powers. She firmly believed that the incidents were due to a young woman who had been killed somewhere in the building. Her soul had been trapped and Margaret suggested that peace might be restored if it could be released. It was even thought possible that there were several trapped spirits. And that might explain the intensity and extent of the haunting. Although no exorcism took place, the number of incidents gradually dwindled to nothing leaving, as is often the case where hauntings are concerned, many unsolved questions.

DOWSING

Does dowsing belong in the realms of the paranormal? Scientists would say that it does, in that it is an unproved technique which is not repeatable. You can switch on an electric kettle and know the water will boil, but no two dowsers can get an identical reaction. Nor can dowsers always detect buried water pipes.

Most familiar is the water dowser with his Y-shaped twig, searching for an underground spring or stream. These days, however, most dowsers use metal rods, often made of copper. There are several well known dowsers in Scotland who have gained considerable reputations as water finders—Cyril Wilson is perhaps the best known.

Dowsers do not actually have to visit a site to look for

water—many simply use a map in the first instance, swinging a pendulum (which could be as simple as a lead weight on a string) over it to see if they can discover a water source in this way. This will be followed up by a visit to the site to dowse the area and pinpoint the actual spot where the water is flowing. A dowser should be able to tell you the depth and strength of the water flow.

In theory, dowsers can detect anything—gold, oil or diamonds for example. Oil companies have made use of dowsers, but only as an addition to conventional scientific methods. Dowsing is also widely used on an informal basis—on a building site you might well find electricians dowsing for cables, and plumbers dowsing for pipes. Archaeologists even use it for detecting underground remains and, in spite of scientific scepticism, it seems to work.

However, it is in more controversial areas that Scottish dowsing has made its impact. Investigators like Crieff-based David Cowan have really pushed forward the practice of dowsing so that it has become a potential tool for a wider variety of activities, including healing.

Central to the Scottish philosophy of dowsing is the idea of energy lines running beneath the surface of the Earth, energy lines which can be detected by techniques such as dowsing. This form of energy flow usually crosses the Earth in straight lines, although you also find energy spirals, rather like whirlpools. This flow can be of different strengths and types, some of which can be classified as 'good' or 'bad', i.e. beneficial or harmful. Dowsers claim it is possible to detect these energy lines and then to enhance or decrease their effect. This can be especially important where energy lines are running through a house or workplace, as most buildings have them and at one time or another we all experience their effect. Dowsers like Cowan can, through various devices, change the direction of the flow or block the effect altogether.

Dowsers have visited many historic sites to map the energy lines flowing through the area, and see standing stones as being of particular significance. Harry Bell has mapped a network of lines criss-crossing Glasgow and, according to David Cowan, the pattern of lines form a 'Star of David' around Crieff.

Experienced dowsers do not need rods or other tools for their work. Whatever causes the dowsing effect runs through the human body. It can apparently be blocked by wrapping tin foil around the shoes, suggesting that there is some kind of force radiating from the Earth.

DOYLE, SIR ARTHUR CONAN

Born in Scotland's capital in 1859, Doyle, the creator of Sherlock Holmes, spent most of his professional life outside the country of his birth. It is difficult to be sure of the extent to which his Scottish background contributed to Doyle's fascination with the paranormal. His own family came from Ireland, a nation with its own tradition of nature spirits and communications with the 'other side'. It is highly likely that England's well documented folklore was absorbed by Doyle, a voracious reader. However, as Doyle was brought up in Scotland by

Irish parents it seems safe to assume that the traditions of these countries had the greatest influence on his thoughts on paranormal matters. Even so, to complicate matters, it was in England that he actually took up the cause of spiritualism.

In his lifetime Doyle was one of the best known people in Britain. He involved himself in a range of cases, but his interest in spiritualism and his belief in the existence of fairies has always caused unease amongst devotees of his detective stories. The analytical forensic expertise which made Sherlock Holmes so successful seems to some an unhappy contrast with Doyle's enthusiasm for the intangible, unscientific nature of spirits and communications from the 'other side'.

Doyle did not see it in that way. He was convinced that the messages mediums produced were accurate and that physical demonstrations of mediumship—such as the production of 'ectoplasm'—were evidence of another world. However, even in his lifetime his involvement in the notorious case of the 'Cottingley Fairies' photographs exposed him to ridicule. These pictures, taken in 1917 by 15-year-old Elsie Wright and her cousin, 10-year-old Frances Griffiths, allegedly showed nature spirits—gnomes, elves and fairies. The photographs looked far from convincing—leading psychic investigator Sir Oliver Lodge called them 'obvious fakes'—but Doyle seemed strangely willing to accept uncritically the account of the children involved. No doubt he wanted to believe in the reality of nature spirits, but his acceptance of the photographs as genuine was a serious error of judgement. As the participants later admitted, they had carried out a very simple hoax using pictures of fairies cut from a storybook. However, in Doyle's favour (and usually ignored in accounts of the case), those involved were adamant that not all the photographs were hoaxes. The children claimed they really had seen nature spirits in the area and simply wanted to prove to adults that these entities actually existed.

Doyle's interest in spiritualism was not a passing fad. From 1918 till his death in 1930 it dominated his life. In his memoirs he wrote: 'the psychic question . . . has now come to absorb the whole energy of my life.' He later claimed that 'this revelation [spiritualism] is the most important that mankind has ever had.' Doyle went to his death convinced that it was possible to lift the veil between this world and the next, and that the world was a far stranger place than science would have us believe.

Doyle's participation in spiritualism certainly raised its profile, although even in Scotland it did not bring in many converts. Spiritualism was, and still is, a fringe religion. Nor did his involvement encourage belief in fairies. Far from it—the publicity given to the 'Cottingley Fairies' case damned the phenomenon to a level of ridicule from which it has never really recovered. People still claim to see fairies, but are usually unwilling to speak openly about it. The world has never forgotten Sherlock Holmes, but it has largely ignored those activities for which Sir Arthur Conan Doyle would most probably rather be remembered.

DRAGONS

The idea that a creature like the dragon walked the Earth and even survived into relatively recent times seems hard to believe. But just because there are no dragons around today, can we be so sure that such animals did not once exist? Several accounts of these bizarre creatures have come down from the Middle Ages, although they may well be based on an older tradition. What we have today may simply reflect the time when the details were finally written down. Naturally those who first wrote the stories down put them in a contemporary context, reflecting the spirit of their own times.

Even in Scotland, when we think of a dragon the story of England's St George comes to mind. Distinctly Scottish dragon stories have not survived. In his fascinating book *Dragons of the West* mystery author Nigel Pennick fails to mention a single Scots dragon, and his lack of awareness of the myth in Scotland probably reflects that of the Scots themselves. One reason may be that in times past dragons were called 'worms'. And the meaning of that word, which still occurs in place names, has changed so drastically that the ancient links have more or less been forgotten.

But that was not always the case, and we need look no further than the parish of Linton, situated close to the Cheviot Hills in the ancient shire of Roxburgh. Although it is now buried deep in the annals of local history, the Linton dragon or 'worm' was once as famous as the Loch Ness monster. It is probably more than coincidence that the dragon of Linton was confronted by a 'George'—George de Somerville, the king's falconer. And the king in question was William the Lion, who reigned from 1143 to 1214. The destruction that the monster was inflicting on the local community had been brought to William's attention and de Somerville volunteered to take on the beast. According to tradition he brought back to the king 'the worm of Linton's huge and hideous tongue.'

The Linton dragon lived in a cave at a spot still known as Worm's hole. That the tradition of the dragon is an old one is shown by a Norman carving of the dragon over Linton kirk door. It shows a knight on horseback with his lance confronting the beast. But if it was not a real dragon that was being dealt with, then what is the story about? A clue might be found in a part of the tradition where de Somerville tells disbelievers to 'go and see the hill that bears the marks of this worm's coils where it twisted and clung in its last agony. The furrows will be there for many years to come.'

Twisting paths around hills are a noted phenomenon, and have been linked to pre-Christian religion. The tradition of the destruction of the dragon may therefore be a story referring to the triumph of Christianity over paganism. The Anglo-Saxon word 'vyrm' or 'wyrm' can mean either a dragon or serpent, so tales of dragon/snake/serpent hills may all be legends originating from the same source. It is noticeable that Linton kirk is built on a mound, and it is more than likely that the mound was itself the original pagan place of worship which was later taken over by Christianity. So the death of the dragon may refer to the hill where the Christian place of worship now stands.

And while it is certainly true that Scotland has forgotten its dragon tradition, the 'monster' legend is alive and well in the form of the loch monster. Christianity, in the shape of St

Columba, confronted a monster at Loch Ness [qv], although we can only speculate as to whether this was a 'real' monster, or the symbolic dragon of paganism. In the case of Loch Ness, however, the monster has apparently managed to survive long after Christianity became the country's dominant religion.

Although several hundred miles separate Linton from Sutherland, a very similar dragon story can be found here. It too is generally dated to the Middle Ages although its origins may be much older. As at Linton, William the Lion was again instrumental in organising the slaying of the creature, this time through the efforts of a down-to-earth character called Hector Gunn.

The hill which the dragon coiled itself around was known as Worm Hill (Cnoc na Cnoimh in Gaelic). And in fact there are several places with worm in their name, for example 'Worm Law' in the Pentlands. Perhaps these were all sites where at one time pagan society could feel the strength of the dragon's breath.

It has been speculated that dragons may have been the last relic of a dying breed of dinosaurs, and perhaps this is not without the bounds of possibility—several hundred years ago Scotland's landscape was much wilder than today. Wolves survived till the 1740s, and it may be that other more ancient creatures inhabited the forests that at one time stretched in a dense carpet all the way from the Scottish Borders to Edinburgh and beyond.

DREADNOUGHT HOTEL

The Dreadnought Hotel in Callander is one of Scotland's oldest hotels. It is still in business today and has a reputation as a ghostly 'hot spot'. The building was extended in 1896 when a new wing was added, but the original part is still in use and it is that area where apparitions have been regularly noted.

It was founded in 1802 by Francis, the Chief of the Clan McNab, a man with a fiery temper. Legend has it that he bricked up his wife in one of the rooms and left her there to die. This could be in the 'black window' room, so called because the original window was covered over with black paint. It is now separated from the room by a later partition, and new windows have been put in, but paint is still visible on the older outside wall as an ominous reminder of past events. However, another account has it that McNab threw his pregnant mistress out of the window to avoid a scandal.

In a bedroom close by, people have heard the cries of a child—is this the echo of an ancient tragedy? In the basement there is an old well used in the days before there was running water. It seems that a child may have drowned here, and it is the toddler sobbing for help that people hear. The image of a child has also been seen to appear on a bedroom wall. But no one can be sure it is the same child who drowned in the well. Francis himself is said to appear as a kilted figure stalking the corridors. His portrait hangs in the bar, and when it moves out of place it is taken as a signal that the ghost of Francis is on the prowl.

The black window room seems to be the centre of activity. Staff report that guests regularly ask to be moved out of it as it can feel freezing even in summer, and shadowy figures have been witnessed in the early hours of the morning. But most disturbing is the chilling experience recounted by a number of guests—the end of the bed is felt to sink suddenly, just as if an invisible figure had carefully sat down on it.

There are other hotels in Scotland which have suffered periods of intense paranormal activity [see Hotel Ghosts], but the Dreadnought can fairly lay claim to the longest continuous haunting.

DUNCAN, GILLIE

Gillie Duncan earned her brief footnote in history because her arrest marked the beginning of a chain of events which led to the unravelling of a plot to murder King James VI by supernatural means. Her involvement shows how easily a 'white' witch could become suspected of black magic.

While working as a servant in 1590, sometime during her teens, Gillie developed miraculous healing powers. One of those she helped to cure was her employer, David Seaton from the village of Tranent. Far from feeling grateful, Seaton suspected her of having received these abilities from the Devil and on no other authority than his own he arrested and tortured Gillie, forcing a confession that she had indeed entered Satan's service. Thrown into gaol, Gillie admitted being part of a coven which included Agnes Sampson, a well known healer or white witch, John Cunningham (better known by his nickname 'Dr Fian' [qv]) and several others. Cunningham was the Earl of Bothwell's [qv] secretary, and when Agnes Sampson confessed to attempted regicide the chain was complete and a massive witch hunt unleashed.

Gillie's fate is unknown, but she will be remembered as an ordinary serving lass who became involved in a most notorious occult scandal which changed the course of Scotland's history.

DUNCAN, HELEN

Helen Duncan, who was born in Callander in 1897, was a well known medium who became famous (or notorious) because of her prosecution during World War Two.

Mrs Duncan claimed she received messages from the spirit world—standard fare for a medium—but in addition she had a reputation for physical mediumship. She produced a substance called ectoplasm which, it is said, allows a spirit to take on a solid form in this world. More than all other types of psychics, those who claim physical mediumship are regarded by sceptics as nothing more than calculating frauds.

But it was not this more controversial aspect of mediumship that led Helen Duncan into trouble. She hit the headlines because she was taken to court for fraudulently claiming the ability to communicate with the spirits of the dead. It is a case which reverberates today among spiritualist groups, who continue to feel a sense of outrage. And even today people are still campaigning to clear her name. But why should a medium who was quietly going about her own business and attracting modest audiences be considered worthy of the attention of the authorities?

The answer lies in the circumstances surrounding her activities. Mrs Duncan gave public demonstrations of her mediumship during the Second World War. As a large part of the male population was serving in the forces, months often passed by without families hearing from their husbands or sons. They did not know if their loved ones were dead or alive, and some tried to find out through contact with the world of spirits.

One evening in Portsmouth in 1941, Helen Duncan informed a member of her audience that she had a message from the woman's son. Through Duncan he told his mother: 'My ship has been sunk.' The woman had no idea that her son's ship had gone down. Nor as it turned out did any other relatives of the crew as, obsessed with secrecy, the authorities had kept the fact quiet. Helen Duncan's message was uncannily accurate—the ship in question, *HMS Barham*, had been torpedoed by a German U-boat.

News of Mrs Duncan's clairvoyance reached the ears of officialdom, who took the view that the medium posed a threat to the security of the nation. Of course, they did not present it in that way, and the charge under the 1735 Witchcraft Act was of 'pretending to raise the spirits of the dead.' But if secrecy was not their concern, why go to the lengths of prosecuting one medium who before the trial was unknown outside spiritualist circles? And why wait three years—until 1944—to take action? Even in the climate of the Second World War and with the approaching landings in Normandy, it seems an overreaction. At first glance it seems to be taking paranoia to an extreme, but some suggest that the real reason for Duncan's prosecution has never been revealed.

Spiritualist circles claim that Helen Duncan was a confidante of Winston Churchill and leading military figures, and that she was used (just as the Third Reich used their own mediums) to detect the movement of enemy warships and troops. It is a fact that Churchill was enraged by Duncan's prosecution and wrote to the then Home Secretary: 'What was the cost of a trial to the state in which the Recorder was kept busy with all this obsolete tomfoolery?' If Duncan had indeed been consulted by members of the government they could never afford to admit to it at the time, nor are we likely even now to discover the truth behind the prosecution.

Duncan was found guilty and sentenced to nine months' imprisonment in Holloway gaol. A stiff sentence which points to the fact that contacting spirits was not the real motive behind the prosecution. After all, spiritualists had been active since the 1850s and had largely been left to carry on without serious hindrance. That was particularly true as the 20th century moved away from the Victorian age. Helen Duncan's prosecution was a strange blip in a generally more religiously tolerant age. It is also noticeable that Duncan was kept under observation after her release and police officers attended a number of her séances. Spiritualists believe that it was a confrontation with police at a meeting in Nottingham in 1956 which led to her death later that year. She was cremated at Warriston crematorium in Edinburgh.

Decades later Helen Duncan continues to stand as a beacon for spiritualists and those who believe in religious liberty. A campaign has recently been revived to have Helen Duncan granted a posthumous pardon. A close friend of hers, Alan Crossley, described her as 'the most gifted person I have ever seen in the field of psychic phenomena.'

E

EARTHLIGHTS

'Earthlights' have been put forward as a potential solution to UFO sightings. The idea originated from earth mysteries researcher Paul Devereux, drawing on research carried out by Canadian scientists Michael Persinger and Gyslaine Lafreniere. It is well known that most UFO reports are of strange balls of light seen in the sky. Could there be a natural explanation for this? Devereux drew attention to the fact that rocks under pressure produce balls of energy which emerge from the earth and shoot into the atmosphere. These events occur particularly in association with earthquakes and earthquake-prone areas. So, Devereux not unreasonably decided, it was this scientifically based phenomenon rather than unproven extraterrestrial visitation which explained UFO reports.

It is hard not to see the force of Devereux's argument. But it is difficult to see how earthlights can be applied to all UFO incidents particularly where there is a close-up sighting. So while offering an explanation for 'lights in the sky' it does not bring us any nearer solving the phenomenon itself. And it has to be asked whether Devereux's theory can be applied in Scotland. If for example we examine UFO sightings in 1996 and compare them to areas where rock is under greatest pressure—that is, where earthquakes are recorded in Scotland—we find that there is no obvious connection. The areas where most UFO incidents are reported do not correspond with areas where earthquakes occur. Of course, there might well be rocks under pressure but no earthquakes. Nevertheless, if the theory is correct, some link would be expected. So as far as Scotland is concerned, earthlights remain an interesting but unproven solution to the UFO phenomenon.

EILDON HILLS

The Eildon Hills in the Borders are one of those landmarks which seem to ring of magic. Today they boast three distinctive peaks, but it is said that in remote times there was only one. A wizard conjuring up supernatural aid broke it into three with a massive thunderbolt. The alleged wizard was Michael Scott [qv], a 13th-century figure, but it is more than likely that his name became attached to an ancient tradition which long pre-dated him.

Throughout recorded time the number three has possessed a magical connotation: the three witches of Macbeth, the

Christian Trinity (Father, Son and Holy Ghost), the pagan threefold death, and there are many other examples which confirm the mystic force of a simple number. This sacred force took on a physical presence in the three peaks of the Eildons.

Visible for miles around in the low-lying countryside, there can be no doubting that to our pre-Christian ancestors these hills had a special religious significance. For a long time in folk tradition the Eildons were held in awe as a place where strange rituals and sacrifices took place. One small hill on the north side is known as the 'Bourjo', and according to legend it was at this spot that pagan priests lived and held religious ceremonies in an oak grove which once stood on the site.

As with many place names, the origin of 'Eildons' is uncertain. One translation is 'hills of fire' which, even if not accurate, is at least correct in the sense that fires would have burned on these hills during pagan celebrations.

There are many mysterious accounts connected with the hills. The best known is that of Thomas the Rhymer [qv], who was abducted by the Queen of the Fairies. The incident involved a real person—Thomas, Laird of Ercildoune—so may be based on events that he himself related. The Eildons may also have at one time played a part in the Arthur and Merlin tradition.

One legend, handed down through countless generations, is that a great king lies in a magic sleep beneath the Eildon Hills. He will wake up at a time when his people are in need of his help. That sounds very much like the legend commonly linked to King Arthur's return and it is a romantic, if highly unlikely, possibility that, far inside the Eildons, the supreme knight and his retinue of warriors lie in a deep sleep waiting for a cry for help.

EYNHALLOW

On 14th July 1990 a party of 88 set out to spend time touring Orkney's inner islands. Part of the day's events included a landing on Eynhallow, a tiny isle less than two miles across lying within sight of the Orkney mainland. The trip, which had been arranged by the Orkney Heritage Society, went as planned until the group reached Eynhallow. But as the party of visitors tramped back on board the ferry after their walk round the island they discovered that two of their number were missing. Crew members had counted 88 people out but only 86 had returned.

The rest of the tour was abandoned as an immediate search of the area was launched, but as time went by it became clear the two missing people were not going to be found on the island. No one even knew their names or were sure, with the large numbers on board, exactly who had disappeared. As confusion reigned, a major search swung into operation. Both police and coastguard teams combed the shores of Eynhallow and the Orkney mainland in an operation which lasted several days. Shetland's coastguard rescue helicopter, which had the latest in heat seeking equipment, was sent up but no definite traces were found. The police considered the possibility that the crew had made a simple mistake but were taking no chances. Chief Inspector John Ratter of Kirkwall's Northern Constabulary commented: 'We must keep an open mind. We have corroborative statements from the crew members and yet we do not have a missing person—it's a strange one.' He also made it clear that it would be 'very foolish' to put the incident down to a simple counting mistake when there was a chance that two people might be missing or dead.

Eynhallow certainly has a reputation. In ancient tradition it was a mystic 'vanishing isle', a land which could appear and disappear or even change shape. In pagan eyes such a place would be the point of entry into other dimensions where humans could come in contact with the inhabitants of other worlds. It was also known as the haunt of mermen, entities who live half in and half out of the sea but who, at certain times of year, can take on human shape. So were the missing visitors abducted by beings from another world? Or did they cross the threshold into another dimension? Eynhallow is said to be criss-crossed by mysterious lines of energy [see Ley Lines], and it has been argued by mystics that the strange couple must have gone to the island with a definite ritual purpose in mind. But if that was so, why did they disappear so quickly? There is really nowhere on that small island where they could have remained hidden for long. And if they had a secret plan, why travel there in such a public way.

It should be remembered that reports of people mysteriously vanishing are not uncommon. What made the Eynhallow incident so remarkable was the public nature of their disappearance. Part of the puzzle is that events were quickly overshadowed by more dramatic news—the murder of MP Ian Gow and the invasion of Kuwait. Against that background it became easy to bury events at Eynhallow within the claim that there never had been 88 on board—it had been a simple counting error. This convenient 'solution', rejected by the crew of the ferry, leaves a mystery which remains to this day.

F

FAIRIES

Fairies were the 'alien entities' of their day. Although there was widespread belief in their existence, only a few people would ever meet them. They were invisible to most people. Those with special abilities might be able to see and speak to them, but the world inhabited by the fairies was usually closed to mortals.

So how were fairies different from us? Their long life marked out fairies as a separate race, as they were reputed to live for ever in their own land. But, strangely, that world bordered on ours. We talk today of other dimensions, other 'Earths' sharing the same space as our own planet although normally unseen by us. This modern idea fits with traditional views of fairy life—their land seeming to exist alongside our own, yet in another place.

However, to our ancestors the fairy land had a physical

reality. And you might encounter it unsuspectingly at any time. There were particular spots like the fairy knowes or hills where entrance to the fairy domain was guaranteed if the 'wee folk' allowed it. There were deep caves and if you strayed too far you would find yourself within the fairy realm. But as they lived in an invisible world you could find yourself straying into it wherever you might be. Especially if you wandered into strange or isolated parts of the countryside.

You might be taken away (or 'abducted') by fairies for whatever reason [see Abduction]. And if you were, you might not return. Or if you did return you might find that, though you felt you had only been away a short time, years had gone by in the land of mortals. You had entered a different time frame, and this is a theme which has returned today in alleged alien abduction incidents. In fact 'missing time' has emerged as a key part of these events. Abductees find that unaccounted hours have disappeared from their lives while they have gone through an experience which appears to have lasted for only a short time. However, there is an important difference. In fairy lore men are often 'missing' for months or even years. In current abduction events the time lost is measured in hours and only occasionally days, but never for longer. Even so, the similarity has led some to suggest that alien encounters are simply a modern version of traditional fairy stories, updated and injected with technology for present-day tastes. For example, the Meigle incident in 1976 involved small, blue-coloured beings encountered by a young girl in a wood, who then beamed her aboard what seemed to be some kind of craft. It is a strange mixture of traditional fairy lore and current alien entity encounter incidents.

Fairies were seen as very human-like in appearance, although smaller in height and possessed of supernatural powers. You could never be sure of how they would behave towards you. They might decide to help you, but could also turn nasty. Humans had to be very careful in their dealings with fairies.

The literature on fairies is vast and covers almost all of Europe. Fairies in various types, and under different names, could be found across the whole of the British Isles and eastwards into Russia, taking in Scandinavia to the north. Does this prove that fairy people were a reality? Perhaps it is best to start by asking whether some of these traditions are based on actual events. Whatever the truth, certain themes run through the incidents, revealing common fairy characteristics. An underground entrance was a likely place for an encounter. A tale told by George Ross from Sutherland starts in this way: 'A Harris woman was walking along the sea shore when, on passing a rock, she noticed an opening in its side, leading into a spacious cavern. A fairy woman was standing by the opening, dressed in green, and invited the woman to accompany her and visit a sick person inside the cave.' The woman foolishly agrees and finds herself caught up in a magic spell—fairies were not to be trusted. Incidents abound of individuals being enraptured by hearing fairy music which comes from below ground, or of fairies appearing inside a house as if by magic. They apparently had the ability, shared by ghosts and aliens, to walk through solid walls. Fairies might also steal a baby and put another in its place, often one of their own sickly kind. Or they would disguise themselves as a baby and could only be revealed in their true form by magic means.

It would be wrong to think of these entities in the past tense—they are still met with today, but many of these encounters are ignored or unreported, because the merest suggestion of a belief in these entities exposes individuals to ridicule. Psychic Ian Shanes reported seeing several of these creatures around Loch Morar in the 1990s. They were elf-like creatures about eighteen inches tall, with human heads and lizard-like tails. The elves were apparently using the streams that ran through the loch as canals. Their homes were, as in traditional accounts, beneath two small humps which rose up from the surrounding land. Robert Crombie [qv], one of the Findhorn [qv] Foundation inspirers, claimed to have talked to a similar being in the Royal Botanic Gardens in Edinburgh and several other places, including the island of Iona. And in 1992 a man exercising his dog on a hill outside East Kilbride had an encounter with an entity which he could only describe as looking like a 'goblin' [qv]. So perhaps the fairies are still there for those with the eyes, or good luck, to see them.

FAIRY KNOWE

Almost every hill or mountain in Scotland has its fairy knowe. Just glance at a local map. But the best known in Scotland is undoubtedly that situated just outside the village of Aberfoyle. It was here 300 years ago that the Reverend Robert Kirk [qv] met and talked with his fairy friends and, it is claimed, disappeared with them. The knowe remains a haunting spot still visited by those who believe that fairy folk continue to inhabit the area. At the summit of the hill you will find cloths hanging from trees and bushes, some with messages to the fairies on them regarding people's illnesses. It is an old belief that as the cloth rots, so the illness to which it refers also passes away—thanks to the fairies' intervention. A cloth made of fabric that will disintegrate must be used, otherwise the spell will not work.

A knowe was believed to be an entrance to the fairy kingdom. They lived beneath it occupying what was in effect an underground village. It could also be a gateway to the wider fairy domain, a truly fantastic location where no one ever grew older. But the fairies inside their knowes lived more down-to-earth lives with machinery and workshops. This fitted the traditional view held of the 'little people'—that although they were a mystic race with supernatural powers, they were also very human-like in their appearance and way of life.

FESTIVALS

In recent years there has been a revival of pagan festivals. The celebration associated with May 1st never quite died out, but in the 1990s it began to be referred to quite openly as Beltane again, a pre-Christian name. Edinburgh, Stirling and other towns began to hold Beltane festivals. The pagan aspect of these celebrations was quite openly admitted, although the challenge to Christianity was muted and not appreciated by people who attended these events purely as a spectacle.

In ancient tradition May 1st marked the rebirth of Spring after the death of Winter. In Scotland a variety of figures were linked to the extensive festivities at the time, including Robin Hood [qv], Little John, the 'Abbot of Misrule', the Queen of May and the Green Man [qv]. These were elected 'posts' chosen either by the working men's associations of the time or the burgh councils. 'Robin Hood', perhaps with his elected 'Maid Marion', would preside over the day's events and be carried in procession to the spot where the festivities would take place. In Edinburgh this was the 'Greenfield', close to where the Playhouse Theatre stands today and at one time proposed site of a new BBC headquarters. Fire played a prominent role in Beltane celebrations and bonfires were lit on key landmarks. As at Halloween it was a time of change when the veil between the different worlds was lifted, and a time of activity for witches and fairies.

Scotland had a rich calendar of such festivals until the 16th century when the protestant reformers began to ban them as relics of a superstitious past. Most of these festivals have long since been forgotten, and the survival of Beltane as May Day is all the more remarkable. Perhaps it continued because the date is used to mark other events. More recently we have come to think of it as a day for celebrating manual labour, the May Day holiday. This is certainly a link to the past as it has an ancient tradition as a holiday when the old workmen's guilds like the goldsmiths and tanners would organise huge pageants and compete for prizes.

Most festivals we celebrate today have a long history rooted in pagan religious rites. Some have been incorporated into Christianity and others gradually forgotten. October 31st (Halloween as we know it today) was the converse of May Day—a time when life and light gave way to death and darkness. November 1st was closely linked with the Cult of the Dead—as 'Imbolc' it marked the start of the Celtic year. And December 25th, now celebrated as the day of Christ's birth, is in reality of pagan origin. It records the end of the Celtic 'five dark days', which begin on December 19th and mark the time when the sun seems to stand still in the sky and time itself stops.

Lammas, August 1st, was originally the Celtic festival of Lughnasadh, in honour of the god Lug, one of the key pre-Christian deities. The same is true of the Christian festival of Candlemas (February 1st), which began as the Festival of Light in honour of Brigit, the original Earth Mother. It was the first day of Spring in the pagan Celtic calendar and Brigit, who under Christianity became St Bride, was the goddess of Spring.

Celebrations on midsummer's eve or at the summer solstice have also undergone a revival in recent times. This has been partly due to the growth of druidism with the publicity given to annual gatherings at Stonehenge and to the general spread of 'New Age' ideas which, in linking man more to the environment, inevitably bring pre-Christian beliefs back into focus. In times past, midsummer was a key festival in the year and was celebrated with torchlight processions and bonfires which emphasised its link to the ultimate fire in the sky, the bringer of universal life, the sun.

FIAN, DR JOHN

John Fian has gone down in history as one of Scotland's most notorious witches. But was he really part of a satanic conspiracy to murder a king, or just an innocent victim caught up in another person's demonic plot?

John Fian was a schoolmaster in the Midlothian village of Tranent who in the 1590s acted as secretary to the Earl of Bothwell [qv]. It was Fian's confession that he was a practising witch which directly implicated Bothwell in an alleged plan to assassinate James VI. The reliability of Fian's confession has to be questioned, as it was extracted under torture.

And Fian was certainly put through a terrible experience. At first, he steadfastly proclaimed his innocence of the accusations of witchcraft which had been levelled against him following the earlier arrest of another alleged witch, Gillie Duncan [qv]. But as a suspected follower of Satan, any means could legally be used to 'encourage' him to confess. So he was put into the 'Spanish Boot', an extreme form of torture whereby the legs were enclosed in metal jackets and then hammered. The effect on bone and flesh was gruesome, and Fian lapsed into unconsciousness. Or so it seemed. But seasoned witch hunters suggested that it was all a clever ruse. They opened his mouth and discovered 'two pins thrust into the head', as they reported to the king. It was a charm to prevent the witch confessing, they explained. According to their account, when they took the pins out Fian broke down and made a full admission of his guilt.

Fian told the King that he acted as secretary to Satan's coven and stood at His side when they held their gatherings at North Berwick kirk. He had also attempted to raise a storm to sink James' ship when the royal armada had sailed to Denmark. There was no doubting that a gale had sprung up and pushed the King's ship off course, but was that anything more than a common peril of travelling through the North Sea? James seemed to think so, and was more than willing to believe that factors other than the weather had been in action that day.

Fian was sent back to his cell to sit alone and contemplate the unfortunate hand that fate had dealt him. The following day he reported a strange conversation. He claimed that the Devil himself had visited him, dressed in black and carrying a white wand. He challenged Fian to keep his word 'according to his first oath and promise'. Fian retorted: 'I have listened to you too much and by the same you have undone me [therefore] I utterly forsake you.' In a chilling response the Devil informed him: 'Once you die you shall be mine.'

Not long after, in the early hours of the morning, someone or something passed Fian a key and, miraculously, he not only slipped his gaolers, but got clean out of Edinburgh Castle without being spotted. His movements thereafter appear bizarre. Instead of heading off to an isolated area, of which 16th-century Scotland had plenty, he made for the familiar territory of Tranent where he was bound to be immediately recognised. Was he looking to Bothwell to save him? Or had he been released by his 'Master' to perform one last task? Did he set out to contact another coven member or destroy incriminating evidence? We will never know. But one thing is clear: following his escape and recapture Fian was a changed person. He withdrew his earlier confession and repeatedly denied any involvement in witchcraft.

Now the confession had to be dragged out of him once more. The Spanish Boot was fitted and Fian's legs pounded mercilessly till, as a contemporary witness recorded, 'his legs were crushed and beaten together, as small as might be, and the bones and flesh so bruised that the blood and marrow spouted forth in great abundance. They were unserviceable forever.' His continued refusal to confess had moved beyond the heroic and bordered on madness. However, his protestation of innocence meant that legal formalities had to be followed and a trial was arranged. There could be no doubting the guilty verdict and Fian's fate. He was taken by cart to the execution spot where he was strangled then burned on 13th January 1591.

Innocent or not, it seems that Dr Fian had been involved in some aspects of the occult. 'Dr Fian' was a nickname—his real surname was Cunningham. 'Fian' comes from Feanne, Fianne or Fean, all of which are Gaelic-Irish derivations pointing to a fairy connection, suggesting someone with second sight or with the psychic power to dabble in areas denied to ordinary men. Such then was 'Dr Fian', a man whose reputation was established in his name. But just what he and Bothwell had been involved in we will probably never know, although the circumstantial evidence does point to it being some murky involvement in the practice of the Black Arts.

FINDHORN

The community of Findhorn, an early New Age 'green movement', started in a very small way. Indeed it is hard to understand why it has gained such a worldwide following. Findhorn is a small outpost on the north-east tip of Scotland, although its isolated situation has been exaggerated. It is less than a couple of hours' drive from the city of Aberdeen and forty minutes from Inverness, the 'Capital of the Highlands'. Just down the Findhorn peninsula is RAF Kinloss, one of Scotland's most active military bases. However, when Peter and Eileen Caddy set up their caravan at a deserted spot at Findhorn in November 1962 it must have seemed to them that they had reached the ends of the earth, particularly as their home was in England.

What happened in the following year is a subject of controversy. Eileen Caddy claimed to be getting messages from 'higher forces' including the spirits of nature. There was a strong religious or Christian motivation underlying Eileen Caddy's activities. The direct result of Eileen's contacts with the 'spiritual kingdoms of nature' was that vegetables she had planted in her patch grew to enormous proportions. Or so Eileen (who had been assisted by another psychic, the Canadian Dorothy MacLean) claimed. However, the only person who could actually see the elves, gnomes, and pixies that were reputedly present and encouraging the vegetables to grow was the mystic R O Crombie [qv].

There is no doubt that the Caddys' activities covered a range of ideas which were growing in popularity at the time—the 'drop out' culture, 'small is beautiful', the move away from mass-production to 'real food', community versus anonymity, the yearning for spirituality, and certainty against disorder. Findhorn was successful to an extent beyond anyone's wildest dreams, and in a 30-year period it attracted tens of thousands of followers and many more who just wanted to savour the atmosphere of the place. And having visited Findhorn the author can confirm that it does, even in its contemporary state, have an air of detached calm. Whether that is down to the pure chance of having selected a 'good energy' site or the continuing legacy of the Caddys is hard to tell. Its influence waned a little in the 1990s as tastes changed, but it has left a mark on 'New Age' and other thinking. As one writer noted on the death of Peter Cuddy in 1994. 'The potential for the restoration and healing of the Earth through conscious, practical collaboration with these kingdoms of nature was glimpsed and the creation of the Foundation's garden will be seen as a landmark.'

Its relationship to the rest of Scottish society has been somewhat casual and it has made little effort to link up with Scottish mystic movements. An example of this has been the tendency of Findhorn to play down the role of Scot Robert Crombie in its formation, so that it has come to be seen as almost a completely Caddy-inspired institution.

One strange aspect is that Findhorn had an ancient tradition that the fairy folk ('nature spirits') were particularly attracted to the area. There is no evidence that the Caddys, Crombie or Dorothy MacLean were aware of this local lore before they settled there, so perhaps the influence of nature spirits did work in a mystical way to show the world what co-operation with the world of nature could achieve.

FLANNAN LIGHTHOUSE

It is one of Scotland's most enduring mysteries—the disappearance in December 1900 of three lighthouse keepers from their isolated tower on the Flannan Islands, situated in the Atlantic Ocean some twenty miles off the tip of the Outer Hebrides.

The lighthouse had been opened in December 1899 as the area was a notorious spot for shipwrecks. Everything had gone smoothly till the dramatic events of a year later. The keepers on duty at the time were James Ducat, Thomas Marshall and Donald McArthur. A fourth member of the team, Joseph Moore, was taking a week's rest in Lewis where he had his home.

It was his return to the Flannan Islands on 26th December which led to the discovery of the tragedy—whatever it was. Everything in the lighthouse seemed in good condition and the lighthouse beam was ready for operation, the gates and doors were properly closed, and the kitchen table was set for a meal. However, the fire was cold—clearly, the place had been unused for some days. There was no sign of disturbance, other than one chair, which had been tipped back and was lying on the floor.

A log had been kept by Marshall until 15th December. It indicated that the men were terrified by the fierce storm that had raged for days. On December 12th he wrote: 'Sea lashed to fury. Never seen such a storm. Waves very high. Tearing at Lighthouse. . . . James Ducat irritable.' And later: 'Storm still raging. . . . Cannot go out. . . . Ducat quiet. Donald McArthur crying.' On December 13th, further reference to the agitation of the keepers was made: 'Ducat quiet. McArthur praying.' There was no log entry for the 14th. The entries for the 15th read as follows: *'Noon:* Grey daylight. Me, Ducat and McArthur praying. *1 p.m:* Storm ended, sea calm. God is over all.'

It was discovered that Ducat's and Marshall's oilskins and boots were missing, but McArthur's gear was still there. There had been fierce storms during the month, and it was suggested that Ducat and Marshall had gone outside to check that everything was secure, and had been swept away, perhaps by a huge wave. McArthur might then have gone to search for his colleagues, and also been swept or blown into the sea.

The island, Eilean Mor, was only forty acres in extent, so a search quickly revealed that there was no sign of them. Had they been washed into the Atlantic? The lighthouse was 200 feet above sea level, so to be hit by a wave all three keepers would have had to have gone down the cliff side to the jetty. But why would they have done that in rough weather? It made little sense—all were experienced lighthousemen.

Other suggestions were put forward: for example, that one man killed the other two and then committed suicide. But there was no evidence of a fight, no bloodstains on wall or floor, no implements lying about which could be linked to a struggle.

Were they attacked by a some sort of sea monster? There was, it was said, oddly-glowing seaweed found in the men's quarters. Had it been dragged up from the depths by an unknown creature? It was all speculation and nothing was proved. Recently, it has been mooted that the men could have been abducted by extraterrestrials. Whatever the truth, their disappearance remains an enigma which, a hundred years on, is unlikely to be solved.

G

GIBBS, PETER

Some incidents defy explanation. Almost forgotten now, the mysterious death of wartime Spitfire ace and orchestral conductor Peter Norman Gibbs in 1975 is one such incident, and remains one of Scotland's strangest cases.

On Christmas Eve 1975, the 55-year-old Gibbs was holidaying on the island of Mull, and decided late in the evening to take a flight in a single-engined Cessna he had hired. He was staying at the Glenforsa hotel near the village of Salen, and claimed that he wanted to test the local airstrip for a night landing. The strip was unlit and Gibbs asked a group of guests to shine torches to mark it for his descent.

He took off, but never returned. A massive search was launched for the missing Cessna and its pilot. Starting with a sweep across Mull, it gradually broadened till it took in large areas of the Highlands and Islands, went as far south as

Glasgow and across the central belt to Stirling. Gibbs, however, had vanished into thin air. There was no sign of either the pilot or his aircraft.

Four months passed. Then, on 21st April 1976, Donald Mackinnon, a shepherd rounding up lambs, made a grim discovery. It was the body of the missing Peter Gibbs, slumped over a fallen tree, as if he had simply collapsed on an afternoon stroll. There was no sign of the Cessna. His body appeared undamaged and later examination showed that there was no salt water in his clothes. The police claimed that the pilot had parachuted from his plane. But this was contradicted by the assistant manager of the Glenforsa Hotel, who reported that Gibbs was not wearing a parachute harness. Strangest of all, however, Gibbs had been found only a mile from the Glenforsa Hotel. An area which the rescue services had already searched thoroughly.

So how had Gibbs arrived at that spot? He did not jump into the sea, as the lack of salt water on his clothes showed. Even if he had brought the plane down to stalling speed and thrown himself out he would surely have sustained some significant injury. But his body was unmarked. And the plane, without a pilot, would surely have been found not too far away. On top of that, it is hard to believe that Gibbs, in the pitch black of a December night, and flying over unlit countryside, would have managed to bring down his plane to a height from which he could safely jump.

It was a puzzle which deepened twelve years later with the chance discovery of the downed Cessna in the Sound of Mull. In 1987 George Foster, a scallop diver, came across the wreckage of Gibbs' plane about 300 yards offshore at the entrance to Fishnish bay in the Sound of Mull. So the aircraft had definitely crashed, but how had Gibbs managed to abandon it before it sank, swim ashore and then climb a hill only to die from exposure. And in doing this he would have had to cross a main road when the obvious thing to do would be to wait for a passing car.

Unless information has been kept back by the authorities or witnesses, it is hard to make sense of the sequence of events. Something is wrong somewhere.

So should we look beyond the normal into the supernatural for a solution to these bizarre events? The Gibbs incident has strange echoes of the mysterious and still unsolved death in 1929 of Norah Fornario, the young occultist whose unmarked body was discovered on open ground on the nearby island of Iona. Dressed in a ritual cloak it has been believed that Norah was the victim of psychic murder [qv]. And the road through Glenforsa leads in only one direction, straight to the Iona ferry.

There is no evidence that Peter Gibbs was interested in the paranormal or UFOs, but then people do not usually choose to meet ghosts or confront strange entities. These encounters just happen. And there certainly are weird aspects to Gibbs' disappearance. In the first place, there is the day that Gibbs took off and vanished, Christmas Eve, a significant date long before the arrival of Christianity. In the ancient druidic calendar it marked the end of the five dark days when the sun stood still in the sky and time came to a stop before the world was born again. It was a time when this world and the next came closest.

Perhaps not on its own significant, but it could be when

linked to the day on which Peter Gibbs' body reappeared. Incredibly, April 21st is the holy day of Mull's key saint Maelrubha, after whom Tobermory, the main town on the island, is named. It was Maelrubha who, centuries ago, travelled down the west coast of Scotland driving the druids out of their old religious sites.

Then there is the area where Peter Gibbs' body was discovered, at a spot known as Pennygown. In past times this was a well known haunt of fairies who were supposed to live beneath the hill. It is also curious that Gibbs' Cessna was last seen flying over Pennygown before it vanished. And though today we link strange lights up above with UFO sightings, traditionally they were known as 'fairy lights' and as a phenomenon have been reported over a long period of time. Lights in the sky were reported at the time Gibbs disappeared. James Hewitt, manager of the Glenforsa hotel, said following the discovery of Gibbs' body: 'My wife and I maintained all along that we saw lights dying out in the Sound of Mull which could have been the plane, but at the time we thought he was still in it.' If those lights were not the stricken Cessna then what were they? And why did the plane end up in the water when the last sighting was of it heading away from the sea over Pennygown?

Could it have been a case of alien abduction, with Peter Gibbs removed from his plane by extraterrestrials—then days, or even weeks later, left on a Mull hillside? The 'open' verdict at the fatal accident inquiry may simply be evidence that though all normal channels of investigation had been followed, the solution lay in a different dimension altogether.

GHOST ROADS AND RAILWAYS

Most religions believe in some form of afterlife. It is a common belief that we all have a spirit which survives death. But what of those objects which were never alive in the first place? Reports of ghost cars, lorries, ships and planes may be less frequent than spirit entities, but it is a real puzzle that they are reported at all.

In August 1989 Brian Maddison and his wife were driving along the A84. It was a dark but clear night as they approached a caravan park near the hundred-year-old station at Balquhidder Junction. The silence of the hour was suddenly broken by the distinctive sound of a steam train. Glancing in the direction of the noise they caught sight of a row of lights like those of a railway carriage, moving in a northerly direction. In fact, as they later learned, the line had been closed to railway traffic in 1965, a full twenty-four years before the incident. It seems hard to understand why a ghost train should continue to travel up a long-disused track. But it seems that phantom vehicles appear all over Scotland.

On Skye's A863 a notorious car thunders down the road, headlights blazing, causing oncoming cars to pull in hurriedly to the side of the road. When the driver glances up the lights have vanished and the mystery vehicle never appears. At the opposite end of the country, on the A7 near the village of Stow, cars find themselves following a vehicle whose driver seems to know every bend like the back of his hand. It is so dark they keep their eyes on his rear lights, but are suddenly forced to swerve to avoid running off the road as the phantom car drives through the countryside on a route which went out of use decades ago.

But in these cases are we dealing with ghost vehicles or haunted roads? A Kilwinning couple starting out on a journey to London were heading along the A71. It was around 2 a.m. and they found themselves driving through a wooded area on a bend. As they came out of the bend they saw directly in front of them a strange white shape stretching across both carriageways. There was no way to avoid it so they drove right through, relieved to come out unscathed on the other side. They were startled to discover, some weeks after, that the incident happened close to the site of the battle of Drumclog fought in 1679. The area is well known as a site where spirit figures regularly appear.

One of the most famous spirit roads is found in the Borders, just outside the village of St Boswells. Its eerie reputation led the Society for Psychical Research to label it as 'one of the best-authenticated hauntings of modern times.' Matilda Scott was the first to catch sight of the strange figure in May 1892— a man dressed all in black walking in front of her. Naturally cautious to see a stranger in the area, she decided to stay behind rather than pass him, but suddenly he simply vanished. As Matilda continued walking she rounded a bend and saw her sister standing a couple of hundred yards down the road. Louisa too had spotted the stranger and had been just as amazed as Matilda to see him disappear. Over the next 20 years several others witnessed the appearance of the mystery man in black. The identity of the ghost, however, was never discovered.

You do not have to be on a deserted road to encounter the supernatural. One of the best known haunted highways is Glasgow's Sauchiehall Street, where a phantom tram was for many years regularly seen. It is even said that a member of the public tried to hail it, but that its ghostly driver simply nodded and smiled as he drove by before the whole vehicle vanished like a gentle mist.

Phantom trams have been reported from all our main cities, but ghostly stagecoaches make the most regular appearances. At Inverbervie on the north-east coast the phantom of the Aberdeen to Glasgow mail carriage, complete with horses, travels on a still-visible track down a hill to the site of a former inn. And on the old Edinburgh to Kirkliston road a stagecoach, complete with crew, is still seen thundering along this ancient trackway.

However, some of the more frightening encounters have been experienced in West Lothian. Here motorists have encountered a strange figure, glowing white, who seems able to run at an incredible speed. In one reported incident a passenger in a car caught a movement from the corner of his eye and, glancing out of the rear window, saw a silver-coloured being chasing down the road after the car. The vehicle hit sixty miles per hour, but the entity ran fast enough to keep up and followed them along at this speed for almost two minutes.

What causes a road to become haunted? It cannot be simply because several accidents have taken place. There have been a number of fatal accidents connected with the Forth Road Bridge, but it has so far remained free of apparitions. It may be that rather than seeing 'ghosts' we are in fact looking into the past, and that certain stretches of road act as windows through which we may see dramatic events of years gone by.

Of all the paranormal phenomena experienced in Scotland, encounters with ghosts occur most often. Scots have seen strange phantoms which have appeared in almost every location imaginable. There are haunted hotels, pubs, houses, castles, trains, planes, ships, woods, hills and roads. The list is endless. But what are people seeing? Are these creatures really the spirits of the dead?

If the world is populated by spirits, we might well ask where they all are. They should be appearing everywhere. So it is a puzzle why we are not meeting ghosts every day of our lives. Mediums have an answer—most ghosts move to another world or 'plane' of existence. Only those spirits that for some reason become 'earthbound' are seen as ghosts. They may not want to leave the area where they lived, or they may not understand that they have died. They may have gone through a traumatic death, an incident which roots the soul to the site of death. But if that is the case why do they not appear at the same spot every day? The truth is that 'daily' ghosts just do not exist. There are many ghosts which are seen regularly, but there is no location in Scotland (or anywhere else) where you can be guaranteed to see a ghost, however long you wait.

Few people can see ghosts at will. Psychics, on the other hand, might enter a house and see a dozen. However, as ghosts are invisible to others, any medium's claims have to be taken on the individual's say-so. There are no definitive ghost photographs, although there are many strange images which are hard to explain.

The experience of psychics seems to suggest that, although

some spirits may simply be 'earthbound', other ghosts may be the spirits of friends or relatives who are trying to contact us, maybe even acting as 'guardian angels'. Those who have tried to explain ghosts in ways more palatable to science suggest that by some unknown process an inanimate object can somehow 'photograph' or 'record' an incident. This might explain why so many Scottish castles are haunted. If this theory is correct, what we see from time to time is a replay of the event, when conditions are right.

Scotland can fairly lay claim to being a long-standing ghostly 'hot spot'. As a result it has a lengthy history of dedicated investigators of the ghost phenomenon, from William Linskill [qv] in the 19th century, to Professor Archie Roy, who set up the Scottish Society for Psychical Research in the 1980s. There have been countless Scottish mediums—including the world's greatest, Daniel Home [qv], who died in the 1880s, and Helen Duncan [qv] in the 20th century—who have provided substantial evidence of the reality of ghosts as spirits of the dead. A great deal of Scotland's ghost history has been reported but, as elsewhere, especially England and the USA where interest has also been intense, substantial case reports have led to no firm conclusions.

Many people firmly believe ghostly apparitions do appear. But what they are and why they suddenly make themselves known to us remains as elusive and controversial as ever.

GLAMIS

Glamis Castle, near the town of Forfar in the ancient county of Angus, has become an international byword for a haunted building. There have been numerous witnesses to its many ghostly presences and these, it is claimed, have included members of the royal family.

The present Queen Mother, Elizabeth Bowes-Lyon, lived in haunted Glamis as a child. No doubt she saw the bloodstained floor where Malcolm II allegedly died, Macbeth having dealt the fatal blow so he could claim the Scottish kingdom as his own. However, Malcolm's ghost is not, apparently, seen. Or perhaps there are simply so many spirits and strange incidents that one more phantom—even if it is a king—simply goes by unremarked. For the castle has witnessed since its origins, which date from at least as far back as the 15th century, many an unnatural death. Feuding between local families connected with support for or opposition to Scotland's ruler of the time often led to fighting and murder.

But if violence creates a ghost then it has not happened at Glamis. Many of the apparitions have a sad and tragic tale attached to them, but lives lost on a battlefield have not been the main source of these earthbound spirits. The phantom most often reported is that of a 'Grey Lady', frequently seen in Glamis Chapel. It has been suggested that this spirit could be that of one of the ladies of the castle who was accused of witchcraft by James V and, after a staged trial, burnt in 1540. She is said to appear when a tragedy is about to strike the family. Less is known about a 'White Lady', although she has been said to make regular appearances—as does the 'Black

Boy', seen sitting quietly on a stone bench. His identity is also unknown. A phantom has been seen floating across the castle grounds, and inside the building a tall figure wearing an overcoat, and a soldier dressed in armour, have also appeared. The most pitiful tale is that connected to the ghost known as the 'Tongueless Woman', an unfortunate lass who supposedly had her tongue cut out to prevent her telling of crimes carried out by one of the castle's less law-abiding owners.

But most mysterious of all is Glamis' secret room. It is suggested that there is a locked room in the castle which no one is allowed to enter. There are two different explanations for this. One is that the room supposedly holds some strange secret, perhaps a revelation about the afterlife or other worlds. The alternative is that the room has simply become too dangerous to use. A century or more ago, it is said, a previous owner engaged in black magic rituals and succeeded more extensively than he dreamt of. Weird demons were conjured up with other strange spirits and he found that he could not get rid of them. The demons may even have killed some of those who were foolish enough to get involved in this dangerous activity. Since then, it has never been possible to clear the room of its evil atmosphere and make use of it in a normal fashion.

Walking round Glamis you do feel a sense of heavy foreboding. But is that due to Glamis' reputation or your own mind tuning in to malevolent energy running through the castle? It may be this, rather than a bloody past, which has led to so much ghostly activity and earned Glamis the reputation of being Scotland's most haunted building.

GLASGOW

Today we tend to think of Glasgow as an industrial and commercial centre. But that is to ignore the city's origins.

Glasgow started life as a spiritual centre. Christians saw it as a key spot which probably reflected the fact that when the new religion arrived the area around the Clyde River was a prominent focus for pagan belief. Nearby was the stronghold of Dumbarton Castle, which may have played a significant part in the life of Merlin, that figure from Arthurian legend whose lifetime marks the boundary between paganism and Christianity. Tradition has it that Glasgow Cathedral was built on the site of a druidic temple. We should then be less surprised to learn that Glasgow has a hidden mystic past and an active paranormal present.

Investigator Harry Bell has been a key figure in unravelling the mystery of Glasgow's secret history. Through his research, brought together as *Glasgow's Secret Geometry*, Bell has shown that many strange alignments created thousands of years ago between ancient monuments can still be followed today in the modern city, and still have something to tell us. According to Bell: 'there's no doubt that Bronze Age people built forts and other sites to line up with prominent landmarks on the hills that surround Glasgow.'

Bell himself has not suggested that there was anything mystic in this arrangement, but others using the results of his work have claimed to be able to dowse these lines which they call 'ley lines' [qv]. Bell believes that he has shown that the alignments starting and finishing at distant summits around the city lead to four main sites in Glasgow—including

Camphill, the Necropolis, and Carmyle Fords. These alignments may have influenced later builders, or it may be that the lines represent a strange energy force within the Earth which unconsciously affected our ancestors.

One of the lines discovered by Bell runs through King's Park, an area of Glasgow where several UFO sightings have been recorded. This was the site of Tom Coventry's amazing 'flying carriage' encounter in 1983, during which a UFO shaped like a railway carriage passed less than twenty feet above his head in broad daylight.

Although the UFO phenomenon appeared early in the Glasgow area, with incidents reported from as far back as 1948 and 1952, Glasgow has not yet reached world UFO 'hot spot' status. But it has experienced a substantial number of reports including the largest Scottish UFO ever recorded—the one and a half mile monster seen in 1992 over Bellahouston Park at night. It can also boast the fastest travelling—a strange cigar-shaped object, reported in 1984 by an experienced private pilot, moving at an estimated speed of 45,000 miles per hour.

An interesting aspect of Glasgow's UFO experience has been the way in which spiritual matters and UFO incidents have intertwined. In 1971 a witness in the King's Park area heard a strange noise, followed immediately after by a silver beam of light which entered her house and the appearance of a Christ-like figure—an incident which seems to show that the division between UFO encounters and the spiritual domain is not a clear one. It forces us to think again about how UFOs and the spirit world may relate to each other. In the area of Westbourne Gardens in the 1950s a group of children encountered a number of strange entities. Twenty years later in the same area in the early hours of the morning a group of friends saw a silver-coloured UFO take off. In the 1990s a UFO witness looking from the Campsie Fells watched in amazement as two strange objects moved over the city in a definite pattern as if they were mapping the whole area.

UFOs are a regular city phenomenon, but so also are ghosts and poltergeists. It is clear from individual investigators, and groups like the Scottish Society for Psychical Research, that this 'traditional' paranormal phenomenon is more common than we might like to admit. And ghosts are not just to be found in private houses. The Kelvingrove Museum has a well known ghost, as has Pollok House. The Royale Snooker Club in Rutherglen has been plagued by ghostly visitors—according to Glasgow psychic Ian Shanes, the place is 'jumping with spirits'. The apparitions were being kept under control by 'a tiny priest in black robes and a skull cap'. According to investigator Arlene Russo: 'the club may be haunted because it was built on land which was an old cemetery.'

A similar connection might explain a ghostly presence in the Ramshorn Theatre, which was once a church. A woman called Edie supposedly haunts the toilets where the minister's vestry was located. Strange footsteps have been heard and powerful unpleasant smells. There is evidence that the building was constructed over an ancient crypt so this may be a very old haunting indeed.

However, in recent years the greatest focus of paranormal activity has been in an unlikely spot—Glasgow Transport Museum. The strange incidents that have occurred there have been brought to public attention thanks to the interest of Bill Mutch who, while working in the museum as a security assistant, has had the opportunity to note the many unexplained events. Mutch has recorded 'the sighting of a headless female', a 'pale blue wave' travelling through the exhibits, and the sound of children screaming late at night next to the display of train engines—an incident that may be linked to a past railway accident. Strange footsteps have been heard repeatedly and the sound of voices when the museum is closed and empty. Shadowy figures have been seen walking through solid walls.

The focus for the incidents appears to be within one area of the building, which houses a famous reconstruction of a 1930s street with shops, cinema and underground station—although there is no obvious explanation as to why this should be the centre of supernatural activity.

GLENLUCE DEVIL

Although generally referred to as the 'Glenluce Devil' this incident was, in fact, Scotland's earliest well documented case of the poltergeist phenomenon [qv]. Dating from 1654, it contained all the ingredients that became more familiarly known through later incidents and which have been popularised to 20th century audiences through films such as *The Exorcist*. The public of four hundred years ago would have no difficulty in recognising events portrayed in such films, as the phenomenon of poltergeist activity has not changed over the centuries.

And, almost in the style of a Hollywood script, events in

the village of Glenluce in Dumfriesshire were sparked by the anxieties of an adolescent, the youthful Thomas Campbell, a weaver's son. A beggar, Andrew Agnew, came to the home of Gilbert Campbell, Thomas' father, looking for a handout— which was refused. Agnew then cursed the Campbell home. Thomas was at school in Glasgow at the time, but when he returned he learned of the beggar's threats, which probably had not been taken too seriously by his parents. It appears that Thomas did take them seriously, however. And, coincidence or not, his return from his distant school appears to have set off the first poltergeist manifestations. Stones were thrown at the windows of the cottage and into the house, blankets were pulled from the beds, cupboards opened and the contents thrown about the room.

The family turned to the church for help and a day of prayer was held. It did not stop the disturbance, but what did bring a halt was the removal of the children from the house. When the children returned, and Thomas was among them, the phenomena started again with renewed intensity. Small fires flared up in different parts of the house. They were kept under control, but it was clearly a worrying escalation.

People began to suspect that perhaps the events were linked to Thomas. He was taken from the house and lodged with a local minister. But the poltergeist activity did not cease in spite of Thomas' absence. So had Thomas himself been carrying out these supposedly paranormal acts, and had the other children followed suit? Thomas, it seems, was quite happy to be out of the place and claimed that a voice had told him that he must not enter the house again as long as his father was in it. This may point to tension between Thomas and his father, a not unusual situation in adolescence, but does not prove that Thomas was creating the poltergeist effect.

The incidents continued from November 1654 to September 1656, so it was a lengthy infestation which reached its height when the voice of a spirit who called himself the 'Devil' was heard several times. Sceptical adults expressed the view to the 'Devil' that 'this voice speaks out of the children', to which the spirit replied: 'You lie. God shall judge you for your lying.'

Whoever or whatever was responsible for events at Glenluce, they stopped as suddenly as they had begun. To some this was because Thomas Campbell had resolved his differences with his father. To others the hanging of the beggar Andrew Agnew brought the curse to an abrupt end. With the benefit of hindsight, we know that poltergeist incidents usually have a beginning and an end—even if we have no better explanation to offer than had the witnesses to the 'Glenluce Devil'.

GOBLIN

Although traditionally recognised as grotesque members of the fairy tribe, goblins appear to be very seldom encountered. They are generally believed to belong to myth along with the whole band of nature spirits. It is astonishing, therefore, to learn that as recently as the 1980s a man out with his dog was confronted by what he could only describe as a 'goblin'.

Understandably, in view of the nature of the event, the witness wishes to remain anonymous, but as he is fully aware that what happened was unusual and bizarre, he has freely talked about the evening in question. 'Martin' had been given a springer spaniel for his fortieth birthday, which he intended to train as a working dog. He chose as the training ground a site just outside East Kilbride, which whilst easily reached was in open countryside. Events, however, did not work out as planned, as he recounted.

'The dog had gone into the scrub woodland to my right and started chasing what I took to be a rabbit or hare. The dog was barking as it ran in a wide circle. I could see something in front of the dog. But I was surprised to see as I watched that there was something red on whatever it was he was chasing. A dark blood red. I thought maybe it was an injured animal, but it was going at some speed. The dog could never quite catch up with it and chased it round four or five times. They covered quite a bit of ground. The animal was moving closer to me by now and I realised that it was completely red. That was obviously puzzling. I whistled the dog over to me. But instead of the dog the creature he'd been chasing came over. I think it could have been the sound of the whistle that attracted it. I don't know where the dog went to at this time. He just fell quiet all of a sudden.'

Martin then experienced a unique and direct encounter. 'The creature came towards me through the heather. As it approached I could see that it was an owl-like shape. It had a rounded head on a very thick set neck. But the head was sunk into its shoulders. My mind was trying to tell me it must be an owl, but I knew it wasn't. It had square shoulders like a person. And as it got within 15 yards of me I thought "it's made of leather." It wasn't smooth. It was partly wrinkled like

a diver's suit when it comes out of the water. It didn't have
any arms or legs that I could see and just seemed to be gliding
along. It didn't seem to be making any sound. There was no
noise of it brushing against the heather as it passed by. It just
glided up towards me. I remember, however, that it was
bobbing up and down when it was being chased by the dog.
It moved as if it was bent forward. But when it came up to me
it was definitely standing upright. It had square shoulders
like a person, not falling away like a bird's. It just seemed to
be a body with a head and looked like something that had
been skinned or plucked. It was about 20 to 22 inches in
height. It wasn't skinny. It looked sturdy, in fact. It was a little
fat thing. And ugly. There were wrinkles on its face. No nose
or mouth. It had a large head compared to the body. It
looked completely solid, not like a phantom or ghost'.

In keeping with the rather fearsome reputation of these
entities the creature showed no fear, as Martin explained. 'It
came within six feet of where I was standing and looked up
at me. Two blue eyes just appeared out of nowhere on its face.
The eyes were almond-shaped, but up and down and not
sideways like a human's. There were no eyebrows or lashes.
And the thought went through my head: "it's a goblin!" I'd
seen something that shouldn't be here. Then it turned side on
and went off through the heather in the shrubland, in the
direction of a nearby farm. It went off fast. I headed for the car
and at that point the dog turned up. So I left the area right
away. I wasn't frightened, but I was concerned.'

Holding down a professional job, the witness had (and still
has) nothing to gain from recounting this experience. There
can be no doubt that he encountered a weird entity. But as we

have no sure way of telling one nature spirit from another we cannot be certain that the creature he saw that evening was a goblin and not another being from the normally invisible worlds around us. It should be borne in mind, though, that according to tradition goblins sometimes dressed in leather, which would be consistent with the description given by the witness. [*See also* Fairies]

GOLDEN TRIANGLE

Following the success of the book by Charles Berlitz on the 'Bermuda Triangle', every spot where there seemed to be a special focus of paranormal activity was deemed a 'triangle'. We had the 'Welsh Triangle', the 'Warminster Triangle', the 'Bonnybridge Triangle' and the 'Falkirk Triangle'.

The 'Golden Triangle' in Scotland refers to the area in West Lothian where there have been a disproportionate number of National Lottery winners. It achieved such fame that people from far and wide would drive to the area just to buy their lottery tickets.

But is there a paranormal explanation for this phenomenon? It has been suggested that perhaps those who win have 'seen' the numbers in advance through enhanced psychic powers. The area is well known as a UFO 'hot spot', so could there be a force (earth energy has been suggested) which affects people so that they become more psychically aware, and unconsciously catch a glimpse of the future, allowing them to choose the forthcoming winning numbers? It has all been very much in the realms of newspaper speculation, and only time will tell if the high success rate continues.

GOWDIE, ISOBEL

Though she lived in the 17th century Isobel Gowdie has become a key figure in the history of modern witchcraft [qv] or 'Wiccan' belief. She earned notoriety during her lifetime as a central figure in the Auldearn village [qv] witch trials.

At a time when witchcraft mania, having swept Europe for two centuries, was fading fast, her confessions made in the 1660s did not appear significant to her contemporaries. But to 20th-century writers who came to believe in the reality of witchcraft, the Gowdie confessions were of major importance in the understanding of an alleged religion centred around the worship of a horned god.

Isobel provided an amazing amount of detail in her confessions, which were made on four separate occasions between April 13th and May 27th 1662, apparently voluntarily without the customary application of torture. This fact, coupled with the extensive descriptions she gave of her activities, convinced later writers that she could not have invented all the incidents. She must have been talking of events that had actually taken place.

Isobel claimed that she had become a witch 15 years earlier, in 1647, when she was re-baptised with the name Janet by the

Devil himself, in a macabre ritual after she had renounced her Christian baptism. The ceremony which took place at Auldearn Church was said to involve the Devil sucking Isobel's own blood from her body and using it in the place of holy water. Isobel also explained to her interrogators that she would fly to the Sabbat, a regular ceremonial gathering of witches, after muttering an incantation. Here she would take part in various sexual acts with the Devil, as well as plotting mischief such as raising storms or ruining the crops of farmers who had displeased Satan. Isobel also told of how Satan would punish the witches of her coven with a beating when they failed him.

Many of these details could be found scattered within other witches' confessions, but the most significant aspect of Gowdie's statements was the suggestion that witchcraft was organised into covens of 13 witches. Her account is the only evidence that such groups existed, and has put a completely different slant on the idea of witchcraft, suggesting that witches could be active in small, local but determined groups, almost like a secret sect.

It was this detail within Isobel Gowdie's confession which convinced later writers—such as Margaret Murray, author of the ground-breaking but still controversial *The Witch Cult in Western Europe* and Montagu Summers, who wrote extensively on the subject—of the reality of witchcraft. Their conclusion was that what was being dealt with was an organised religion rather than a mass hallucination or mania. It was the writings of Murray in particular which provided a historical basis for witchcraft to which 20th-century followers of the craft could point as justification for their beliefs. Isobel Gowdie, through

Murray and other writers, sparked the modern revival of Wiccan religion with its covens of 13 witches.

Strangely, in spite of the details in the confessions we do not know Isobel's eventual fate. Her trial, if there was one, went unrecorded. Her statements, however, did survive largely intact, although parts have mysteriously disappeared— including any evidence which would allow us to identify the person who originally branded Isobel a witch.

GREEN LADY

If you saw a ghost would you expect it to be anything other than white in appearance? In fact, female ghosts of distinctive colour feature widely throughout the British Isles. Grey ladies, black ladies and even pink ladies have been regularly reported from various parts of the land. However, the legend of the 'Green Lady' appears largely confined to the castles and houses of Scotland. Green ladies can be found in all parts of the country from Comlogon Castle in Dumfriesshire to the Castle of Mey at the north-eastern tip of Scotland.

The green lady phenomenon is often linked to tales of heartbreak and young love unfulfilled. A broken relationship or a refusal to obey parental wishes leads to suicide or even the murder of the lass caught up in the tragedy, whose ghost then lives on as the green lady. However, despite her own personal unhappiness, the green lady is generally a friendly spirit, having no ill intent. A good example of this is the ghost known in folklore as 'Lady Greensleeves'.

Lady Greensleeves is a green lady who haunts not only Huntington tower on the outskirts of Perth but the surrounding estate. It has been recorded that on one occasion a young boy lay ill, close to death in a cottage on the estate. His widowed mother left him to fetch medicine from Perth, a return journey which in those days took at least three hours. When she arrived back at the cottage, she was amazed to find the lad sitting up in bed looking better than he had done in months. When he was asked what had happened, he told his mother that a 'bonnie lady' dressed in green had stroked his forehead, making him feel better straight away.

And in the tradition of the pagan 'Green Man' [qv], the ancient god of the forests, Lady Greensleeves protects as well as heals. An old man who lived outside Perth was rumoured to have a hidden store of cash. One day a band of thieves broke into the cottage and forced the old man to give them his savings. He handed over what he had but, not satisfied, they dragged him outside intending to beat out of him the location of his secret hiding place. As he lay on the ground he gazed over to Huntington tower. The robbers saw the stunned look in the old man's eyes and followed his gaze to the castle. There they saw the image of a beautiful women dressed in green silk, her eyes ablaze like fire, standing at an open window staring directly at them. The terrified gang immediately ran off.

Although many of Scotland's green ladies are benevolent spirits, there are exceptions. At Stirling Castle a green lady wearing a flowing dress is reputed to appear as a prophet of doom. It has been said that she is the ghost of one of Mary,

Queen of Scots' ladies-in-waiting who, according to legend, was burned to death while saving the Queen from a bed fire. In the 1820s a guard on sentry duty was found dead, his face fixed in a mask of terror at some unknown sight, just in the area where the green lady was known to appear.

Sometimes, however, the green lady turns up in unlikely places. In the early 1990s Lorraine McAllister was driving her mother home on the A91, which runs alongside the Ochil Hills. As they approached the village of Dollar a ghostly shape suddenly flew across the road in front of the car, almost hitting the windscreen. Although the incident was over in seconds, Lorraine was convinced that for a terrifying moment she had encountered the phantom of the green lady who has for decades been reputed to haunt this spot.

One explanation for so many sightings of the green lady may be the reputation of the colour green. It is regarded as unlucky, especially when worn by women. Do theses spirits, unfortunate in love when alive, carry a badge of their unhappiness into the afterlife? Or is the green glow around them simply an effect often reported by mediums, a phosphorescence, which appears when spirits 'come through' from the other side. But for an answer we may have to plunge into the realms of pagan mysticism. As well as a 'Green Man' there may be by his side a 'Green Woman'.

GREEN MAN

The 'Green Man' may be unfamiliar to us today, but at one time he was a key figure in traditional religious belief. In many places—particularly on tombstones—representations of the green man have survived into the present time as testimony to his former importance. On the simplest level he represents vegetation in all its forms—flowers, crops, fruit and forest. He was often visualised as a real person, a god become human. Such well known figures as Robin Hood [qv] and Herne the Hunter, people to be found living in and looking after the forest, can in fact be viewed as the green man. That may explain why Robin Hood was at one time as closely linked with Scotland as he was with England, though that link has largely died out north of the border.

The green man also represents life, and one of the most memorable stories associated with the King Arthur legend involves the 'Green Knight' who, having had his head cut off, picks it up and puts it on again—and becomes as good as new. So the 'green' of Summer is beheaded by the arrival of Winter and re-born again as the greenery re-emerges in Spring.

Clearly the green man is a figure from our pagan past. So why then do we find his likeness carved in churches and castles dating from a much later period? One notable example of this is Rosslyn Chapel [qv], near Edinburgh. There can be no doubt that it is an atypical church—the many pagan symbols carved all round its interior walls and ceiling bear witness to that, and there are many stone heads of the green man to be found there. But Rosslyn is merely one of the best known example of the type of green man carvings that can be found elsewhere in many older churches. Where you see a figure with vegetation sprouting from its mouth you know you are seeing the green man, a very ancient pagan symbol surviving within a Christian society.

But is the green man not simply a myth? So it might have been thought—until the 1990s when Adrian Cerrone took an amazing photograph. A picture of the green man himself, taken on that island of mystery, the reputed Avalon of legend and ancient druidic centre, the Isle of Arran. Cerrone's experience of the incident is down-to-earth. He was renting a cottage in the town of Lamlash and took a few photographs in the back garden. He saw nothing at the time, but when he developed the film an astonishing figure could be seen in one of the photographs. A green entity whose shape can be made out yet at the same time who seems to blend into the greenery of the hedge from which he is emerging. It could be astonishing, unique proof that the god of vegetation is not a myth and may still be among us, watching over the living fruit of the land. Arguably we need his presence now more than we ever did before.

GREY MAN OF BEN MACDHUI

Ben MacDhui in the Cairngorms is Scotland's second highest mountain. It is also the possible home of Scotland's answer to the yeti [qv], the 'Big Grey Man'. The mystery of Ben MacDhui stretches back into the last century, but it was first brought to widespread public attention by an incident involving Professor Norman Collie in 1891, although he did not talk openly about his experience on the mountain for over thirty years.

Collie was a veteran of climbs in the Alps and Himalayas, but his experiences on Ben MacDhui forever stood out in his mind. Climbing solo, he reached the summit just as a thick mist descended. As he began to make the descent, he heard loud crunching in the snow behind him. He assumed it was a fellow climber, although he was surprised that he had not noticed anyone on the way up. But as the footsteps continued, Collie realised that the strides being made were enormous. Several times the length of a human's. Collie was overcome with a terrible fear: 'I was seized with terror and took to my heels, staggering blindly among the boulders for four or five miles nearly down to Rothiemurchus Forest.' Collie concluded that there was 'something very queer about the top of Ben MacDhui', and he refused to go back there again alone.

Collie did not catch sight of an entity of any description, but other witnesses have reported encounters with a huge grey phantom-like being that appears out of the mist, and then disappears, leaving no clear tracks. Sceptics put this down to odd reflections caused by sunlight playing on mists and clouds, although it is not clear why such a natural phenomenon should strike so often in the one place.

In the years following Collie's experience, numerous people came forward with strange stories to tell—Peter Densham, who had worked in the Cairngorms during the Second World War and afterwards as a forester, Wendy Wood the Nationalist activist, Dr A M Kellas, another Himalayan climber, and Alexander Tewnion, the naturalist and photographer.

Recently, a possible solution to the phenomenon has been put forward in *Trail* magazine. In certain conditions the snow on high Scottish peaks thaws and freezes in such a way that, when walked on, an effect known as a 'double footfall' can be produced. Essentially, the impression made in the snow by a boot collapses a few seconds after the walker has moved on. The sound thus produced could explain the many reports of being followed by a creature which remains invisible and keeps pace with the person who is being 'followed'.

The 'giant figure' which has often been glimpsed may also have a fairly simple explanation—a phenomenon known as the 'Brocken Spectre' which occurs when, as a result of unusual weather conditions such as a temperature inversion, a person is standing between bright sunlight and a bank of mist. The resulting shadow that is cast on to the mist is often very large and, given the right circumstances, could easily be seen as a terrifying apparition such as the legendary grey man.

Those who have encountered the grey man generally disagree that there can be any natural explanation for what they have witnessed. Some say that the grey man is the spirit of the mountain, guarding its domain against intruders. Or the phantom of a dead, never discovered, mountaineer. Others suggest it is an ape-like being, a remnant of an ancient race, like the yeti of Tibet.

GREYFRIARS

Greyfriars Kirkyard in the heart of Edinburgh is one of the most famous sights of the capital's historic Old Town. Built in 1620 and restored in the 1930s, Greyfriars Kirk stands on the site of a mid-15th-century Franciscan Friary. Many famous, and some infamous, Scots are buried here—including the Earl of Morton, Regent to James VI; James Craig, the designer of the New Town; William Creech, publisher of Robert Burns and Adam Smith; and Sir George MacKenzie, the notorious prosecutor of the Covenanters who came to be known as 'Bluidy MacKenzie'.

More recently Greyfriars has become something of a spectral hot spot. Certain tombs within the Kirkyard—most notably that of Bluidy Mackenzie—have long been reputed to be haunted, but from late 1999 onwards witnesses have been reporting a spate of ghostly encounters within the Kirkyard. The media, both local and national, have become involved in this developing story, with mediums and psychic investigators being brought in to try to discover exactly what is going on. Many reports have highlighted the concentration of paranormal activity in the part of the Kirkyard known as The Covenanters' Prison—the place where Covenanters taken prisoner at the battle of Bothwell Bridge in 1679 were incarcerated. The conditions they endured were extremely harsh, and many did not survive their imprisonment. It has been suggested that this melancholy period of the Kirkyard's history is at the root of the modern day haunting.

The ghostly activity that has been reported recently includes strange noises and smells, but by far the most disturbing phenomena have been attacks by unseen assailants. *The Sunday Telegraph* reported the experience of a college lecturer who felt as though a hand was being pressed over her mouth as she walked through The Covenanters' Prison. She fainted and awoke to find herself sitting on the ground. The following day she noticed a strange bruise on her cheek and neck. She did not believe she had hurt herself when she fainted and attributed the marks to 'something to do with a ghost'. The report went on to claim that many other people had experienced similar assaults—49 visitors having been 'attacked', nine of whom had passed out.

In November 1999 an exorcism was performed in the Kirkyard, and during the ceremony a dark shape was seen moving inside the Kirk—even though it was locked and empty at the time. The exorcism itself seems to have had little effect on the ghostly inhabitants of Greyfriars and, as yet, the best efforts of the press, psychic investigators and mediums have failed to solve the enigma of Edinburgh's most haunted kirkyard.

HAMILTON, PATRICK

Set into the cobbles outside the entrance of St Salvator's College in St Andrews are the letters 'PH'. These are the initials of Patrick Hamilton, the first martyr of the Scottish Reformation, who was burned at the stake on this spot on 29th February 1528.

Born in 1504, Hamilton was a young aristocrat who had studied at Paris and Louvain and had been influenced by the teachings of Martin Luther. On his return to St Andrews, he began to preach these heretical doctrines. He was soon arrested, tried in the cathedral, and condemned to be burned at the stake. His executioners, however, were incompetent and the fire kept going out, with the result that Hamilton survived for several hours, before the flames finally caught hold and his terrible ordeal came to an end.

But it would seem that Hamilton's cruel fate has left an

indelible mark on St Andrews. Tradition has it that, at the moment of his death, the image of the martyr's face was supernaturally etched into the stonework of the tower directly above the place of execution. It is certainly the case that a strange image of a human face can still be seen on one of the stones at the front of St Salvator's Tower, just above the coat of arms of Bishop Kennedy.

Whether or not this is the death-mask of Patrick Hamilton, to this day it is considered bad luck for students at the University to step on the letters PH, which lie under the watchful gaze of the face on the wall.

HILL MAZES

Hill mazes remain a controversial phenomenon. If they exist what were they for? The word 'maze' is perhaps misleading— the ones that occur in Scotland were formed by a path which snakes its way around the hill in a number of encirclements, starting at the bottom and ending at the top.

The most obvious purpose for a path made in this way would be as a ceremonial road. Many ancient festivals were celebrated on the summit of a hill, and hilltops often had a special significance, being seen as nearer to the gods. Lugh or Lug, whose name survives in so many areas—Lugton in Ayrshire being the most obvious—was particularly associated with festivals of celebration held at a spot which looked over the surrounding area. As the son of the sun god, Lug's connection with hilltops is self-evident.

Locating examples of hill mazes is difficult. The snaking path around the mound at Dunkeld typifies the way a hill maze should look, but caution is necessary. The origin of the mound, which sits near the centre of Dunkeld, not far from the cathedral, is uncertain. It looks artificial, at least in part, and the path around it may or may not be of any considerable age. The same qualification applies to the Bass motte or hill at Inverurie. It is cut round by a steep path. But the motte may date only from Norman times and the path may be even more recent.

However, the link between paths, snakes and hills is traceable. Several traditional stories have come down to the present which have as their theme a hill guarded by a snake. In these accounts the animal wraps itself around the hill with its tail at the foot and its head resting on the summit. One tradition from Galloway concerns a white snake which took over a hill in the village of Dalry, on the bank of the River Ken. As described in *Tales from Galloway* (1979): 'a great white snake like a dragon took possession of the mote. It curled itself around the hill . . . its tail trailed down the hillside. Every day at the same hour the snake raised its head to the top of the mote'. The connection between the snake's body, the encircling path and a ceremony on the hilltop seems clear. But identifying hills where we can say with certainty that these events took place is now almost impossible—too much time has passed and too much knowledge has been lost. After 2,000 years of Christian practice we can only speculate over where and what our ancestors worshipped. [*See also* Dragon]

HOME, DANIEL

Daniel Home, a Scottish medium who achieved worldwide recognition, has come to be regarded as one of the key figures in the history of the Scottish paranormal.

From humble origins Home became, in a relatively short time, the most famous spiritualist medium of all time. The friend of royalty and the international élite of the time, his activities were reported in newspapers around the globe.

Born in 1836 near Currie, then a small village near Edinburgh, Home claimed descent from the aristocratic Home family of the Scottish Borders. His father, he said, was the illegitimate son of a relationship between his grandmother (a maid) and one of the young Homes. Research by the author has shown that Home's father was indeed paid regularly through a firm of Edinburgh solicitors by the Home family. So Home's account, which has been generally regarded as mere pretension, may well be correct. Such incidents are hardly unique in the history of the British aristocracy.

Home emigrated to the United States at a young age, and his psychic abilities developed suddenly when he was just 17. His fame developed rapidly and he was quickly taken up by the upper echelons of local American society including the élite in Boston. Contacts between America and Britain even at this period were extensive, and Home's abilities soon became known in Britain. He came to London via Liverpool and quickly developed a circle of upper- and middle-class admirers. As his fame spread, he gave séances for the Tsar of Russia and the rulers of France and the Netherlands among others. He himself married a Russian aristocrat.

Home exhibited a remarkable range of psychic talent. He regularly levitated, floating up to the ceiling of his sitters' drawing rooms, claiming that the spirits were pulling him towards Heaven; he could increase his height by several inches at will; he made phantom hands appear, and musical instruments play without anyone touching them; he could change his appearance so that he appeared to have taken on the form of dead relatives of his sitters. If he was the fraud some claim, he had a supreme ability to deceive because no one ever caught him in the act of cheating.

Throughout his life, controversy followed Home. He was seen as the standard-bearer of spiritualism, which in the 19th century seemed to be threatening established Christianity. Robert Browning wrote a poem bitterly attacking Home as 'Sludge the Medium'. He believed Home to be an expert conman who tricked people into believing that he could produce paranormal phenomena. But Home had important supporters, including the scientist Sir William Crookes who conducted experiments on Home which seemed to prove that he possessed paranormal ability, in particular psychokinesis— the ability to move objects without touching them. However, Crookes eventually abandoned these experiments after criticism from the scientific establishment.

Home's best known (and needless to say most controversial) demonstration of his supernatural power saw him floating out of a window only 17 inches wide, and back in through another window, thirty or more feet above the ground. Although this was witnessed by three of London's social élite sceptics refused (and still refuse) to accept that it actually took place. It is argued that it was another of Home's tricks. As recently as 1975, a book bitterly attacking Home as a fraud was published—proof of his continuing impact.

Home visited Scotland to give public séances, although he never returned to live in his native land. He always regarded himself as a Scot and in the books he wrote on spiritualism made much of his Highland blood which, he believed, had given him the power of 'second sight'. When he died in France in 1886 he was rightly viewed as the founding father of modern spiritualism. He remains the greatest medium of modern times.

HOOD, ROBIN

Robin Hood was at one time as closely linked to Scotland as he is now to England. In fact, some of the earliest written references to Robin Hood—such as that of the medieval chronicler John of Fordun, in his *Scotichronicon*—place him in the woods of southern Scotland. Up to the 16th century the May Day festivals regularly featured Robin Hood and Little John as leading participants in the celebrations, and it was a great honour to be chosen for these positions. Their significance, at least in the Lothians, can be judged by the fact that two stone towers of Roslin Castle near Edinburgh were named 'Robin Hood' and 'Little John' in honour of the men in green.

Religious pressure gradually brought about the end of many festival days, and the tradition of Robin Hood died with them. The memory of Robin as a Scottish hero has now completely vanished from our consciousness.

This appears to have been a general trend throughout England and Scotland, with many sites south of the border at one time claiming a link with Robin Hood. Only Nottingham and Sherwood forest have maintained that connection.

The widespread celebration of Robin Hood suggests that he was not a real person, but a mythical entity—a god of the forest. And it was Robin Hood's link to a pagan past which brought about his fall. A Church led by preachers in the mould of John Knox rejected the mystical side of life which they regarded as mere superstition. The recent revival of pagan celebrations on the ancient festival days has not yet included the reappearance of Robin Hood, but it is surely only a matter of time before he resumes his rightful place.

HOSPITAL GHOSTS

Hospitals are an area where you would expect to see many ghosts—they are places where people die, often in unpleasant and tragic circumstances. While there is no doubt that ghosts are regularly seen in the hospital environment, there is a reluctance amongst staff to talk openly about supernatural events they have witnessed. It is noticeable that the press and television do not publicise such incidents in the same way as they do hotel, domestic or castle hauntings. However, that hospitals do experience paranormal incidents is clear from the following cases. The identity of each witness has been withheld for obvious reasons.

A medical student reported the following event which took place in the 1990s in a Scottish hospital.

'As a medical student I had to do an "on-call" session one evening. Mine had run over, so it was about 12.45 a.m. by the time I was ready to leave. At that time of night, the corridors had minimum lighting and were deserted. I walked down to the main foyer area, continuously glancing around me due to the silence which was only broken by the sound of my own footsteps. I decided to phone a taxi. As I was waiting for someone to answer I looked back towards the corridor where I had just come from and there, standing about three metres away, was a young child. He couldn't have been more than four years old. It was a cold misty February and he was standing smiling at me, wearing only a pair of shorts and a T-shirt. I tried to think of all the possible reasons why he would be there on his own at that time in the morning. The paediatric ward was a locked ward, so he couldn't have got out from there. And anyway it was situated on the other side of the building through many heavy fire doors. The hospital didn't have an Accident & Emergency unit so he couldn't have accompanied anyone in an emergency. Even if he had, it wouldn't explain how he had managed to come behind me down the corridor silently. Or why he was dressed in only a T-shirt and shorts on such a cold night. I do not know where he went to after this as I turned and walked away. I wish I hadn't now, but that's easier said than done when you find yourself in a situation like that!'

The following odd events were reported by an experienced nurse as having occurred in 1991 at an Edinburgh hospital.

'I was on the 4 p.m. to 9 p.m. shift. At 4.30 p.m. the nurse

I was on with asked me if I could hear a high-pitched whistling noise in my ears. I told her that I could, but that it did not bother me as there was a patient at the top of the ward receiving oxygen which made a similar noise. About half an hour later the nurse became rather distressed. She had taken two patients to the toilets which are situated at the far end of the ward. The high-pitched whistle had become very intense inside her ears, like a hearing aid. It could not have been due to the oxygen all that distance away at the top of the ward. She stated that she felt strange and dizzy. We both went down to the toilets to check. Our ears were now receiving an extremely high-pitched noise like a signal of some sort. Internal rather than external.'

Both nurses now experienced a 'bleeping' noise, and both sounds continued for several hours without anyone being able to detect the source. It was a disturbing situation, as the witness reported. 'We began to feel strange and rather alarmed. My nursing colleague asked me to check if any of the visitors had a hearing aid, security device or . . . digital watch . . . but all of this drew a blank. Staff nurse was by this time rather flustered . . . visibly shaken and looked frightened, but said she was not afraid. She kept putting her hands up to cover her ears. At one point in the dining room a very loud whistle in my left ear nearly knocked me off my seat. The bleeping and whistling continued all of the shift even at the bus stop, but began to fade away on the bus home.'

Whistling is associated with poltergeist activity, as are strange noises in general. However, there is no evidence that, apart from the unexplained sounds, anything odd was happening on the ward at the time. Perhaps the incident had a natural explanation, although it is hard to know what that could be. Or maybe it was the result of a build-up of the mysterious 'earth energy' which we know can affect people in many different ways. It is interesting that the effect on the witness gradually diminished the further she travelled from the hospital. Would apparitions have begun to appear had the phenomenon continued? There is no way of knowing, as there are no circumstances under which ghosts inevitably appear. But these incidents do show that the paranormal is no stranger to hospitals. It is simply reported less.

HOTEL GHOSTS

Ghosts appear as often in hotels as they do in castles. Which is reasonable if these apparitions really are spirits of the dead. A hotel or pub seems as good a place as any to haunt. Some argue it is too good—sceptics have voiced the suspicion that claiming a bar is haunted is generally good for business, so experienced 'ghost hunters' tend to investigate such reports especially carefully. A house owner experiencing ghostly incidents might be less prepared to call for help as he has no desire to attract attention to his home, whereas for obvious reasons those restraints do not apply to owners of hotels and pubs.

It is clear that hauntings do affect these places, a large number of which have stood on the same spot for many years, perhaps for centuries. And given the nature of the hotel and pub trade, which encourages general social chat, it is likely that incidents which might go unreported elsewhere do become more widely known. The pub ghost is a well-established facet of the paranormal phenomenon.

There does not seem to be a 'typical' hotel or pub ghost. The Dreadnought Hotel [qv] in Callander has experienced a long period of ghostly events. But perhaps the most unusual is that of the Campsie View Hotel in Lennoxtown. Here the ghost of a previous owner is still believed to haunt the place. Incidents typical of ghost and poltergeist activity regularly disturb the routine of the staff, who try their best to carry on as normal. The juke box would be playing music in the morning when the cleaners arrived, and cans of drink would be lying on tables as if someone had been having a party. Room lights have been switched on and off. The telephone might be constantly engaged at the same time every day.

In March 1999 the hotel owner, Ian Currie, had an encounter with the ghost who was thought to be the source of the haunting, a past owner called Norrie Smith who died in unfortunate circumstances. According to Currie: 'the incidents seem to be concentrated in the upper bar. When Norrie was here this was the main area of the hotel. He had accommodation just off it. It was here that I saw a white figure of some kind. It was like a thick cloud of fog. It just floated by. It moved along a straight line from one corner of the bar right across to where Norrie used to live.' Norrie had apparently claimed: 'This place won't work without me', and his attachment to the hotel appears to be so strong that his spirit refuses to move on to the next world.

In the case of the 'P J Lyles' bar in Edinburgh, the source of the disturbance experienced in 1996 was attributed to a disgruntled regular whose spirit had returned because of changes made to the layout of the pub. The landlady, Elaine Christie, claimed that as she and the staff were clearing up one Friday evening they 'heard footsteps running across the ceiling above us. The footsteps continued running right through a wall.' They were understandably unnerved by the incident. Poltergeist activity was also in evidence when the assistant manager, Rick Flett, had to turn out one night to switch off an activated burglar alarm. According to Rick: 'When I got there the alarm had turned itself off and been reset. Upstairs some curtains stuck over windows had been ripped down and a potted plant moved. There's no way anyone could have got into the pub because it was securely locked.'

Hotels and pubs clearly do not escape the attentions of the spirit world. Events in these places up and down the land add weight to the argument that ghosts and poltergeists are not the product of an over-imaginative mind, but genuine phenomena. But as with domestic incidents, the inquiring mind has to wonder why a haunting starts and ends at the hotel door. Why does an apparition appear at the foot of the stairs or in a particular room, but not move off the premises, just as a house ghost does not normally follow the occupant to work? It may possibly be due to currents of energy which build up within a confined space. This intense energy, helped perhaps by the human activity inevitably found inside a hotel or pub, may allow what we regard as phantoms to appear.

HOT SPOTS

Why do we have 'hot spots', areas where there are intense and prolonged bursts of paranormal activity? In recent years the village of Bonnybridge [qv] near Falkirk became well known as a world UFO hot spot. It has been claimed that during the 1990s there were thousands of sightings of unidentified flying objects in its vicinity, although it now seems that this was an exaggeration. However, there is no doubt that UFO hot spots do exist and that Bonnybridge was one of them. If the area between Edinburgh and Stirling (and Bonnybridge lies at the heart of it) is compared to the rest of Scotland, then the startling figure emerges that this part of the country accounts for over 50% of all UFO reports. On the basis of population alone you would expect a much lower figure.

Attempts have been made to explain the phenomenon of the Bonnybridge UFO hot spot from a number of different angles—from a straightforward rational approach, relating incidents to air traffic movement (Edinburgh and Cumbernauld airports are close by), to the out-and-out psychic theory that the area is a 'window into other dimensions'. However, there has been no conclusive solution. Just as baffling is the fact that UFO hot spots move around the country. In the 1950s East Lothian experienced a wave of sightings, as did the city of Aberdeen. In the 1970s an area stretching from Moffat into Dumfriesshire was allegedly visited by several hundred unidentified objects [see Byers, Joyce]. So why do hot spots switch from one area to another?

Does each type of paranormal phenomenon bring with it a particular focus of activity? Phantom pumas [qv] have been reported from most parts of Scotland. However, as with UFOs, there were a few areas—notably Ayrshire and Inverness—which witnessed more than their share of incidents. Both locations reported numerous sightings in the 1970s, but while those further north gradually died down Ayrshire has remained an area where phantom pumas regularly appear.

Loch monsters [*see* Ness, Loch; Morar, Loch] might be viewed as inevitably more likely to be seen where deep lochs are to be found. So would it be wrong to think of 'hot spots' in this context? If, however, we consider loch monsters in the context of large, unexplained creatures, the 'shifting hot spot' phenomenon re-emerges. Dragons [qv] were once far more numerous than inland monsters of the deep are today—they were reported in considerable numbers from various locations across central Scotland. Now, of course, these creatures are seen as pure myth. Dragon hot spots have long disappeared, to be replaced in the 20th century by water monsters and their closely defined areas of activity.

Ghosts [qv] and poltergeists [qv] are widely distributed—more widely than any other unexplained incidents—and might be regarded as an exception to the rule. There are no hot spots, only widespread activity which touches almost every town and village and every aspect of life. Nevertheless, if there is an area where they seem to occur with greater regularity, then it would have to be Glasgow [qv]. Not only because of its numerous cases of domestic spirit encounters, but also its many public places where hauntings are regularly reported—museums, theatres, gaming halls and railway stations—Scotland's biggest city appears to be a thriving forum for spirits of the departed.

One curious aspect is that hot spots involving different

phenomena often seem to re-occur in the same area after intervals as long as hundreds of years. The witch craze of the late 1500s focused strongly on the Edinburgh area, especially East Lothian. In the 1950s the same part of the country was hit by the UFO phenomenon, and Edinburgh today can be regarded once more as a UFO hot spot in its own right. And in the 1990s witchcraft [qv] as 'Wicca' made a reappearance in the capital with, it was claimed, at least a dozen covens—far more than the rest of Scotland put together.

HYPNOSIS

Hypnosis has become a tool used by paranormal investigators in a variety of contexts. It has also led to much controversy. Its main application has been in relation to the alien abduction phenomenon, although it is also extensively practised in delving into people's alleged 'past lives'. However, in Scotland it is its use with 'abductees' which has hit the headlines.

Hypnotists have been brought in to draw out, it is claimed, an abductee's lost memory of his or her experience. Key to the use of hypnotism in these circumstances has been the assumption that alien entities have the ability to erase or block the memory of those they have taken away. Hypnosis, so it is argued, releases the blocked memory. Colin MacKerracher, who has had extensive experience using hypnotic regression, describes an incident with an abductee he 'put under': 'When I tried asking him for more information about the entities he suddenly reacted and told me "You're not to know." This was a block left in his mind by the aliens to stop us finding out things about them they don't want us to know.'

Although hypnotism has been used extensively in the United States, in Britain the longest established UFO organisation, BUFORA (the British UFO Research Association), long ago banned its use by field investigators on the grounds of its unreliability. The argument is that there are no guarantees that hypnosis is revealing memories that have been 'lost'—it could instead be creating them, something that has come to be known as 'false memory syndrome'. Under hypnosis the abductee may be bringing together a whole variety of events, from fiction as well as fact, and turning them into a UFO encounter. This is not to say that an abduction incident has not occurred. Only that we cannot be sure that the 'recovered' memory accurately reflects the real events.

In Scotland the use of hypnosis was central to the A70 abduction case of August 1992 involving Gary Wood [qv] and Colin Wright. Although a strange object was encountered on the road while both witnesses were fully conscious, there was no memory of an abduction incident till Colin and Gary were hypnotically regressed. All the details that emerged from these sessions, such as meeting skinny grey aliens and other entities, were brought out by hypnosis—they were not consciously recalled. A number of ufologists have, therefore, expressed doubts that they accurately reflect the events of that night. That is not to say that the witnesses did not encounter extra-terrestrial beings, but that hypnosis does not provide real evidence.

Hypnosis as a means of recovering memories of past

lives, or as proof of reincarnation [qv], is used by several Scottish practitioners. As with the abductee experience, the same criticism is made: can we be sure that the memories of living in past centuries are genuine recollections, and not mere fantasy? However, it is perhaps too hasty to dismiss the link between hypnotism and the paranormal out of hand—there may be a use for it under properly controlled conditions. And should not those who have been hypnotically regressed be the best judges of its benefits or failings? According to A70 abductee Gary Wood: 'before the hypnosis I was scared to sleep at night. I realise now that whatever took me away wasn't going to hurt me, and I learned that through the hypnosis sessions.'

I

IONA

Now seen solely as an important Christian centre, bizarre incidents on the small island of Iona suggest that it has had a strange past. It is well known that Christian missionaries took over sites which had been centres of the pagan worship they replaced, and although linked to the Christian zeal of St Columba, Iona may well have been one of these. Islands situated just off the mainland were often attractive to druids—Anglesey (Ynys Mon) across the Menai Straits from north Wales, and Arran off the west coast of Scotland, were key pagan centres, and Iona might have served a similar purpose.

The meaning of the name 'Iona' is uncertain. It may or may not have some link with Columba. Allegedly, its 'older' name is correctly Icolmkill ('isle of Columba of the church'). But tradition has it that the island was inhabited for many centuries before Columba arrived, though we have no idea what it was called in the remote past. It may be useful to remember that the word 'ion' was in fact once used to describe horses of around one year old. We know that the Iceni, a horse-worshipping tribe, had associations with groups up the west coast of Scotland who also worshipped the horse god. This is not to argue that this is how Iona's name came about. But we should be careful before assuming that Christianity completely erased earlier memories, even though the physical remains of our pagan past may have long gone.

A centre of Christianity though it may be, Iona's pagan links continue to re-emerge from time to time. While visiting Iona in the 1960s, the mystic and psychic Robert Crombie [qv] described how he saw the ancient pagan god Pan 'in the Hermit's cell, a ring of stones which is all that is left of the cell where St Columba used to go in retreat.' According to Crombie, Pan told him: 'I am the servant of almighty God, and I and my subjects are willing to come to the aid of mankind in spite of the way he has treated us and abused nature, if he affirms belief in us and asks for our help.'

More dramatic and tragic was the unsolved case in 1929 of Norah Fornario [see Psychic Murder]. Its significance lies in the contrast between the circumstances of Fornario's death and the spirit of the island. Her death is the only case in Scotland where psychic forces have been openly suspected. Fornario's body was found on open ground dressed only in a cloak used in ritual magic, a knife clasped in her hand. She had been involved with psychic groups, but did she go to Iona hoping for spiritual protection, or as part of someone else's plan to raise psychic power for a purpose never discovered?

Whatever the answer to the mystery of Norah Fornario,

there can be no doubting one fact: those who believe in a mystical aspect to life are convinced that there is a special power running though the remote island of Iona.

J

JACOB'S PILLOW

The 'Stone of Destiny' has a strong hold on the imagination of Scots. But is it simply sentiment or is there something more powerful at work?

There is a long tradition that the Stone of Destiny was the same rock which in Biblical legend Jacob used one night as a pillow. As he slept he dreamt of a ladder which reached from Earth to Heaven, and he heard God's voice. In modern times, this tradition has been interpreted in different ways. To some Jacob was in touch with beings from another world. To others he was making contact with spirit entities. But it is widely agreed that the rock must have acted as a key of some kind.

Legend has it that the Stone of Destiny came to Scotland by way of Egypt and Ireland. It had a reputation as an object possessing great paranormal powers. Some say it still has, and point to the fact that within three years of the Stone's return to Scotland a parliament—the first for 300 years—was set up. Interestingly, this parliament held its first meetings a short distance from where the Stone now sits on display in Edinburgh Castle.

Central to the role of stones in magic is the belief that where they are situated is the key to their influence. It is argued that lines of invisible energy run across the Earth [*see* Ley Lines], unrecognised by science but tracked by modern dowsers [*see* Dowsing]. Stones tap into this energy, then release and control it. The Stone's energy might have been untapped while it lay in Westminster Abbey, where it was taken by Edward I in 1296, because it was put in a place it was never intended to be. All that would change when in 1996 it was returned to Scotland by the then Conservative government.

Following this argument leads to the conclusion that the choice of Scone [qv] in Perthshire as the site of the coronation of many Scottish kings would have been no accident. The Stone of Destiny, on which the king sat to be crowned, would be at its most powerful at this exact spot. The monarch would perhaps feel, as Jacob before him, strange currents flow into his body—the power of the Earth would have passed through him, channelled by the stone. There is an ancient tradition that the land and the king are one and the same, that as the monarch thrives so does the land. An object like the Stone of Destiny would serve as the mystical link between the two.

JERUSALEM

Could scholars have got it wrong when they placed the Jerusalem of the Bible in the Middle East? According to William Comyns Beaumont, journalist and author, previous writers were thousands of miles out and the true site of the Biblical Jerusalem was actually Edinburgh, with Arthur's Seat identified as the Mount of Olives of the gospels. Beaumont reached this extraordinary conclusion after studying ancient Biblical texts, with the help of clues derived from a wide variety of sources, including Greek writings and Pictish carved stones.

Beaumont, at least to his own satisfaction, rewrote ancient history, arguing that the people we call the Phoenecians and Greeks lived not in the Mediterranean but in Scotland. Mount Olympus was not to be found in today's Greece, but was in fact located in Scotland—the mountain we know today as Ben Nevis. A cataclysmic natural disaster, possibly a comet strike, which occurred as recently as 2,000 years ago, had driven the inhabitants from this country to settle in Egypt and Greece. They had taken with them their accounts of past events and renamed the places they moved to with the names they were familiar with in Scotland. According to Beaumont, that was how Jerusalem came to be handed down the generations as a Middle Eastern city, when the religious events forever linked to it actually took place on land overlooking the Firth of Forth.

In two densely argued books, *The Riddle of Prehistoric Britain* and *Britain the Key to World History* published in the 1950s, Beaumont backed up his unlikely claims with extensive evidence. Understandably, his arguments were not accepted by orthodox historians, and have been dismissed out of hand by the Christian Churches. If Beaumont was correct, it would mean rewriting the last 3,000 years of Western history. Despite the outlandish nature of his theories, Beaumont did, however, gain a following in both the USA and Scotland and, at least up to the 1970s, a William Comyns Beaumont Society flourished in Edinburgh trumpeting his views. [See also Jesus]

JESUS

Could Scotland have closer links to the life of Jesus than we have been led to believe? Might Jesus even have been a Scottish druid? And could Pontius Pilate have belonged to the same sect and helped Jesus to escape after he supposedly died on the cross?

In fact, there is a long-standing tradition that Jesus was born in Scotland, and that Pilate was born at Fortingall, Perthshire. But a more reasonable (though still astonishing) version of events is that Jesus as a young man was involved with various mystic sects, travelling through Europe to learn from them. And it is at this point that Jesus' uncle, Joseph of Arimathea, enters the picture. Joseph is famous as the man who in legend took the Holy Grail, the vessel used at the last supper, to Glastonbury in England. But it is possible that Joseph, who was a merchant, visited both England and Scotland and brought the young Jesus with him on his travels. So Jesus could have come into contact with British druids from an early age, and returned in later life to learn their mystic ways.

The latest thinking on Jesus' involvement in Scotland, inspired by the research of writers Gordon Strachan and Barry Dunford, fits in with a growing belief in advanced mystic circles that Jesus was not only married with children, but may even have escaped death on the cross. In the aftermath of the crucifixion, it is claimed he fled to Europe and possibly came to Scotland. Even if Jesus did die on the cross his followers may—like the Knights Templar of later years—have found Scotland a safe haven. At Fortingall there is an ancient yew, said to be 5,000 years old, which may be an indication of how this area was sacred to pre-Christian religious groups. If Pontius Pilate was connected to this area and was linked to Jesus, it may explain why Jesus' followers made it their new home.

Though the evidence for a Scottish connection is there— Barry Dunford has drawn attention to a carving of Christ on the cross wearing a kilt—it is so at odds with the traditional account of Jesus' life and upbringing that it is likely to remain highly controversial. [*See also* Jerusalem]

K

KIRK, REV ROBERT

Robert Kirk (1641–1692) can be considered as one of Scotland's earliest known abductees. And an unlikely one at that. A Church of Scotland minister at Aberfoyle in the 1680s, Kirk claimed that he had regularly met and communicated with fairy folk [qv]. His meeting place was a wooded hillside situated a mile or so from the village, a spot still known today as the 'Fairy Knowe' [qv]. In 1691 Kirk published a book entitled *The Secret Commonwealth* in which he described his contacts with the fairy people, and some of their characteristics.

His account can sound strangely familiar. The description he gave of the fairies' capacity to enter a house unseen are echoed today in the appearance of entities which we label 'extraterrestrials' inside an abductee's home. Other features recalled by Kirk, such as the fairies' fires which blazed without wood or coal, and strange lights which burned without an obvious power source, would be less puzzling to contemporary society. Even so, they do open up fresh mysteries as to what fairies really are.

To Kirk, however, the fairies were real people and he wrote how they would 'remove to other lodgings at the beginning of each quarter of the year', that the food they ate was 'exactly clean, and served up by pleasant little children like enchanted puppets' and that 'their apparel and speech is like that of the people and country under which they live.' Kirk claimed that the fairies were 'distributed in tribes and orders and have children, nurses, marriages, deaths and burials [and are] in appearance even as we.' However, their bodily structure was not the same as humanity's, as they possessed 'light changeable bodies (like those called astral) somewhat of the nature of a condensed cloud and best seen in twilight.' Kirk made a powerful attempt to explain the nature of fairies with the aim of convincing the sceptical world of his time that they did exist.

Little is known about Kirk's life or why he became so involved in communicating with fairies. And the manner of his death has remained controversial. According to some accounts he died a natural death and lies buried in Aberfoyle Kirk. Others, however, have claimed that he was taken away by the fairies one day as he sat with them on the Fairy Knowe. This last incident might well be invention, although abduction by fairies was as well established then as abduction by aliens is today. Whatever the truth it is clear that Kirk himself had a genuine belief in the existence of fairy people.

KNIGHTS TEMPLAR

A medieval military order, founded during the Crusades, the Knights Templar were once an important part of Scottish society. Largely forgotten today, a measure of their former influence can be seen in the many place names with 'Temple' in them found throughout the country—a sign that the land was once owned by the Templars. It is only in the last 20 years, with the revival in Scotland of the Templar movement, that there has been greater appreciation of the role they played in our history. The Templars played a significant part in the Battle of Bannockburn, and some have suggested that the battle's date—24th June, the Feast of St John, and a key date in the Templar calendar—was chosen for its mystical significance.

There is no doubt that the story of the Knights Templar is swathed in occult rumours and arcane mystery. The movement had an odd relationship with Christianity, sometimes giving the impression of having more interest in other religions—a strange attitude, as the Templars were founded in 1191 to protect Christian pilgrims and wage war on those opposed to Jesus' message. Large areas of eastern Europe were still pagan at this time and the Holy Land was under Muslim control. So did the Templars, as they came into contact with pagan worshippers and the sophisticated Arab world, gain mystical knowledge about the spirit domain and learn lost secrets of their own religion?

On Friday 13th October 1307, the vast Templar empire of wealth, land and property was destroyed in one night by Phillip IV of France, working hand in hand with Pope Clement V. The leaders were arrested and, allegedly, confessed to being Devil worshippers and engaging in various bizarre occult activities. While it would be unwise to take these alleged confessions at face value, it is nevertheless clear that the Templars, at least at their higher levels, saw Christianity in a broader context—and held beliefs that did not fit with the narrower view that the Church had developed of the faith.

Many individual Templars managed to escape, or were allowed to escape, the persecution and made their way to Scotland, and a Templar fleet sailed into the port of Leith. Scotland was a key destination, but the reason for this is not immediately clear. It is true that in those days, as an independent country, Scotland had its own voice in international affairs. But this does not explain why the Templars decided to set up home here, or why they were made welcome. It is likely, though, that Scotland had a strong mystical attraction, and there must have been many influential people here who shared the Templars' interest in the supernatural aspect of religion.

Rumours have continued down the centuries that, when they fled to Scotland, the Templars brought with them several astonishingly important objects. These included the Holy Grail, discovered during their crusades in the Holy Land, and the 'head of Christ', probably a representation in stone or marble of Jesus of Nazareth. Most important of all, and the alleged reason for the Pope's determination to see them destroyed, they also took with them 'proof' that Jesus, far from being celibate, was married, and that Jesus' blood line continued through his direct descendants. It is claimed that these artefacts and perhaps even the documents are hidden away at secret locations. Rosslyn Chapel [qv] in Midlothian has emerged as a favoured location, as it has well-documented links with the Templars. However, so many sites have Templar connections (and more are being discovered) that it is not yet possible to reach a firm conclusion as to the nature of the Templars' secret insights into the worlds of mystery, Christianity and the paranormal.

L

LEWIS INCIDENT

An unsolved mystery began off the coast of the Outer Hebrides on the afternoon of 26th October 1996. It started at 4.10 p.m. when several witnesses on the island of Lewis observed a massive explosion in the sky. Strangely, according to the Stornoway coastguard, no one rang up about the sighting till 5 p.m., almost an hour after the incident. RAF Kinloss later claimed that it was around this time that they had been alerted by the first reports of the incident.

Initial accounts seemed to indicate that a large object, perhaps an aircraft fuselage, had been seen crashing into the sea. One witness also claimed to have seen an orange ball in the sky with a solid object beside it just before the explosion. In spite of the evidence that a serious incident had occurred, there followed a two-hour delay before an air search got under way. And it was not till 10.35 p.m. (six hours after the first

Above: When Avril McGuire photographed a painting on her living room wall, this extraordinary image was produced. It bears no resemblance to the actual painting (*right*), and seems to be a view of an old shop, later identified as having once been part of the building in which the photograph was taken

Above: The 'Green Man', captured on film by Adrian Cerrone, outside a cottage at Lamlash on the Isle of Arran

Left: Aleister Crowley, master of the occult and self-styled 'wickedest man in the world'

Right: Boleskine House, near Foyers on the shore of Loch Ness—once the home of Aleister Crowley, and now reputed to be haunted

Opposite above:
Glamis Castle—Scotland's
most haunted building

Opposite below:
Bob Taylor identifying the
site of his close encounter
with a UFO on Dechmont
Law near Livingston

Right: The extraordinary
'Apprentice Pillar' of
Rosslyn Chapel near
Edinburgh

Below: Rosslyn Chapel—
said to be the last resting
place of the Ark of the
Covenant and the
Holy Grail

Opposite above: The Haunted Tower, St Andrews, where a grim discovery was made by a group of antiquarians in 1868

Opposite below: Warner Hall's paranormal painting, a print of *The Bombardment of Algiers*, in which demonic faces have been seen

Right: The sheet of scrap paper on which a ghostly face mysteriously appeared during a pub quiz in Falkirk in June 1998. *Inset:* close-up of the face

Below: Flannan Lighthouse —the disappearance of the keepers in December 1900 remains one of Scotland's most enduring enigmas

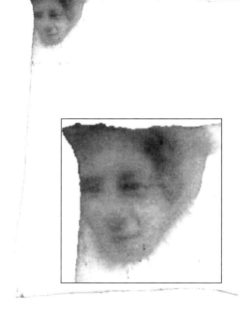

Above: The Royal Mile 'ghost' (*circled*), photographed close to a doorway on Castle Hill in Edinburgh by David Knott in August 1987.
Inset: close-up view of the ghost

Above: Loch Morar—home of an ancient monster? *Below left:* Iona—scene of a fatal 'psychic attack' in November 1929. *Below right:* Callanish stone circle

Above: Is this the face of Patrick Hamilton, who was burned at the stake in 1528?

Right: St Salvator's Tower in St Andrews, site of Patrick Hamilton's execution. The strange image above can still be seen, etched into its stonework

Opposite: Greyfriars Kirkyard—one of Edinburgh's most haunted places, currently witnessing a series of disturbing spectral visitations, including attacks by 'unseen assailants'

Above: St Rule's Tower, St Andrews—the site of Victorian
ghost-hunter William Linskill's lonely Halloween vigil

reports) that an emergency alert was broadcast to ships in the area.

So what had crashed? If the military are to be believed, it was simply a false alarm. But how could so many witnesses be mistaken? Several reports indicate that the explosion was strong enough to light up the sky with an orange glow— evidence which must cast doubt on the military's version that nothing of any interest occurred. And was the delay between the time the incident took place and the alleged receipt of the first reports an attempt to hide the fact that the military were aware of what had happened? Suspicion was further fuelled by a massive NATO exercise held in the same stretch of water on Monday 4th November, just a week after the Lewis incident. It was argued that this was just coincidence, and that the exercise had been planned for some time. But it would also have provided an excellent cover story if Western governments wanted to carry out a detailed search of the area

The authorities went to extraordinary lengths to play down these events. The military issued a statement claiming that nothing had shown up on radar. This was clearly intended to cast doubts on eyewitness reports that an object of some kind had been seen. Was the object able to avoid radar detection? If so you would think it would lead the military to ask questions, and there can be little doubt that they have, in fact, done so. However, as it is a matter of routine for the military to cover up such matters, in the understandable belief that secrecy is essential in matters of national security, the public is unlikely to discover the truth for a long time.

However, this in no way proves that an alien spacecraft penetrated our air space near the Butt of Lewis. At the moment there is no evidence that this incident was Scotland's underwater Roswell, but the question of exactly what it was that crashed into the sea on 26th October 1996 remains unanswered.

LEY LINES

Are there strange lines of energy, unknown to science, running beneath the surface of the Earth? And did our prehistoric ancestors choose precise locations for monuments so that they would be aligned with one another?

The evidence that standing stone circles, forts and other prehistoric sites had been deliberately built on a common alignment was produced as far back as the 1920s by an amateur archaeologist, Alfred Watkins. Watkins made the discovery while investigating the countryside of Herefordshire, but what he learnt could be applied to our ancient heritage throughout the British Isles. Watkins called these lines 'leys' and saw them as a system of ancient trackways linking sites by the shortest, most direct, route.

Later generations interpreted his ideas in a more mystical way, and it is in this context that Scotland has made a contribution to the idea of leys. Watkins, a businessman, saw nothing mystical about the lines he had discovered. To him they had a practical purpose, but there is nothing incompatible between his discovery and the way that his ideas have been developed north of the border.

Watkins' original ideas have been applied to the Scottish landscape and there is no doubt that the pattern he first recognised in Herefordshire can also be found in Scotland. Harry Bell in Glasgow, the author in Edinburgh, and David Cowan in Perthshire have uncovered many instances where several buildings and historical sites all lie on straight lines. Stretching across Glasgow, one ley starts at Cadzow Castle, runs through Coatshill (a bronze age cist), then to Carmyle Ford, continues to a bronze age burial site, cuts through the Necropolis, on to Cairn Hill, then Castlehill Roman Fort and ends at Duncolm—a total distance covered of around 20 miles. It is noticeable that the sites linked cover a variety of historical periods. A similar pattern occurs in Edinburgh, where a ley runs from a prehistoric monument on Arthur's Seat, passes through two Christian churches, touches the wall of Edinburgh Castle, bisects Queensferry Road at the crossroads where it meets Princes Street and Lothian Road, cuts through Dean cemetery and terminates at Blackhall Church. A distance of several miles.

Sceptics have argued that these alignments are all pure chance, particularly as the straight lines run through sites of varying ages. You might start with an ancient monument and on a ley running for several miles have a medieval church, a castle, a well of unknown date, and so on. In other words a pattern has been created by the modern mind where one does not exist. It certainly casts doubt on Watkins' belief that leys formed an ancient roadway, as thousands of years of history might separate one site from another.

However, it is in responding to this criticism that Scottish thinking about leys has come into its own. The view north of

the border is that though Watkins was right about the alignments he was wrong about the nature of leys. These are in fact
lines of energy or 'force' running underneath the surface of
the Earth, which we respond to consciously or unconsciously.
Our prehistoric ancestors were aware of leys and deliberately
planned buildings to lie over them. Medieval builders may or
may not have been consciously aware of this, but responded
just the same. More modern people were probably not aware
of them as society has lost the feeling of being at one with
nature. But architects, builders and planners still cannot help
linking into the energy, so that contemporary buildings, even
football grounds, may be located so as to benefit from the
strange forces beneath the Earth.

Scottish dowsers [see Dowsing] like David Cowan have used
the idea of leys as underground lines of force to explain various
incidents, from the state of an individual's health to the
appearance of ghosts and poltergeists. Ideas on the subject
have been germinating for a long time. As far back as the
1920s investigators in Germany linked water flowing beneath
the ground in hidden streams to high rates of illness. It was
believed that energy fields were created which injured the
body's defence systems. The hard-headed Germans still take
these invisible forces into account when siting public buildings.
The Chinese have for thousands of years made use of Feng
Shui, a system which seeks to bring the earth spirit into
harmony with the heavenly spirit through balancing beneficial
and harmful energy by the careful location of buildings and
domestic objects. Scotland's mystical leys seem to combine
aspects of these ways of thinking, although Scottish energy
dowsers deal with leys almost as if they were electrical

currents. They claim the ability to turn the energy off or redirect the flow by relatively straightforward means, including the placing of stones or insertion of metal rods into the ground.

LINSKILL, WILLIAM

The Victorian ghost-hunter and antiquarian, William T Linskill, was one of Scotland's first, and most dedicated, investigators of paranormal phenomena. A well-known and respected resident of St Andrews in Fife, he collected a great many ghost stories and legends relating to the history of the town, but his abiding ambition was to encounter a ghost himself. This ambition, however, was never fulfilled, as he admitted in 1921: 'It is a sad, nay, a melancholy fact (for I have been told this by the very best authorities) that *I am not psychic*, despite the fact that I have spent days and nights in gloomy, grimly-haunted chambers and ruins, and even a lonesome Hallowe'en night on the summit of St Rule's ancient tower (my only companions being sandwiches, matches, some cigars, and the necessary and indispensable flask), yet, alas! I have *never* heard or seen anything the least abnormal, or felt the necessary, or much talked of, mystic presence.'

Yet this personal disappointment did not dampen Linskill's enthusiasm for all things paranormal, and one particular mystery became a lifelong obsession—the search for 'Underground St Andrews'. After visiting the Catacombs in Rome, Linskill became convinced, despite a singular lack of evidence, that a similar complex of underground passages and chambers existed beneath St Andrews, connecting the ancient castle with the cathedral and the surrounding ecclesiastical buildings.

Towards the end of the 1870s, Linskill was staying with friends in Edinburgh when he met a Mr Ashton, who told him a very curious tale of an encounter on the Fife coast. Ashton had been staying near St Andrews in one of the small coastal towns of the East Neuk of Fife—most probably Crail or Pittenweem. One evening, as he walked alone on the beach, he met a strange old man who showed him a cave or cleft in the rocks along the shoreline. Following the old man into the cave, Ashton found himself at the foot of a staircase which ascended, via some thirty or so steps, into the cliffs, and appeared to have been hewn from the solid rock. At the top of the steps was a narrow passage which the old man informed him had been used by the monks of a nearby monastery that had long since disappeared. Ashton went on to describe all manner of terrifying sights and experiences in the darkness of the tunnels and chambers the old man led him through—at one point he even claimed to have heard the tolling of bells, which the old man said were ghostly echoes of the bells of the ruined Cathedral of St Andrews. After they had covered a considerable distance underground, Ashton suddenly lost sight of his companion and found himself completely alone in the darkness. Confused and by now very frightened, he stumbled, fell down a flight of stone steps and lost consciousness. When he regained his senses, Ashton was astonished to find himself above ground once more, just inside the old gateway to the Pends—part of the medieval walls that surround St Andrews Cathedral.

Clearly, this story fitted in with Linskill's ideas about 'Underground St Andrews', and he set about finding the entrance to the cave Ashton had described. He found the place easily enough, but the cave had fallen in and obliterated any trace of the staircase Ashton claimed to have ascended. Similarly, Linskill was unable to find any evidence of the exit from which Ashton had emerged in the Pends.

Then, in 1879, a startling discovery close to the castle walls seemed to back up Ashton's story. During the demolition of the old Keeper's cottage adjacent to the castle, an extensive and previously unknown subterranean passage was uncovered. Linskill's hopes were soon dashed, however, when it was revealed that this was not the entrance to the lost passages of 'Underground St Andrews'—it turned out to be the remains of a mine and counter-mine, dating from the siege of the castle of 1546-7. This was to be as close as Linskill got to the secret he believed lay hidden beneath the town. No other significant discoveries were ever made, despite his best efforts and his relentless exploration of St Andrews' many ancient buildings and ruins.

Of the many other investigations Linskill undertook—including a phantom coach, various spectral monks and the screaming skull of Neville de Beauchamp—perhaps the strangest case he investigated was that of the White Lady and the Haunted Tower. Situated within the medieval walls of the cathedral, one of the thirteen fortified towers that originally guarded the precincts of the cathedral had long been reputed to be haunted. The ghostly figure of a 'White Lady' was said to roam the walls in the vicinity and many locals claimed to have seen her—indeed, Ashton claimed to have seen a similar apparition during his underground experience. Linskill set out to uncover the story behind this haunting, and his enquiries soon led him to make a strange discovery. For many years, the two-storey rectangular tower had remained sealed, its evil reputation dissuading those who may have been curious about whatever secrets it contained. Then, in 1868, a group of antiquarians had broken into the tower. This is the account Linskill was given by Jesse Hall, one of those present:

'Mr Smith, watchmaker, and Mr Walker, the University Librarian, who were both antiquaries, pressed me frequently to allow them to open the vault. I did not care about it, as I did not like to disturb the dead; but I at last consented, and early one summer morning before six o'clock—as we did not want to make it public—the three of us, Mr Smith, Mr Walker and myself, went to the place and made a small hole, just enough to admit a man's head and shoulders. The doorway opened into a passage, and round the corner to the left was the vault proper. We all scrambled in, and by the light of a candle which we carried, we saw two chests lying side by side. I cannot say how many chests there were. There would be half a dozen as far as I can remember. I saw the body of a girl. The body was stiff and mummified-like. What appeared to be a glove was on one of the hands. . . . After we went in the first time we shut up the hole and kept the matter a profound secret, and I did not know that anyone knew of it except ourselves. People had been in the habit of calling the place the Haunted Tower and when going to the harbour they ran past it. No one had any idea that it was a place of burial till we opened it.'

Although he had no idea why this fortified tower had been converted into a tomb, Linskill did put forward several theories

as to the possible identity of the 'White Lady', suggesting that
what Jesse Hall and his companions had seen could have been
the mummified remains of a Celtic saint, a princess, or even
a nun who had once been a lady-in-waiting of Mary, Queen of
Scots and had retired to a nunnery at St Andrews after a
scandalous affair at Court.

Whatever the true identity of the 'White Lady', when Linskill
himself reopened the vault in the tower at midnight on the
21st August 1888, he found nothing more than scattered
fragments of coffins and a few skeletons. For Linskill, the
quest for the truth continued, but the mystery of the 'White
Lady', like that of 'the wonders that lie in Underground St
Andrews', was to remain unsolved. As Linskill himself wrote:
'We may know some day. Or never.'

LIVINGSTON UFO

The encounter at Livingston is Scotland's best known UFO
incident, having received worldwide attention.

On 9th November 1979 forestry worker Bob Taylor, then
aged 61, was walking through the woods on Dechmont Law
near the new town of Livingston. As he came round a bend in
the track he was astonished to find ahead of him, in a clearing
in the wood, a strange object which seemed to be hovering
slightly above the ground. He came nearer to the object, noting
that it was about 20 feet across and that whilst parts of it
looked solid other sections were transparent. He could see

right through to the vegetation behind. The upper part was dome-shaped and a thin flange ran around the centre. Overall it appeared grey in colour.

Suddenly two smaller objects dropped from the craft and moved towards him. They were shaped like Second World War mines with spikes all around. As they came near him Taylor could hear a distinct plopping sound. He tried to move but felt frozen to the spot, so the objects were able to come close up. He felt something grab hold of his trouser leg near his thigh, and was immediately aware of an overpowering smell. Taylor then appears to have passed out and remembers nothing till he came to some 20 minutes later. He staggered back to the lorry he had parked at the top of the path and tried, but failed, to start it. He then set off for home on foot— a journey of a mile or more.

When he reached home he immediately informed his wife that he had been attacked by a spaceship. She replied: 'there's no such thing' but, concerned by his physical state, called the doctor and Bob's boss, Malcolm Drummond. Because it looked as if Bob had suffered a physical assault, the police were also involved—they treated the incident as a crime and conducted a search of the area. It was suspected that Bob might have been attacked by youths or vagrants who had been sleeping overnight in the woods. No evidence, however, was discovered to account for the incident and the events remain on police records as an unsolved crime.

The doctor who examined Bob confirmed that, apart from the obvious upset caused by the encounter, he was in generally satisfactory physical condition. On the surface he did not seem to have suffered an epileptic fit or seizure of any kind.

Back at the scene of the incident, examination by police revealed tracks and marks on the ground where Bob said the encounter had occurred. These were of two kinds: ladder-shaped and round depressions. However, their relationship to the events of that morning remains unclear. They did not fit easily into the scenario described by Bob Taylor, and in particular there was nothing in his account which provided an obvious link with the ladder marks. The suspicion is that they may simply be a red herring and have no connection with the event, though it does seem strange that marks were found just at the spot where the incident took place.

Scottish sceptic Steuart Campbell [see Sceptics], who produced the earliest authoritative account of events, believes that the physical evidence had a natural explanation: the marks had been due to material left lying by workers laying cables in the area.

Even if there is no connection between the ground marks and the sighting, Bob Taylor's encounter still presents a puzzle. No one has ever doubted Bob's sincerity (even the sceptics), so it remains a mystery. Twenty years after the event Bob was still adamant about what he saw that morning, dismissing all 'natural' explanations.

Various solutions, however, which deny the UFO hypothesis have been put forward, most persistently by Steuart Campbell. His suggestion that Taylor experienced a hallucination as the result of an epileptic fit deserves serious consideration. Although he did pass out, and he experienced symptoms that might be associated with a seizure, Bob Taylor had no history of epilepsy, nor has he suffered a fit of any kind since 1979. And, it might be asked, why hallucinate a spaceship? Taylor had no interest in the subject, even after his encounter. He was quickly bored with all the media attention and, though always polite and co-operative, never gave the impression that he felt deeply involved with the general topic of UFOs.

As the years passed by, evidence gradually emerged that several UFO incidents had occurred in the area either on the day itself or within a short space of time. Although the link with the Taylor encounter can in no way be proven, it does place Dechmont in a wider context. Far from being an isolated incident, it may be a part of a broader episode, though it is possible that the rash of sightings at this time may have been pure coincidence.

Whatever the truth, the events at Livingston are unlikely to be forgotten. In 1992 Livingston Development Corporation marked the site with a cairn and plaque to commemorate the encounter. A unique recognition by a public authority of the significance of the UFO phenomenon.

M

MACHRIHANISH

Machrihanish, an RAF base on the Mull of Kintyre near Campbeltown, has long been rumoured to be 'Scotland's Area 51'. With a runway a mile long it would be an ideal landing spot for aircraft utilising advanced technology. But has Machrihanish been used for more sinister purposes—even for testing secret alien discs? In the United States there is a vast military base known as Area 51 located in the Nevada desert where, it is claimed, alien spacecraft have been stored and their technology copied. It has even been suggested that the products of this alien-inspired technology have been tested outside the USA, and one of the places chosen has been Machrihanish.

It should be said that much of this is simply hearsay, although there is at least one eye witness, a former employee, who has reported seeing a disc-shaped UFO in the skies close to the base. However, there is no direct evidence that anything obviously 'alien' has ever been kept on the base itself. And there are doubts about how 'top secret' Machrihanish really is. The land on which it stands would not be suitable for underground storage, so anything of a reasonable size, or needing to be worked on, has to be kept above ground. The whole area is easily overlooked by anyone who happens to be around the base, and the level of security in operation at Machrihanish is not high.

There are, of course, counter claims. Individuals have reported that in the early 1990s, if not at other times, a strict state of security was in force around the base. Anyone who came near it without authority was immediately challenged. And it has been suggested that this could have been linked to the testing of the stealth bomber or other even more extraordinary technology—genuine alien spacecraft.

It would certainly be possible to use Machrihanish as a testing ground. With a long runway and situated directly over the Atlantic from the USA it would be a convenient landing ground. It does occupy a relatively isolated location and it would be easy, by imposing stricter security, to seal it off completely from the outside world.

In 1993 a spate of UFO incidents were reported along the west coast of Scotland which could be linked to secret testing at Machrihanish. The west of Scotland has also been a key area for sightings of black triangular objects [see Black Triangles]. Some have linked these reports to stealth aircraft, although it has also been argued that the way these UFOs behave suggests that they were constructed using techniques that are way beyond the scope of our current technology.

There is no documentary proof that Machrihanish has been

a landing site for extraterrestrial craft, and some conspiracy theorists argue that the military have deliberately tried to focus attention on the base knowing that there is no foundation to the speculation—a 'double blind', intended to conceal the fact that any secret testing is carried out at more remote sites whose very existence is kept hidden from the public.

MARY KING'S CLOSE

In 1685 George Sinclair, Professor of Moral Philosophy at Glasgow University, published his treatise on witchcraft, spirits and other strange occurrences, entitled *Satan's Invisible World Discovered*. Containing numerous examples of supernatural or paranormal happenings from all over Scotland, England and further afield, it was a best-seller in its day and was reprinted often throughout the 18th century. It included one chilling story which has endured right up to the present day, concerning a street in Edinburgh which is still said to be haunted.

Mary King's Close is a very steep, narrow close running from the High Street down to what used to be the Nor' Loch, but is now Princes Street Gardens. Built in the early 17th century, it still survives although it has long since been built over. Named, probably, after the daughter of a proprietor, Alexander King, it became notorious as a place infested by the plague of 1645, the last great outbreak in Edinburgh, which wiped out thousands of citizens. The Close was in fact sealed off in this year, and food and water passed in from outside to those unfortunates, whether infected or not, who were thus condemned to live on there. It never shook off the ill-repute of that time, and was largely abandoned by the end of the century. In the 1750s the City Chambers were constructed above it, and the last inhabitants moved out. But their houses remain more or less intact 250 years later. The exodus was apparently hastened because the Close was also believed to be haunted. In modern times, its unwholesome reputation has led to renewed public interest, and guided tours regularly explore the abandoned houses, gaining entry from a door leading down steps from the Chambers, and arriving in due course at the bottom end, which is blocked up, above Cockburn Street.

The following case of haunting is recorded in George Sinclair's book. Around the year 1680, a lawyer, Thomas Coltheart by name, took a house in Mary King's Close and moved in with his family. One Saturday an inhabitant of the Close, seeing Coltheart's maid taking some light furniture into the house, warned her that if she intended living there, 'I assure you, you will have more company than yourselves.' The maid took fright, and informed her mistress that she would not stay there, because it was haunted by a spirit or ghost.

The mistress informed her husband, asking him to reconsider the let, but Coltheart calmed her and said that he had no intention of changing his mind. Indeed, he insisted that they stay in the house that same night, which they did.

The next day, after attending church in the morning, Coltheart felt unwell, and in the afternoon took a nap. His wife sat reading the Bible, having sent the maid out to church (she never came back). Mrs Coltheart glanced up at one point, and saw, by a 'little Chamber Door just over against her', 'the head and face of an old man, grey headed with a grey Beard, looking straight upon her' from a cupboard door above the fire. She fainted, and did not come round till she heard the noise of her neighbours opening their doors after church. She roused her husband and told him what she had seen, but he dismissed it as 'some fancy or delusion of her Senses'.

After his wife had gone to bed, Coltheart sat up alone by the fire. He too saw the same old man's head in the same place. He woke his wife, who fell into a passion, and then together they prayed for God's protection. After an hour 'they clearly perceived a young child, with a coat upon it, hanging near to the old man's head.' Terrified, the Colthearts lit more candles and tried to wake their neighbours, but got no answer. As they watched and prayed, another apparition manifested itself: 'a naked Arm . . . in the air, from the elbow downward, and the hand stretched out, as when one man is about to salute another.' It approached as if it sought to shake hands with the lawyer, who retreated into bed with his wife, but the arm followed, 'still after a courteous manner, with an offer of acquaintance'. Now drowned in sweat, the Colthearts prayed more fervently, but to no avail, as next appeared a little dog, 'which after a little time looking about, and towards the Bed, and the Naked Arm, composed itself upon a Chair, as it were with its nose in its tail to sleep.' There followed a cat, which seemed to leap from the door of a small adjoining room, where all the apparitions had come from, and started to play in front of them. 'Then was the hall full of small little creatures, dancing prettily, unto which none of them could give a name, as having never in nature seen the like.'

The Colthearts continued on their knees in bed, there

being nowhere left on the floor for them to kneel, and prayed yet again. 'In the time of prayer,' says Sinclair, 'their ears were startled with a deep, dreadful, and loud groan, as of a strong man dying, at which all the Apparitions and visions at once vanished . . . and the house was quiet.'

The Colthearts, understandably, refreshed themselves with a drink after this awful experience, and in the morning went about their business, making no secret to anyone of what had happened to them. However, they did wonder, looking back, why they had not simply unbolted the door and fled, rather than lighting the first candle. They concluded that they had been meant to undergo the trial, and this gave Coltheart the courage to stay on in that house, until the day he died, which as it turned out was not too long in the future.

After going to Corstorphine one day, to hear a sermon, Coltheart was taken ill on the way home, trembling and aching in his joints, and with a pain in his head. Meanwhile, in Tranent, seven miles the other side of Edinburgh, one of his clients, being in bed one morning with his wife, saw a cloud-like figure like a man floating in the room, and was so startled that he jumped out of bed and drew his sword. After a while, he, his wife and a nursemaid to their child all saw the cloud take the definite form of a man walking up and down. 'At last this Apparition looked him fully and perfectly in the face, and stood by him with a ghastly and Pale countenance. At which the Gentleman with great courage said to the Spectre, what art thou? Art thou my dear Friend Thomas Coltheart?' The ghost held up its hand three times, waving and shaking it, and then disappeared. It transpired that at almost this exact time Thomas Coltheart died.

How much of this is credible is of course open to question. Certainly none of it is now verifiable. However, many visitors to Mary King's Close in recent years claim to have seen or felt presences of some kind. One room is often described as being inexplicably cold, despite the fact that it leads off another room which is noticeably much warmer. The most frequently experienced presence is the ghost of a little girl, believed to have been a plague victim, to whom an unofficial shrine has built up in a room of one of the old houses. Many witnesses have reported eerie encounters in this particular room. Mediums and clairvoyants have been down the Close and confirmed that the place is full of ghosts of various kinds, mostly from the period of the plague. As to the weird procession of apparitions observed by the Colthearts, a possible connection was made in 1995, as reported in the *Evening News* on 24th June of that year. A Glasgow architect called David Roulston spent an entire night alone in the Close in order to raise money for charity. He took a camcorder down with him, and recorded a mysterious image on film during the course of his stay. As Roulston explained, at one point he felt quite cold. It was not until he played back the video at home that he saw what looked like a head on a wall. To him it was like the head of a dog, which just turned and disappeared. It might also be the image of a human head.

It would seem that some of the old inhabitants of Mary King's Close are still around.

MERMAIDS

It would be wrong to think of Mermaids as no more than ancient myths. As recently as August 1949, several mermen were reportedly seen by a number of witnesses near Craigmore in the parish of Kinlochbervie. And this raises an interesting point: although many tales have a mermaid as their central character, as many sightings of mermen have been reported through the years. Sceptics, of course, explain mermaids away as mistaken natural phenomena, usually seals—and there certainly has been a link even in folklore, some accounts telling how mermaids are disguised as seals throughout the year, only assuming human form on certain days.

But could it be, as critics argue, that people have simply mistaken seals, dolphins and other animals for half-human entities, and that a great myth of the mermaid has been built up because witnesses misidentified what they saw? If that is all there is to it, then why are there descriptions from individuals of encountering these beings at close quarters?

In 1830, on the island of Benbecula, Alexander Carmichael and several others were cutting kelp on the seashore when they 'saw some feet away in the sea the form of a woman in miniature'. Even as they watched, the creature played about and turned somersaults. When they waded into the water to capture her she swam away. But a stone thrown by one of the group hit and injured her as she made off. A few days later, what was assumed to be the same entity was washed up further down the coast. She was certainly not fully human. As the witness recalled: 'the upper part of the creature was about the size of a well-fed child of three or four years of age, with an abnormally developed breast. The hair was long, dark and glossy, while the skin was white, soft and tender. The lower part of the body was like a salmon, but without the scales.' The creature was put in a small coffin and buried locally.

The Benbecula encounter has been repeated on many occasions in Scotland, and on a greater scale across the world. Understandably, as mermaids strain belief even more than loch monsters, it is asked why there have been no mermaid sightings in recent years. The answer is that seeing mermaids is like claiming an encounter with a fairy—people do still see fairies, they just do not report them.

In our modern technological era, both mermaids and fairies appear hopelessly out of place. Even into the 1900s, however, an area south of Cape Wrath on Scotland's northern coast was known as 'the Land of Mermaids'. A witness at the turn of the century claimed to have seen 'a real mermaid' with 'reddish-yellow and curly hair and greenish-blue eyes'. He added: 'she never moved . . . as she reclined amid the noise of the surf with her fish-like tail dangling over the side of the rock.' A peaceful encounter, but other incidents are more disturbing.

In 1903 a Forfar landowner was seemingly almost drowned in the North Sea at Inverbervie near Aberdeen when he tried to help a drowning girl. The man rushed into the water when he heard a woman—who was out of her depth and struggling to stay afloat—crying for help. He was swimming out to rescue her when suddenly a stone went flying over his head. It landed in the water near the drowning woman who promptly disappeared. The man swam back to shore and demanded an explanation from his manservant as to why he had thrown the stone at the woman. He was told that the drowning woman was in fact a mermaid and that if he had touched her he would have been dragged under the water. As the servant spoke, mocking laughter drifted from the sea to mingle with the gathering gloom.

It is true that many tales have gathered around these water-borne entities. Most persistent is that of the man who captures a mermaid and is granted a number of wishes, usually three—the number 'three' being full of mystic significance. In the 1880s a Ross-shire seaman met a mermaid sitting on a rock near Whiteness point at Tain. He crept up on her and seized her in his strong arms. The mermaid struggled and begged for her freedom but the man held on tight and forced the mermaid to grant him his three wishes of health, wealth and happiness. After that the mermaid dived into the sea and disappeared.

However, the mere fact that fanciful accounts have grown up round these creatures does not rule out the possibility that there are genuine mysterious entities swimming off our coasts. The seas and oceans remain the great unexplored wilderness of the world, and who knows what we will discover at great depths beneath the waves?

MILITARY

Are the Scottish military hiding a great secret about the UFO phenomenon? Do they know more than they have ever been prepared to reveal? That has been the suspicion of UFO investigators.

The military's involvement with Unidentified Flying Objects stretches back a long way. As long ago as 1956, a Sea-Hawk aircraft on a training exercise from HMS *Fulmar* filmed a UFO off the coast of Lossiemouth. As recently as April 1995 three Tornado aircraft were scrambled from RAF Kinloss to investigate a strange object hovering over Edinburgh Airport. In 1996 a major search was initiated after an explosion and sighting of an orange-coloured UFO near the island of Lewis [qv]. And these are only the incidents that have become known to the public. There must be many more encounters which are hidden away in Ministry of Defence and armed services files.

There is no doubt that the MOD has been keeping records of Scottish UFO sightings since the 1950s, but has their involvement gone beyond that? Have our military bases been used for storing and testing alien spacecraft? That has been the rumour particularly linked to Machrihanish [qv] on the Mull of Kintyre. But is there any foundation to this claim, or is it just a repetition of alleged events in the United States transplanted to Scotland? A re-working of the Roswell incident with a tartan flavour.

It might be expected that, at the very least, the Ministry of Defence would be interested in UFO reports, as these incidents represent a violation of our airspace by an unknown object. But they will admit to nothing beyond that. Their stock response is that if the event is of 'no defence significance' then their involvement comes to an end. Ufologists, however, are sceptical about the MOD's stance on this. Their feeling is that the MOD know more than they are admitting to. And while it is no doubt true that some in the UFO community are inclined to accept conspiracy theories uncritically, it is not 'all in the mind'. There is the evidence of the Freeman family in Blairgowrie [qv] that a military helicopter hovered close to their house shortly after a UFO incident, as if it was looking for something. More sinister is the claim made by one witness that a UFO took off from a mountain hillside and followed a Hercules transport aircraft that later crashed. If this account is accurate then the defence organisations should certainly be taking the UFO phenomenon seriously.

It would be surprising if the MOD had not accumulated a far greater body of evidence than they have been prepared to admit to. But it is very hard to know the extent of military involvement, particularly in the controversial area of alien contact. There is no documentary evidence of any kind, and until there is a more open attitude from the armed forces their role in the UFO phenomenon will remain in the shadows. Where they would no doubt like it to stay.

MILLER, HUGH

Hugh Miller was born in Cromarty in 1802. He originally worked as a stonemason, and later as an accountant, journalist and editor of *The Witness*. His pioneering work in the field of geology was recognised throughout the world, while in Britain his writing on many subjects made him one of the best known Victorian literary figures. His interest in the paranormal can be seen in his book *Scenes and Legends of the North of Scotland* (1835), in which he retold many of the traditional ghost stories of his native Cromarty.

Miller's personal experience of the paranormal occurred early in his childhood, in November 1807 at exactly the time his father was tragically lost at sea. This is how he recounted the incident in his autobiography, *My Schools and Schoolmasters* (1854):

'The fatal tempest, as it had prevailed chiefly on the eastern coasts of England and the south of Scotland, was represented in the north by but a few bleak, sullen days, in which, with little wind, a heavy ground-swell came rolling in coastwards from the east, and sent up its surf high against the precipices of the northern Sutor. There were no forebodings in the master's dwelling; for his Peterhead letter—a brief but hopeful missive—had been just received; and my mother was sitting, on the evening after, beside the household fire, plying the cheerful needle, when the house door, which had been left unfastened, fell open, and I was despatched from her side to shut it. What follows must be regarded as simply the recollection, though a very vivid one, of a boy who had completed his fifth year only a month before. Day had not wholly disappeared, but it was fast posting on to night, and a grey haze spread a neutral tint of dimness over every more distant object, but left the nearer ones comparatively distinct, when I saw at the open door, within less than a yard of my breast, as plainly as ever I saw anything, a dissevered hand and arm stretched towards me. Hand and arm were apparently those of a female: they bore a livid and sodden appearance; and, directly fronting me, where the body ought to have been, there was only blank, transparent space, through which I could see the dim forms of the objects beyond. I was fearfully startled, and ran shrieking to my mother, telling what I had seen; and the house-girl whom she next sent to shut the door, apparently affected by my terror, also returned frightened, and said that she too had seen the woman's hand; which, however, did not seem to be the case. And finally, my mother going to the door, saw nothing, though she appeared much impressed by the extremeness of my terror and the minuteness of my description. I communicate the story as it lies fixed in my memory, without attempting to explain it. The supposed apparition may have been merely a momentary affection of the eye, of the nature described by Sir Walter Scott in his *Demonology*, and Sir David Brewster in his *Natural Magic*. But if so the affection was one of which I experienced no after-return; and its coincidence, in the case, with the probable time of my father's death, seems at least curious.'

Miller's fascination with supernatural stories associated with the sea, and his ability to maintain a measure of scientific detachment, can clearly be seen in this extract from *Scenes and Legends*.

'About fifteen years ago [c. 1820], a Cromarty fisherman was returning from Inverness by a road which for several miles skirts the upper edge of the moor, and passes within a few yards of the cairn. Night overtook him ere he had half completed his journey; but, after an interval of darkness, the moon, nearly at full, rose over the eminence on his right, and restored to him the face of the country—the hills which he had passed before evening, but which, faint and distant, were sinking as he advanced, the wood which, bordering his road on the one hand, almost reached him with its shadow, and the bleak, unvaried, interminable waste, which, stretching away on the other, seemed lost in the horizon.

'After he had entered on the moor, the stillness which, at an earlier stage of his journey, had occasionally been broken by the distant lowing of cattle, or the bark of a shepherd's dog, was interrupted by only his own footsteps, which, from the nature of the soil, sounded hollow as if he trod over a range of vaults, and by the low monotonous murmur of the neighbouring wood. As he approached the cairn, however, a noise of a different kind began to mingle with the other two; it was one with which his profession had made him well acquainted— that of waves breaking against a rock. The nearest shore was fully three miles distant, the nearest cliff more than five, and yet he could hear wave after wave striking as if against a precipice, then dashing upwards, and anon descending, as distinctly as he had ever done when passing in his boat beneath the promontories of Cromarty.

'On coming up to the cairn, his astonishment was converted into terror.—Instead of the brown heath, with here and there a fir seedling springing out of it, he saw a wide tempestuous sea stretching before him, with the large pile of stones frowning over it, like one of the Hebrides during the gales of the Equinox. The pile appeared as if half enveloped in cloud and spray, and two large vessels, with all their sheets spread to the wind, were sailing round it.

'The writer of these chapters had the good fortune to witness at this cairn a scene which, without owing anything to the supernatural, almost equalled the one described. He was, like the fisherman, returning from Inverness to Cromarty in a clear frosty night in December. There was no moon, but the whole sky towards the north was glowing with the Aurora Borealis, which, shooting from the horizon to the central heavens, in flames tinged with all the hues of the rainbow, threw so strong a light, that he could have counted every tree of the wood, and every tumulus of the moor. There is a long hollow morass which runs parallel to the road for nearly a mile;—it was covered this evening by a dense fleece of vapour raised by the frost, and which, without ascending, was rolling over the moor before a light breeze. It had reached the cairn, and the detached clump of seedlings which springs up at its base.—The seedlings rising out of the vapour appeared like a fleet of ships, with their sails dropping against their masts, on a sea where there were neither tides nor winds;—the cairn, grey with the moss and lichens of forgotten ages, towered over it like an island of that sea.'

Hugh Miller tragically committed suicide in 1856, only two years after completing his autobiography, *My Schools and Schoolmasters*. Yet the circumstances of his death were curious in the extreme. As James Robertson described in his introduction to the 1993 edition of *My Schools and Schoolmasters*:

'He had latterly become paranoid about his own and his family's safety, and kept an arsenal of weapons in the house. He had also been suffering from terrible dreams, fevers, and fits of dizziness and nausea. The day before he killed himself he told his doctor of the previous night's visitation: "I felt as if I had been ridden by a witch for fifty miles, and rose more weary in mind and body than when I lay down." Early next morning, on Christmas Eve, 1856, he woke in anguish, scribbled a farewell note to his wife which spoke of horror and a burning agony in his brain, and shot himself with the revolver which, in his paranoia, he carried with him at all times. Far to the north in Cromarty, as she afterwards recounted, his mother sat up in bed and saw a ball of bright light suspended in the air, which, after moving round the room as if seeking a place to rest, stopped and faded into nothing, leaving the old woman in utter darkness and convinced of the occurrence of "a sudden and awful calamity." '

MOFFAT

The town of Moffat may seems an unlikely focus for visiting aliens. But, it may well be asked, why not Moffat? In fact, the same question arises every time a place with no great claim to fame suddenly become a target for UFOs—the villages of Bonnybridge [qv] near Falkirk and Warminster in England are good examples. Whatever the reason, in the late 1970s the area around Moffat became a UFO 'hot spot'. A large number of people reported seeing unidentified objects in the sky, of various shapes and sizes. One individual, however, Joyce Byers [qv], claimed to have witnessed over a hundred of these objects. The brief celebrity enjoyed by Moffat came to an end by 1980 and the town has not since then been a centre of UFO activity.

The interest generated in the area for that short period raises several questions about the nature of paranormal phenomena. Was the apparent rash of incidents created by the enthusiasm of one person (Mrs Byers) who claimed more UFO sightings than all the other witnesses put together? Did the media exaggerate the true significance of these events? Was there a genuine explosion of the UFO phenomenon? Or did a combination of all three bring about Moffat's temporary fame?

The way in which Moffat hit the headlines might well be worth a full investigative study—it would shed a good deal of light on the nature of the UFO phenomenon and its interplay with society. But as far as ufologists are concerned, Moffat has forever earned a place in Scotland's list of UFO hot spots.

MORAR, LOCH

In the shadow of the more famous Loch Ness [qv], Loch Morar, on Scotland's west coast, is arguably a more likely candidate for an unknown water 'monster'. Morar is the deepest inland loch in Europe, over a thousand feet at some points, and running eleven miles in length by one and a half wide it would provide plenty of room for a 'monster' to hide. It is also less accessible. There are no hordes of visitors here to disturb the tranquillity, and there is not even a proper track around the circumference of the loch. A single-track road runs less than halfway along the north side, but to travel from one end to the other the only sure way is by boat. The lack of public access may explain why the volume of recorded sightings has been significantly less than at Loch Ness. Even so, the number of reports has been considerable and includes some close encounters.

The legend of Morag, the monster of Loch Morar, stretches back at least to the 19th century. It is probably considerably older as some accounts of the creature describe Morag in a way that gives her almost the characteristics of a mermaid. However, at least from the beginning of the 20th century, witnesses describe a creature that approaches what we would think of today as the 'typical' loch monster, particularly in regard to the long neck and humped appearance of the body. As with Loch Ness, though, it was only after the 1930s that significant numbers of incidents began to surface—perhaps due to the general interest in loch creatures created by the publicity given to 'Nessie'.

Loch Morar, though, remained very much the poor relation. It was not until the 1970s, with the publication of *The Search for Morag*, compiled through the efforts of the 'Loch Morar Survey' team, that a considerable body of material was brought together revealing the true extent of the witness evidence.

And some of the accounts were truly revealing. On 16th August 1969, William Simpson and Duncan McDonnell were cruising the loch in their motorboat. Suddenly they became aware of a loud splashing noise directly behind them. McDonnell looked up and saw an object in the water, heading at speed towards the boat, moving through the disturbance left by their wake. He later claimed that 'it took only a matter of seconds to catch up on us'. The object hit the craft side on. McDonnell had no doubt that the collision was intentional. He was also sure that they had been struck by a large animal of some kind, and although the impact had brought the beast to a halt he was worried that it might try and swim beneath the boat and capsize them.

Simpson had joined his crewmate on deck, having rushed from below when he heard the commotion. He immediately caught sight of the creature which he judged about 25 to 30 feet long, its three humps standing clear of the water. The skin had a rough appearance and looked dirty brown in colour. A snake-like head could be seen above the waves. Simpson took his shotgun and fired in the direction of the animal, which rapidly disappeared below the surface.

The incident might read like a scene from a 'B' movie if we did not have reports from other witnesses who describe a similar creature. In September 1970 Charles Fishburne caught sight of a strange object that 'passed within 35 yards to port'. He claimed: 'I could definitely see that it was not a boat—only three large, black hump-shaped objects moving quickly through the water.'

The sighting was in line with the most recent significant encounter, on 18th August 1990. On that day Alistair McKellaig, with his brother Duncan and young sons Neil and Steven, was fishing on the loch. McKellaig was a frequent sailor on Morar and very familiar with the terrain. However, what followed was totally unexpected. He caught sight of three humps moving together, about 50 yards behind the boat. The objects were keeping pace with the vessel and were clearly visible, standing about three feet out of the water like upright tyres. They were plainly solid, leaving a distinctive wake as they moved.

As with Nessie, it has been claimed that Morag has been seen out of water, though far less frequently, and animal footprints of an unusual kind have allegedly been found in the mud on the loch foreshore. No photographs, however, exist to back up these reports. Speculation that the creature might move in and out of the water intensified when in 1996 a diver brought a collection of bones up from the bottom of the loch. They turned out to be those of a deer, which came as a bitter disappointment to those hoping for proof that Morag was a flesh and blood creature. The discovery also led to speculation that the beast had been dragged into the loch by a large animal, though it is more than likely that the deer had simply fallen in or drowned while trying to swim across. Overall, the discovery did not really add anything to the evidence.

So what is Morag? A flesh and blood beast, or a phantom? At least one psychic who has visited the loch has claimed that the place is alive with fairy people of different kinds. It is also said to be a site which attracts spirits, and a couple using a ouija board on the loch's edge were inundated with messages. Dowsing has also shown that the loch is criss-crossed with energy lines at regular intervals. All of which suggests that the loch generates mystic energy.

On the other hand, the incidents involving Alistair McKellaig and William Duncan point to there being a real creature involved. In Duncan's case the object struck the boat with enough force to rock it, and McKellaig described a definite wake left by the humps. Fishburne's account fits with these two encounters, and all three incidents follow a pattern set by dozens of others. But if Morag is not a phantom, where does she come from and where does she go to? It is a puzzle which at the moment is still being unravelled. The evidence suggests that she is no figment of the imagination, but if she exists only the discovery of a body, dead or alive, will prove it.

MOTHMAN

Mothman has been usually associated with the United States, but a sighting of a similar creature has been reported in Scotland. This entity is described as half man, half bird. Its legs and torso are humanoid, but in place of arms it has wings with feathers. The parallel with an angel is obvious, but the being does not seem to radiate well-being and has a sinister air about it. Scotland's sole sighting of the creature took place in October 1992 in Edinburgh. The witness, a woman, woke up in the early hours of the morning and caught sight of an intense white light clearly visible through the window. She got out of bed to take a closer look, and her attention was drawn to a tree at the foot of the garden. Crouching on a thick branch was a creature which at first glance she took to be a giant bird as big as a man. But as she took a longer look she became aware that apart from its huge size there were other strange aspects to it: it seemed to have a mixture of human and bird-type features. She was certainly frightened by the sighting, although the entity did not seem to be aware of her presence and made no attempt to confront her.

There are no other known sightings and very few strange flying entities reported of any kind. In 1998 a witness travelling through Glencoe late at night encountered what he described as 'a large black bird creature in the sky. It was about eight feet across and resembled a pterodactyl.' There is a vague similarity to 'Mothman', but the differences suggest that we are not dealing here with an identical being. The Glencoe witness has suggested that what he saw might be a 'skree', a mythical creature of doom.

At the moment, however, the evidence from Scotland, relying as it does on one individual, is far too meagre to enable any conclusions to be drawn about mothman.

N

NAZIS

The interest of leading Nazis in the occult is well known. Hitler is said to have consulted astrologers and to have decided a course of action on whether or not it was well omened. Many of his followers were also enthusiastic supporters of pagan cults, particularly those which they saw as of the more manly kind, such as Wodenism. Woden was the Viking god of fighting, feasting and other pagan activities which the Nazis hoped would strengthen the warlike virtues of society—which they were convinced had been undermined by Christianity.

It seems clear, therefore, that leading Nazis were prepared to believe that supernatural acts and objects could influence events. An odd aspect to this was that although they rejected Christian faith, they did accept that certain Christian artefacts possessed mystic power. The spear which pierced Christ's side as he hung on the cross and had, allegedly, eventually passed into the hands of the Europe's Holy Roman Emperor, was seen as being able to generate powerful magic.

So what would the Nazis have given to get hold of the Holy Grail, the cup or plate passed around at the last supper Christ held with his disciples? Its paranormal powers are legendary, as are the tales of its whereabouts. According to one tradition it was taken to Glastonbury by Joseph of Arimathea. But more substantial evidence suggests that it came into the possession of the Knights Templar [qv] during one of their crusades in the Holy Land. They supposedly dug it up from below the ruins of the temple at Jerusalem while carrying out a secret excavation in the 12th century.

It has now been suggested that this event of seven hundred years ago explains the puzzling and unsolved mystery of Rudolf Hess' flight to Scotland in May 1941. Setting off in secret, Hess made a parachute landing near the Renfrewshire village of Eaglesham. It was claimed that he had made this strange mission to try and negotiate peace between Britain and Germany. It seemed such an odd way of going about it that the explanation aroused a controversy that has continued ever since.

But if the story circulated by his British gaolers is not true, what were his intentions? The latest idea is that Hess was, in fact, intent on finding the Holy Grail, which he believed to be hidden at Rosslyn Chapel [qv]. He would have been aware of the tales circulating across Europe about the store of mystical objects taken by Knights Templar when they left continental Europe for Scotland in 1307. It has taken 50 years for the Scottish public to catch up with rumours well known to Europe's leading occultists before the Second World War. So an attempt by a leading Nazi to secure such a prize is not unimaginable.

However, no matter what Hess thought he might gain from his mission, his method of carrying it out seems flawed. He could not have discovered the Grail, even if it is hidden at Rosslyn Chapel, on his own. So he had either been seized with a bout of madness or was on a reconnaissance mission. But sending a figure like Hess ahead to spy out the land seems a ridiculous way to go about such an operation. He was far too well known a figure to risk in an escapade like this. He might have been in charge of a plan to recover the Holy Grail, but he would surely have used trained personnel to carry through the act.

The official account of Hess' journey to Scotland does appear flawed, and we may never know the truth. The link with the Holy Grail is at the moment simply a fascinating but unproven theory.

NESS, LOCH

Loch Ness is Scotland's most famous mystery site, having achieved world fame as the home of a strange unidentified 'monster'. In terms of sightings, the Loch Ness monster is exceptionally well documented, the evidence including an extensive collection of photographs and, more recently, video recordings.

Reports of a strange creature in the loch date back to 565 AD when St Columba, on a mission to convert the pagans, is recorded as having banished a strange creature which was terrifying local fishermen. It could, of course, have been a symbolic incident—Christianity overcoming the 'dragon' gods of the non-believers. (Sceptics have also pointed out that his encounter occurred at the River Ness rather than the Loch itself.) On the other hand, up to the Middle Ages there were many reported incidents involving strange animals—creatures which looked just like the Loch Ness monster might have done if moving out of water. We cannot ignore the possibility that in Columba's case a real incident was being described.

What is without doubt is that the current spate of sightings began in the 1930s when a road was constructed close to the shore of the Loch. There have been hundreds of reports since then, but clearly the initial sightings were crucial in convincing the public that the Loch contained a mystery creature. The most important sighting from this period was that of Donaldina Mackay in March 1933. It triggered mass interest although that was never her intention. She allegedly saw 'an aquatic creature, 12 to 15 feet long with a rounded back'—a description which has been repeated by numerous witnesses down the years.

Donald Campbell was another early witness. He worked for Ness Fisheries Board as the loch's water bailiff, and claimed to have seen the monster on 18 occasions. He became closely associated with 'Nessie'—indeed some believe that he invented some of the initial accounts to boost the popularity of the area. It was through Campbell, who passed local stories to the *Inverness Courier* newspaper, that the Mackay account first saw the light of day. Shortly after Donaldina Mackay's encounter, Campbell claimed his own sighting. He reported that he had seen 'a creature raise its head and body from the loch . . . a small head on a long neck . . . the creature seemed fully 30 feet in length.' The ball was well and truly rolling and in spite of criticism, disappointment and scepticism it has never remotely looked like stopping.

After the sightings came the photographic evidence. The image that has come to be known as the 'surgeon' photograph, dating from 1st April 1934, did a lot to publicise the Loch Ness phenomenon. It seemed to show a creature with a long neck and small head, much like the descriptions given by witnesses. The volume of reports, photographs, cine film and video footage since then has been truly phenomenal.

However, it has to be asked: with so much evidence why has the creature not been filmed close up, or even caught? Especially when there have been several underwater surveys. And for many years a dedicated watch has been kept over the loch by individuals like Frank Searle, Tim Dinsdale and such groups as the Loch Ness Phenomena Investigation Bureau. Sceptics argue that it is because the 'monster' does not exist. Their criticism cannot be ignored: for example, one problem raised is that even though the loch is deep, maybe even 1,000 feet in parts, and at 23 miles long by a mile wide covers an extensive area, could it provide enough food to support a group of monsters over hundreds or even thousands of years? On the face of it, it seems unlikely.

Sceptics have also made a successful attack on the photographic evidence. The surgeon photograph of 1934, which did so much to boost public interest, was recently exposed as a hoax. The steady flow of obvious hoax photographs has not helped Nessie's credibility, particularly as one of the hoaxers was allegedly the dedicated loch-watcher Frank Searle. But false or deliberately exaggerated claims should not be allowed to obscure a key fact: many people have taken a photograph to back up a sighting they have had, and which they believe cannot be easily explained away. They are not persistent loch-watchers, but witnesses who have unexpectedly caught a glimpse of a strange movement or object.

However, sincere belief is not proof, and author Steuart Campbell [see Sceptics] has successfully undermined the photographic evidence in his book *The Loch Ness Monster: The Evidence*. Campbell examined the best of the photographs and came to the conclusion that not one of them stood up to scrutiny. So even though there may be a large number of photographs which together suggest that there is 'something' in the loch, each photograph on its own proves nothing. And thus the case for Nessie collapses like a pack of cards.

It has to be said, though, that Campbell is a campaigning sceptic, and claims in his book *The UFO Mystery Solved* to have proved that all UFOs are mis-sightings of natural phenomena. Others are less sure that the photographic evidence can be so readily dismissed. The photographs may not provide the conclusive evidence that everyone would like, but that is not to say that all they show is either a motorboat, a deer swimming, or unusual wave movement—the explanations that have been put forward to discredit every photograph or film to date.

So does the existence of the Loch Ness monster rest simply on faith? It must depend on what we accept as evidence. There are endless reported sightings. In June 1993 the creature that Edna McInnes spotted came within 20 feet of the loch shore. She could clearly make out its small head, long neck and light brown colour. The McInnes sighting is simply one of the many which have flowed since the 1930s, and it does nothing to explain how a creature could hide away in the loch. True, the waters of Ness are murky, and it is impossible to see more than a few feet beneath the water, but several creatures— and common sense would dictate that there must be, as we are dealing with flesh and blood animals that must be able to reproduce—would surely be more visible.

Maybe the Loch Ness phenomenon should not be viewed in isolation. There are several lochs in the Highlands—Morar [qv], Oich, Lochy, Quoich, Shiel, which contain alleged 'monsters'. Even so it seems unlikely that a group of these creatures could move across miles of open countryside, even though there has been the occasional report of 'Nessie' having been seen out of water. If there is an answer then maybe it lies at the psychic level—that what we have at Loch Ness is a paranormal phenomenon. Perhaps Nessie is an apparition from a distant past which can be seen from time to time if the loch acts as a kind of window into other dimensions. The creature may be a ghost very much like the phantoms of people encountered throughout Scotland. Whatever the truth, there have been just too many sightings of the creature for it to be simply dismissed out of hand. Only one thing is certain: the phenomenon of Loch Ness will be with us for a long time yet.

NIDDRY STREET VAULTS

One of Edinburgh's most haunted sites, Niddry Street Vaults, has been the scene of several paranormal investigations. It seems to be one of the few, perhaps only, buildings in Scotland where strange incidents occur even when researchers are present.

The vaults form the lower floor of an eight storey building built into the structure of the South Bridge, which carries traffic over the now drained Nor' Loch, where the railway station presently stands. During the 18th century the building was divided into flats and shops. The Capital's store of gold bars was at one time kept here under armed guard.

That part of the structure which now rests at street level and below has not been used for a long time. The interior, however, is still remarkably intact and the rough stone walls that once divided it into small shops and living space still stand. It is this area, a network of connecting rooms with vaulted ceilings, where many ghostly figures have been sighted. The rooms have unpaved earth floors, although a large room, called the 'hall' has recently had a stone floor put down with the intention of turning it into a restaurant. It was this room that the group Scottish Earth Mysteries Research used as their base when they conducted an investigation in October 1998. Their experiences are an interesting indicator of the level of paranormal activity on the site, and provide evidence that ghosts do not necessarily vanish the minute researchers arrive, as sceptics sometimes claim.

According to their report, the group had only been on the premises for a short while when they became aware of a distinct drop in temperature. The psychic medium taking part, Katrina McNab, confirmed the presence of many spirits. In particular, she referred to a hooded figure. In one of the rooms—where, it was alleged, occult groups had carried out black magic ceremonies—the medium detected cold spots, a typical sign of spirit activity.

Those present felt that there was a more intense atmosphere in that room than elsewhere in the vaults. One investigator—who was dowsing in the area for 'earth energy', sometimes said to be used by ghosts to come through from the spirit world—noticed a more powerful response on his dowsing rods. A tape recorder, which it had been intended to leave in the room, would not work, but as soon as it was taken into the passageway outside it started recording again. All three of the video cameras the researchers had brought with them stopped operating at one point—and then, again for no obvious reason, started working again. When the footage was reviewed after the investigation, strange faces were seen on the tape. One was of a hooded figure, just as the medium, Katrina, had claimed she had seen—and in the same room. Interestingly, after the investigation, a witness reported that she had seen a monk-like figure in the street close to the area.

Strangest of all, an alien face, just like those associated with UFOs, also appeared on the film, as if a figure was coming through the wall. Photographs of the spot taken by investigator Brian Wilson for comparison after the meeting showed that it was not simply a trick of the light because no face or figure could be seen. However, the presence of a phantom alien is difficult to understand unless the footage was simply mis-interpreted and it was no more than a ghost viewed at an odd angle. On the other hand, psychics do claim that even extra-terrestrials must have spirit bodies and if this was one, it must be a unique piece of film.

There does not seem to be any reason why Niddry Street Vaults should be such a ghostly 'hot spot', but it may be more than coincidence that Scotland's oldest authenticated masonic lodge, Mary's Chapel No. 1, once stood close to this site.

ODIN

The Norse God Odin, also known as Woden, was at one time worshipped in Scotland. Parts of the country were under the rule of the Norsemen from the eighth century AD onwards. The Orkney islands were attached to the Norwegian kingdom until 1468 when they were taken over by the Scottish crown. During that period the Scandinavians nominally went over to Christianity, but the old gods still held sway for several centuries. Very little now remains—apart from the odd ruin and inscription—to remind us of our Viking ancestors' pagan worship. Lerwick's 'Up-Helly-Aa' festival, held in January each year, is of relatively recent origin, despite the longboat and helmets.

In the 1990s, however, an attempt was made, after a gap of a thousand years, to re-establish the worship of Odin in Scotland. It has been the mission of Dutch-born Freya Aswyn, who took over a collection of farm buildings and land near the village of Drumclog as a base for a revitalised cult of Odin. She named the centre 'Gladsheim' after one of Odin's castles in Asgard, the Norse version of the Christian Heaven. Aswyn, author of a key book on the old religion, *The Leaves of Yggdrasil*, has claimed to be a 'High Priestess of Odin'.

Aswyn's decision to come to Scotland is a mystic tale in itself, as is so often the case where cults are concerned. She received a 'trance communication' from Odin which told her that she had to leave London. He had a definite site in mind which would be signalled by an omen of some kind. That signal came in the shape of an advert for 'Bankend Farm', which she glimpsed in a copy of the down-to-earth *Exchange and Mart* that she had bought simply to check on the cost of tea chests for a removal. When Aswyn arrived at Bankend she knew straight away that this was the place she had been looking for. Behind the ruined farmhouse stood an ash and an elm, about two metres apart but with their branches locked together. This, to Freya Aswyn, signified the linking of the gods Ask and Embla, just as Odin had predicted.

The re-establishment of Odin-worship in Scotland is without doubt a formidable task. Aswyn made no great claims for conversions to Odinism and has stated that her movement is not a threat to Christianity. She did, however, aim to have the Odin cult recognised as a religious group if Scotland became an independent nation. It would certainly be 'full circle' as far as the Norse god is concerned, but more curious is the way in which, in the latter part of the 20th century, Scotland exercised such an attraction on a whole swathe of mystic cults, from the Findhorn [qv] pioneers of the 1960s, to 1990s Odinist Freya

Aswyn. The Odinists certainly took their mission seriously, placing a wolf totem pole at the entrance to 'Gladsheim' to frighten away unwanted visitors.

ORKNEY AND SHETLAND

The island of Orkney was certainly attractive to prehistoric man, and the remains of several stone circles can still be seen here and on the neighbouring islands. Then there is the enigma of Maeshowe, a massive chambered cairn, perfectly constructed using gigantic stone blocks which, if we were not bound by the interpretation of archaeologists, would have served as an excellent shelter against a nuclear bomb blast—its similarity to the modern defence bunkers which have been dug at strategic sites across Scotland is striking.

It may be that the village of Skara Brae, a world-famous prehistoric settlement, was also surrounded by a protective layer of earth—although according to the orthodox view it was buried beneath a layer of sand by pure accident. In the past the climate may have been warmer, the land less peaty, but even so it must have been a challenging existence for those who lived on Orkney. There is no evidence that it was a druidic centre of pagan worship, but it would certainly have been suitably located for use as one, in the mould of the islands of Anglesey and Arran.

In spite of their recent development as oil industry centres, there continue to be strange events linked to the islands. Most puzzling on Orkney was a spate of seal killings. The identity of the killer was never discovered, though theories ranged from a deranged local to entities from another world. The deaths stopped as suddenly as they began.

Orkney also earned notoriety through the activities of an alleged 'satanic coven' [see Satanism]. Though reports of witches and Devil-worship turned out to be a simple figment of the authorities' imagination, it might well be wondered if the land itself somehow influenced people's way of thinking. Did bizarre events from Orkney's past somehow put strange ideas into the minds of 20th-century social workers? It is said that houses and even areas of land can have a strange atmosphere, so could a whole island have a mystic influence hanging over it?

For the population size, the number of UFO sightings in Orkney has also been relatively high, but it is to Shetland we have to turn for what must rank as the most bizarre UFO seen in Scotland, and probably in the world. On 6th January 1992 Arthur Moar from Sandwick looked out of his window and saw an object about 40 yards from his house. He described it as 'about five or six feet high with flames all around it . . . in the centre I saw a globe of the world with all the markings on it.' Moar noted that the globe was coloured grey and that the area around the globe was dark red. The globe gave the appearance of being made of a suede-like material which seemed to be crumpled up. It was also connected to a white tube. When the object took off, the tube remained behind and gradually faded away.

In the world of the paranormal, truth is definitely stranger than fiction. This object appears to defy common sense, yet in a land which can boast sightings of goblins, fairies, monsters and flying railway carriages it may simply be yet another example of our bizarre universe at work.

P

PARANORMAL PAINTINGS

Why should a painting start producing paranormal effects? Whatever the answer, it is certainly a very rare occurrence. The only known incident in Scotland involved a picture owned by a retired driving instructor, Warner Hall, from Falkirk.

The painting, measuring three feet by three feet, originally hung in Hall's sitting room. It was a copy of a 19th-century painting entitled *The Bombardment of Algiers*, and it depicted an episode from the Napoleonic Wars. Across a sea bathed in red light, British warships pound the hapless French with cannonshot.

However, the scene painted by the artist appeared to have no connection with the images that 'came through' the painting. Those who viewed the picture saw a variety of faces and figures appearing. Some looked like ordinary people, others looked demonic. Some witnesses even claimed to see alien faces. The canvas had been bought from an ordinary store in Falkirk, and there was no immediately obvious link with anything remotely paranormal.

One possible solution lay in the person of the painting's owner, Warner Hall. Mr Hall clearly possessed psychic ability of some kind, and it may be that he was acting as some kind of channel for images from other dimensions. The painting in his possession was not alone in producing supernatural effects. Old photographs decorating his walls demonstrated a similar ability to allow spirit faces to appear. Furthermore, Mr Hall had taken an extensive series of video footage which seemed to show all kinds of strange scenes, including knights in medieval armour and churches full of kneeling worshippers. But the footage had been taken of everyday objects—including a shed in his garden. These inexplicable pictures had formed on the surface of each object as he videoed and, most remarkable of all, the pictures came out when the film was replayed. One section of footage, taken below Stirling's Wallace Monument, seemed to show a full scale battle scene.

If a psychic link with the spirit world can be ruled out there is another possibility. In the 1960s American Ted Serios was well known for what came to be called 'thoughtography'. He claimed to be able to project his thoughts on to photographic film and produce an image. It is possible that Warner Hall is producing a similar effect, but at a much higher and more complex level.

PARANORMAL PARLIAMENT

The decision to site Scotland's first parliament since 1707 at Holyrood was an interesting choice to those steeped in the history of the paranormal. For the place chosen lies in the shadow of Arthur's Seat, one of Scotland's most mystical hills. It may be no accident that this was the location agreed on. The area has a mass of 'earth energy' swirling through it, and it may well be that those involved in taking the decision were unconsciously influenced by the radiating energy [see Ley Lines].

The design of the new parliament building, curiously-shaped like an upturned boat, will certainly impact on the lines of energy passing across the site. It is unlikely that the architect took into account the need to construct a building which would provide a beneficial flow of earth energy, and the effect, therefore, on individual members of the Scottish Parliament remains to be seen. Too strong a flow will, as other instances have shown, produce a higher than average number of cases of illness, or simply greater irritability. Rather than encouraging a co-operative atmosphere, it may result in a more argumentative assembly. The decision to locate the parliament at Holyrood was no doubt well intentioned, but it may also turn into a warning to the authorities to pay more attention to the knowledge of dowsers [see Dowsing] and those experienced in the ways of earth energies.

Not surprising to those versed in the effects of earth energy, a major row blew up early in 2000 over the cost and delays in building the new parliament. Perhaps the energy vortex in the area was beginning to have an impact on those with an involvement in the project, and the bad feeling generated even before it was occupied casts further doubt on the choice of site.

PHANTOM PUMAS

There have been hundreds of sightings of mysterious 'black cats' in Scotland, over an area stretching from Ayrshire to Sutherland and even including the Isle of Skye. Although the press have labelled these strange beasts as 'black' (or as 'phantom pumas'), many of the animals sighted are fawn in colour, often described as similar in colour to a Labrador. They are usually reported as appearing slightly larger than an Alsatian dog, but distinctly cat-shaped. Sightings may occur typically in the open countryside, but the closest encounter took place on the edge of a built-up area. The witness was oil-worker William McRoberts. The date of the sighting 27th December 1992. Mr McRoberts reported:

'We were driving on the A726 which runs alongside the perimeter of Glasgow airport. The car in front was going slowly, then suddenly came to a complete halt. I drew up behind. Almost immediately after, I was astonished to see a puma plodding along by the side of my car. It was about the size of an Alsatian dog, but more muscular. It was a definite fawn colour. It pounced over the fence the way a cat does. It didn't look at the car or appear to be disturbed by our presence which surprised me.'

For years the standard explanation was that the appearance of these animals coincided with the passing of the Dangerous Animals Act in 1975. This piece of legislation stopped individuals having as pets truly 'wild' animals like lions or tigers. To avoid prosecution, and the cost of disposing of these beasts, owners rid themselves of their unwanted 'pets' by setting them free in isolated places. On the surface it seems an unlikely response given the risks that such a freed animal might pose to innocent passers-by, but it is clearly not impossible. But even if true, would this account for the hundreds of sightings in Scotland alone (never mind the rest of the UK)? And as these reports have been coming in for almost thirty years, can it reasonably be suggested that this same group of freed 'cats' is still going strong? And why, after so many sightings, mangled sheep and alleged photographs, has not one been caught or positively identified? There is a genuine mystery here as elusive and intriguing as that of 'loch monsters', but the solution remains as well hidden as the 'animals' themselves.

PHOTOGRAPHS, GHOST

For over a hundred years, ghost hunters have been searching for indisputable evidence to prove the existence of the spirit world. The one 'ghost photograph' or piece of video footage [see Video Evidence] that will convince even die-hard sceptics. To date, however, such evidence has been lacking. The general view has been that the photographs taken of alleged 'spirits' are either faked or have been caused by a technical fault, particularly in the development process. The number of ghost photos has declined during the last 20 years as other types of phenomenon, particularly UFOs, have come to prominence. However, each photograph of the paranormal should be considered on its own merits. And a number of intriguing images which cannot be easily explained away are worthy of serious consideration.

One which has aroused considerable interest was taken in the early hours of a morning in August 1987. David Knott was walking through Edinburgh's Royal Mile taking, as he stated, 'a whole series of photographs of the old town area . . . ensuring that nobody was in any of the photographs.' The last point is important, as when Knott developed the film he discovered what appeared to be a mysterious figure standing on the pavement at Castle Hill. On seeing the photograph for the first time Knott initially 'thought the figure to be that of a woman dressed in a black shroud'. However, after he had a transparency made his ideas about the picture changed radically as the figure now revealed 'quite clearly a man's head' which appears to be emerging from the shroud.

Given the fact that the picture seems to show a female form in a flowing dress of some kind, and with raised heeled shoes, the contradiction is difficult to account for. Knott's view was that 'there must have been an additional figure standing with the main form.' What is even more puzzling is that the figure, with reference being made to a window in a wall close by, can be no more than three and a half feet tall.

Up to the time the photograph was taken, David Knott had had no psychic experiences. Nor did he experience anything odd at the time he was taking the photograph. If, as Knott says, there were no other persons present when the photo was taken, then it is hard to explain what his camera caught on film. The phantom is more solid a figure than in most alleged ghost photographs, although it is possible to see through the upper part of the 'body'. It is also clearly defined, looking like a human entity, rather than a vague phantom. In the case of the Knott photograph we do not seem to be dealing with a faulty development process, poor film, or quirk of the camera. With no other witnesses to the event, we are relying on David Knott's account of how the picture came to be taken but, assuming his account to be accurate, the photograph may suggest that the age of the ghost photograph is not yet over.

Those who believe without question in the existence of ghosts often argue that spirits simply cannot be caught on camera in the way that normal everyday objects can. It may be that they only allow their image to appear when it suits them. One of the strangest reported Scottish incidents occurred in a pub in Falkirk in 1998 and involved the appearance of a ghostly image on a sheet of plain paper. As the witness directly involved in the event explained: 'It started off in a run-of-the-mill way. A friend and I attended a pub quiz, something we did on a regular basis. Each week the routine was the same. We were provided with pens, a score sheet, an A4-sized piece of paper with pictures of celebrities or famous places, and finally a scrap of paper on which to mark our answers. It was this scrap of paper which was involved in the mystery. On this particular night we were handed the aforementioned items and we each took a small bundle of scrap paper to jot our answers on. My friend put his small bundle in front of himself on the table, but accidentally laid it down in a small puddle of drink. The corner of the bottom sheet became soaked and a picture appeared on it. The wet patch covered one corner and was about the size of your thumbnail. The picture, which is in colour, shows a face though I could not say if it were male or female. We checked in case the picture question sheet had been soaked and the picture transferred, but it hadn't. Besides, the face did not remotely match any of the faces there. The other possibility was that it had transferred from a beer mat, but the pub does not provide beer mats.'

So where could the face have come from? If spirit images do appear, is there any reason why they should avoid pubs? Evidence from across the world reveals that unexplained images have turned up in many odd places, including living-room floors. Sceptics would argue that such facial images are simply chance arrangements of everyday objects. But it may be that some kind of thought transference is taking place so that a human mind, presumably its psychic aspect, projects a mental picture on to whatever happens to be close by.

We should not assume that the only ghostly images are of humans. One of the stranger aspects of the phenomenon is that there appear to be ghost cars, trains and buildings. The experience of Avril and Joe McGuire from Stirling suggests that even phantom images of old dwellings may linger into the present. As Avril McGuire explained: 'I'd taken a whole series of photographs. Most of them were of my baby, but I took two snaps of an old print we had hanging in a frame in the sitting room. This was an antique print my husband had picked up in a junk shop. It is a portrait of a young boy from the last century. I left the film lying for a while but when I had it developed at a local photographers, the pictures I had taken of the print had vanished. There were two completely different snaps in their place. I couldn't understand what had happened. The photos that came out were clearly of the house where I lived, but different. Then I realised they were showing my house as it looked a hundred years ago.' Where the McGuires' flat should have been there was instead the window of an old-fashioned grocer's shop, with the name of the owner visible above the door.

It may be the case that, instead of it being an incident involving a ghost building, the camera itself somehow looked back in time. But if that was the case, why would the image of the house have appeared when a photograph was being taken of a print which seemingly had no connection with the building. It seems that the McGuire flat had witnessed some poltergeist activity, but nothing which appears to have been unusually powerful. So we are left with an image which even sceptics will find hard to explain away.

PHYSICAL EVIDENCE

Is there any physical evidence for the paranormal? In part it depends on what proof we are prepared to accept. It seems clear that the paranormal brings with it physical effects, but the problem has always been in measuring this activity scientifically. On this basis, in Scotland at any rate, the para-normal has failed to produce scientific proof. However, given the range of the paranormal that occurs on Scottish soil and in the sky above, there is a variety of physical evidence for interested parties to consider. How we assess it may depend on our attitude to the paranormal.

Take the UFO phenomenon. There have been repeated claims over the years that UFOs have left behind marks of their presence on the ground, that the vitality of local plant life and even the health of human beings has been affected by their activity.

The most obvious incident which points this way is the case at Livingston [qv] in 1979 involving forestry worker Bob Taylor. There were undeniably physical effects on Taylor himself— tear-marks on his trousers, scratches on his legs, and the fact that he lost consciousness. However, even if we accept that Taylor came into contact with an alien spaceship, were the effects on his person the direct result of an alien assault, or the by-product of energy or chemicals being generated by the 'craft'? Two radically different scenarios follow, depending on which view we accept. The physical evidence was not confined to effects on Taylor alone—ladder-like impressions and circular depressions were found at the 'landing site'. However, their connection with the UFO events has not been proved and they seem at odds with Bob Taylor's account of what happened. On the other hand it is a strange coincidence that these marks should be found at the spot where he claimed the encounter took place. Analysis of the soil area revealed nothing out of the ordinary.

Analysis also drew a blank in the case of an alleged UFO landing in Elgin in 1976, where it appeared as if leaves on trees had been affected near the spot where the UFO was seen standing on three thin legs. Neither has anything been proved from the controversial Fife 'close encounter' case of 1996 [see Abduction]. Gossamer-like material stuck to vegetation near the site had an obvious earthly source, and there were claims of huts made from grass, though whether these had any alien origin (or even existed) remains controversial.

In the USA there have certainly been claims of whole or large parts of crashed alien spacecraft being recovered and stored, although so far nothing has been definitely proved. In Scotland rumours have circulated to link the Machrihanish air base [qv] on the Mull of Kintyre with similar stories. There have been a few claims from Scotland that parts of a spacecraft have been discovered. In 1994 an object was found in the vicinity of the Livingston UFO incident of 1979—an area, incidentally, where there have been numerous UFO reports over the years. However, it quickly emerged that the 'strange object' was actually a religious vessel stolen from a local Roman Catholic church. A warning to enthusiasts to 'gang warily'.

For a while it was claimed that crop circles [qv] were caused by UFO landings, an idea some still hold to. However, the phenomenon has never been definitely linked to any space-craft, although the appearance of strange lights in the vicinity of crop circles has been reported. The most notable example of this in Scotland is of lights appearing before and after the formation of circles on the Ardblair estate in June 1990.

With poltergeist phenomena [qv] we might appear to be on more solid ground. Objects are moved, pools of water and other liquids allegedly form, writing appears on walls. Over the centuries a host of well attested eye witness evidence has been acquired. Again, however, the fact that many incidents of this nature have been reported does not provide physical proof. Analysis of liquids or objects has not revealed structural or chemical peculiarities that can prove that something strange has happened. Certainly the fact that an object has moved on its own is proof that 'something' is going on, but is not by itself going to satisfy sceptics. In the end it comes down, as in so much of the paranormal, to what we are prepared to accept as evidence.

'Energy lines' are a good case in point [*see* Ley Lines]. There have been calls for scientific studies to determine the effect of these invisible lines of force running beneath the Earth, particularly as there are suspicions that some occurrences of this energy can produce serious illness. In addition there is evidence that electromagnetic energy from communication relay towers and electricity pylons can also be a health hazard. However, the principle way in which these energy lines are detected is through the art of dowsing—and at the moment dowsing is not accepted as a scientific technique. It looks likely, then, that it will be a long time before the threat from energy lines beneath our houses is taken seriously by the authorities.

POLICE

To the public the police are often the first port of call where the paranormal is concerned. This is particularly true when a UFO has been seen. The exact role of the Scottish police in tackling the phenomenon, however, remains controversial. The police were involved in investigating the Bob Taylor incident in November 1979 [see Livingston UFO] although, at least publicly, that was mainly due to the initial view that Taylor had been the subject of a physical assault. However, their involvement certainly added to the credibility of the encounter and gave the subject of UFOs a publicity boost. Even so, there is no evidence that their involvement went beyond the level of a standard criminal investigation.

Abductee Gary Wood [qv], of the well known A70 alien encounter case of 1992, considered contacting the police, though in the end he decided not to—he thought it would be hard to convince them of the reality of the incident. However, it is significant that he at least thought of turning to the police for help. When Andy Swan had a disturbing encounter on a road in West Lothian in 1994, he rang the police for assistance. It was the logging of his calls by the police computer which seemed to indicate a discrepancy in Swan's account of events and led to speculation about a period of 'missing time' so often linked to abduction events. And when the Freeman family spotted a UFO above their Blairgowrie [qv] bungalow in 1984, they rang the local police who sent two officers to investigate. These incidents are just the tip of an iceberg of police involvement at a formal level in UFO sightings.

At the unofficial level, individual policemen have been a regular source of UFO reports, on and off the beat. A serving officer, Ben Goodwin, reported seeing a silver UFO over Glasgow in 1976, and as far back as 1957 two officers saw a strange light in the sky as they drove towards Aberdeen. On at least two separate occasions in 1980 in Dumfriesshire, police officers reported seeing strange lights in the sky at a time when the area was a UFO hot spot.

The best known case directly involving a police officer took place that same year in England. While on patrol in his vehicle, Constable Alan Godfrey came across a 'spaceship' hovering over the road. Hypnotic regression [see Hypnosis] revealed that he had been taken aboard the UFO, where he encountered two types of alien entities. There has been no parallel case in Scotland that has been publicly revealed. However, Ben Goodwin, who has now left the police, indicated that many policemen had experienced strange sightings, but were aware of the damage it could do to their careers, and either did not report them, or for official purposes explained them away as misidentified natural phenomena (car headlights reflecting off low cloud is a common example).

Ufologists have traditionally regarded police officers as key witnesses because of their assumed powers of observation. Against this must be set rumours of a controversial, but widely suspected, link between the police, MOD and military. This has become part of ufologist conspiracy theories, reflecting a widely held view that UFO reports passed to the police by members of the public are forwarded to other government agencies, and that the authorities know far more about the UFO question than they are prepared to admit. In general, however, the police have not been unco-operative in their dealings with ufologists, having as a rule shown themselves willing to provide information and their own comments on individual cases. Policemen have even joined UFO organisations, and one serving officer was BUFORA's Scottish representative for a time.

Where ghosts, poltergeists and related aspects of the

paranormal are concerned, the role of the police has to be considered uncertain. A strange unexplained light in the sky could have terrestrial implications. Frightening incidents in a house, if they have no obvious repercussions as a 'breach of the peace', are harder for the police to become involved in—either officially or informally. However, even in these situations the police are often seen as the first port of call for help. Perhaps one day official links will be established between the police and paranormal investigators to tackle events which can be as disturbing to the public as being victims of more obvious crimes.

In the USA at least, police have used psychics to provide help in difficult cases—especially where a murder has been committed or been suspected. Best known for co-operating with psychics at an official level is the Des Moines district police in Illinois. The exact status of such assistance in Scotland is uncertain, although it is at best informal. One well-known incident in Scotland where a psychic became involved concerned the disappearance and presumed murder of Pat McAdam in February 1967. Although the case remained unsolved for several years, a lorry driver, Thomas Young, was later convicted of the crime. Though he had never visited the area, internationally known Dutch psychic Gerald Croiset provided what seemed to be unusually accurate information about the crime. Croiset, however, became involved through the interest of a Scottish newspaper and not at an official level. Nor did Croiset solve the puzzle of Pat McAdam's disappearance, the case finally being solved as the result of down-to-earth detective work.

This seems to reflect a general, though not universal, rule

where psychics are involved—tantalising clues are suggested, but nothing concrete. For example, psychics have not been able to help to solve the still-unexplained disappearance in 1991 of schoolgirl Vicky Hamilton while travelling between Bathgate and the village of Redding. This tragic event might be regarded as exactly the type of incident where paranormal ability might be of use. Janet Hamilton, Vicky's mother, however, commented during the investigation: 'The police have told me . . . that lots of psychics have offered help and no two have come up with the same answers.'

A more official approach to using psychics, including a test of their ability, would avoid the problem of causing distress to relatives where several psychics make claims to have 'solved' a crime.

POLTERGEISTS

Poltergeist phenomena are perhaps the best attested of all supernatural incidents. In Scotland they have a long history, and for at least the last three hundred years there have been many outbreaks which have come to public attention.

The published evidence dates back to the 1650s and the case of the 'Glenluce Devil' [qv]. Two other 17th-century Scottish cases, the 'Bargarran Imposter' [qv] (1692) and the 'Rerrick Poltergeist' [qv] (1695), are regarded as classic examples of the phenomenon and are still often referred to. The Rerrick and Glenluce cases contain all the 'classic' ingredients of a poltergeist manifestation, ingredients which we would find in cases right up to the present—like the strange events which took place at Tillicoultry, and the Bainsford (Falkirk) poltergeist, both from the 1990s.

The term 'poltergeist' comes from the German meaning 'noisy spirit', and it is this which sets poltergeist activity apart from a ghost's haunting. It is certainly true that there are noises associated with the appearance of a phantom—creaking floorboards, voices, doors opening and closing, and there are obviously times when haunting and poltergeist incidents might appear to overlap. However, what characterises poltergeist activity is the indiscriminate nature of the incidents and their intensity.

For example, take the events in Tillicoultry. In this instance a young woman moved into a new flat which had been built in a former mill. She was, in fact, the first occupant of the premises, and had not been in the house long when strange things began to happen. On one occasion, she caught a glimpse of a black shadow flying past her and going straight through the wall as she was kneeling beside her hi-fi. She would come back from work to discover that objects had been moved around the living room. Toothpaste and gel were smeared over the bathroom wall. Most frightening of all, she woke one morning to hear strange footsteps running round her bed, a noise that carried on for several hours and only stopped when the sun rose. The woman was too frightened even get out of bed to try and find out what was causing it. It is interesting to note that, though there was considerable disturbance, there was no appearance of anything that could be described as a ghost. However, a medium who was called in claimed that the spirit of a dead child was causing the problem. It turned out that a child had drowned in an ornamental pond which had at one time been situated near the building.

There are more instances of poltergeist manifestation than is generally realised, and each has its own disturbing aspects. But the events at Bainsford, Falkirk which reached a climax in the autumn of 1990, stand out because of a combination of incidents which simply defy explanation.

The flat involved was situated to the rear of a Victorian tenement block on Main Street, Bainsford. The accommodation consisted of a living room with a kitchen recess, a double bedroom, directly off the living room, a bathroom and an entrance hall. At the time the incidents occurred it was occupied by a single woman, Lisa, who was in her 30s.

Lisa had lived in the flat since 1982, but it was not until the late 1980s that odd things began to happen. On one occasion in 1988 Lisa noticed a strange red light which came into her bedroom from the living room and 'moved about like a torch'. At the same time she noticed an atmosphere 'like a thick fog' in the bedroom, and an aroma of perfume. This was disturbing enough, but then writing appeared on the bedroom wall. This consisted of the numbers 32 and 57, the letters D and E, and three crosses. The significance of this has never been clear. What happened next seems to defy logic. Lisa described lying in her bed one night, and the wall at the foot of her bed appeared to light up. She then saw the image of a ballet dancer appear on the wall. This happened not once, but twice, and the second time the ballet dancer appeared to move across the wall and behind her came the shadow of a man as if he was chasing her.

What happened next terrified Lisa. Writing appeared high up on the bedroom wall. It was light coloured and was in a child-like scrawl. Lisa made out the words: 'You are . . .', noticed there were more words underneath, but simply didn't wait to read the rest. She ran from the house and took a taxi to her mother's.

Although the appearance of writing seemed to mark the climax of events, various other incidents had occurred. On one occasion when plumbers were carrying out improvements in the bathroom, blood was found on the inside handle of the main door. There seemed no explanation as to how it had got there. As in many poltergeist manifestations objects, especially ornaments, had been moved about the house. On one occasion Lisa had seen a man, possibly dressed like a monk, kneeling at the foot of the bed.

Was there an explanation as to why the flat had so suddenly become a focus of poltergeist activity? There was a local tradition that a two-year-old boy had been drowned in the bath—possibly not by accident. At some point in the 1980s the floor of the bathroom had been ripped up to put in a new suite, although this renovation did not seem to coincide with the start of the poltergeist disturbance. Nevertheless, Lisa felt that it had possibly set events in motion, this disturbance being compounded by later improvement work.

Lisa herself was psychic, and perhaps unwittingly acted as a channel. Interestingly, when a medium was brought in he pinpointed a spot in Lisa's bedroom where he saw the body of a child lying soaking wet on the carpet. He had deliberately not been told of the alleged drowning incident. It was not possible to come to any conclusion in this case, as Lisa found events too disturbing and had no wish, at that time, to continue staying in the flat.

The general view of mediums is that poltergeist activity is related to spirits who may not have realised they are dead. They annoy the living in this way for various reasons, including resentment that people have moved into what they still view as their home. However, there is by no means agreement on what causes poltergeist manifestations, and others involved in the paranormal take an opposing view. There are some who argue that 'bad energy' in a house allows malevolent spirits to enter a dwelling and disrupt the lives of the occupants. Though if there really are evil spirits, it is odd that their behaviour should so often appear childish. And many of the actions carried out are at a juvenile level, although when carried out by an invisible hand, these actions become frightening for those who experience them. On the other hand, attempts to burn down a cottage, as was reported during the Rerrick case (1695), seem more deliberately malicious.

Other explanations relate to the phenomenon of electromagnetic energy which dowsers [qv] argue runs below most houses. This theory suggests that the energy fields created produce physical disturbances, which may include the movement of objects. Though that may be true, it is hard to believe that the writing which appeared on a wall during events at Bainsford was produced other than by an intelligence of some kind.

There are some sceptics who would like to dismiss these events as fantasy or fabrication, though even most nonbelievers recognise that poltergeist incidents do require an explanation. Apart from the usual claims that witnesses are either lying or fantasising, one cautionary point should be borne in mind: underground vibrations and rodent activity can account for a lot of the strange noises or odd movements of objects which are reported. So far, though, tests carried out to create vibrations artificially have not been able to bring about the results typical of a poltergeist infestation, and poltergeist activity remains a mystery which even science cannot yet satisfactorily explain away.

POSSESSION

The general view of possession has been coloured by dramatic portrayals in *The Exorcist*, *The Amityville Horror* and other well-known films. However, the idea of an evil spirit taking control of an individual by physically entering his or her body is an old one.

In the past there have been infamous cases—the Nuns of Loudon (1634) is perhaps the best known—in which demonic possession played a key role in events. At this small convent in France several nuns claimed that a local priest, Father Urban Grenadier, was in league with Satan and had sent demons to take control of their bodies. The effect can be seen in the behaviour of one young nun, Sister Clare, who (as described in contemporary records) 'fell on the ground, blaspheming, in convulsions, lifting up her petticoats and chemise, displaying her privy parts without any shame and uttering filthy words.'

Incidents of demonic possession and witchcraft often went hand in hand, with witches being blamed for the torment suffered by those who claimed to be, or were believed to be, possessed by an evil spirit. The possessed person was often a young person, adolescent or pre-adolescent, as events in *The Exorcist* neatly sum up.

Historically, it was often difficult to separate tormenting behaviour by external spirits from behaviour carried out by the possessed person under the control of spirits. At the start of the 18th century, Patrick Morton, a 16-year-old blacksmith's son from the Fife fishing village of Pittenweem, was convinced that he was being tormented by the spirit of a woman, Beatrix Laing, whom he believed to be a witch. In 1704 he began to exhibit the most bizarre symptoms. According to witnesses: 'His belly at some times was distended to a great height. At other times his breast and back were so distended that the bones of his back and breast did rise to a prodigious height and suddenly fell. And in the meantime his breathing was like the blowing of a bellows.' Patrick had clearly lost control of his physical body, but was it a case of possession or an external 'force' exercising control over his mind?

The simple fact of entering the physical body of a person does not, however, qualify as 'possession'. Many spiritual mediums accept as part of the behaviour of spirits that they will enter their body. This is often seen as an essential part of physical mediumship where the spirit communicates through the medium, changes the physical appearance of the medium, or simply uses the medium in order to form a physical presence on what spiritualists call the 'material plane'. 'Possession' implies something more sinister—a malicious intent.

A case in the north of Scotland in the 1990s shows that, although there is a fine dividing line which separates possession from 'spirit entry', there is undoubtedly a difference. In this instance, a woman with a child had moved into rented accommodation. Her husband was often away in connection with his work, so she would find herself retiring to bed on her own, usually around midnight. When she did so she went through a disturbing experience. As she lay down to sleep she had the frightening physical sensation that someone had his hands around her neck as if he was trying to choke her. However, when she got out of bed the sensation stopped. There were no other paranormal phenomena occurring in the house. To mediums there was a straightforward answer—a spirit, probably someone who knew the woman, was trying to contact her. It was his clumsy attempts to do this which were creating the odd sensation that she felt. He was trying to get inside her physical body, but that he was not trying to 'possess' her is suggested by the fact that the feelings stopped as soon as she got out of bed. In other words, when she made it clear to the spirit that she was not responding to his attempts to contact her, nothing further happened until the following night. An attempt at classic 'possession' would not have been so easy to resist.

A case in Perthshire, again dating from the 1990s, draws a step closer to true possession although it also shows how difficult it is to decide what exactly 'possession' is. The woman in question was in her early 20s, but for some years had been plagued by all the traditional phenomena linked to the paranormal. Wherever she lived strange noises could be heard, especially rustling or scratching which are considered to be sounds associated with a poltergeist presence. Unexplained lights appeared in the bedroom. Doors opened and closed, footsteps were heard. The disturbing nature of these events contributed to the break-up of her marriage, or so she felt. More sinister was the fact that she experienced prolonged and unexplained stomach pains. The accumulated incidents were having the effect of depressing the woman and she felt as if a cloud was hanging over her. In a sense it was. According to a psychic medium who was called in, a spirit had latched on to her, and it was the spirit who was wearing her down, drawing energy from her. The medium took action to move the spirit on, and as he did so the effect on the woman was dramatic. It was almost as if she had for a moment lost control of herself, and she ran towards a window which she would have crashed straight through if others had not held her back.

Arguably, this is a case of possession in the sense that a spirit was, over a period of time, using the body of a living person for its own purpose. But it does not approach what we today see as 'perfect possession'—an individual whose whole life has been transformed in a negative way, or who feels that he or she cannot behave in a normal fashion because 'something else' has control over them. There are individuals even today who say that they are in such a situation.

The difficulty for the psychic investigator is in deciding whether the claimed problems are due to mental health difficulties or genuine spirit activity. Even for mediums it is sometimes hard to decide whether an alleged problem with spirits may in fact be the result of a person's mental state. The two may well interact, although those who run psychiatric hospitals will never admit to spirit influence on those in their care. Religious organisations, on the other hand, do have well-established procedures for exorcising demons from those possessed, although they are not ready to admit to what extent they use these rites.

Possession is certainly a difficult area of the paranormal. It is also a disturbing area in that it provides evidence that spirits and humanity may not always live in harmony.

PSYCHIC MURDER

One of the puzzles that continues to intrigue occult circles is why 33-year-old Norah Fornario decided, in 1929, to visit Iona [qv], a historic centre of Christianity. Fornario was a member of the shadowy Order of Alpha and Omega, an offshoot of the Hermetic Order of the Golden Dawn, both organisations created and lead by occultist Samuel Liddell Mathers and his wife Mina. The Mathers were obsessive over control of their Orders—thirty years earlier Mathers and black magician Aleister Crowley [see Boleskine House] had fought a legendary psychic battle for control of the Hermetic movement which Mathers, according to his wife, won. Mathers, an Englishman who liked to claim Scottish ancestry, did not have Crowley's unsavoury reputation, but he was regarded with some awe by those versed in the black arts.

So what was one of his followers doing on the island of Iona, cradle of Scottish Christianity? Had she been fleeing from psychic threats to her life, and was she looking for protection? Given her unexplained death, that might be seen as a real possibility. But there is no evidence that she made any attempt to contact local officials of the Church—whatever reasons she had for coming to Iona they do not seem to have been matters which she felt required Christian help. In fact, Norah spent her days on Iona walking the island's many beaches, reading or writing poetry and contemplating occult matters. At night she would go into a trance, making contact with the many spirits which, she claimed, roamed the island. Although this might appear strange on the surface, many followers of the occult were aware that Christianity had taken over former centres of pagan worship and had even incorporated aspects of pagan religion into Christian belief.

One Sunday late in November, Fornario decided that she must leave the island immediately. However, as it was Sunday she could not get a ferry to take her off the island until the next morning. That night Norah decided to take a final stroll around the island.

The next morning the Cameron family, in whose croft she had been staying, found her bags neatly packed but her bed unslept in. Her clothes were lying neatly folded on a chair. Later that day a party of islanders set out to look for her, but it was not until the following day that Fornario was discovered. She was dead, her body lying in hills south of Loch Staonaig.

But it was the unexplained manner of her death which has continued to raise questions. Had the occult played a part in ending her life? She was naked except for a robe of the Order of Alpha and Omega and a silver chain around her neck. Her feet were bloody and swollen from having walked, run or, as some claimed, been chased across rough terrain. She had a long knife in her hand and when her body was removed from the spot a rough cross was found to have been cut into the turf beneath her.

The doctor who signed Norah's death certificate put heart failure as the cause of death. Considering that she had been out in the open on a cold November night, death from natural causes cannot be ruled out. However, many questions remain unanswered—like her unexplained decision to visit Iona, her sudden wish to get away, and the final mysterious journey on a cold night in full occult dress into the windswept hills of the island.

Fornario may well have set out with the intention of summoning up the phantoms of another world. But was she looking for protection or acting on behalf of other occultists? We may never know whether or not Fornario died because of a psychic attack, but one thing is certain: the look of horror on Fornario's face when she was discovered shocked all who saw it. Had she suddenly realised that the bitter weather had taken its toll on her body, or is it possible that the terror she was faced with that night came not from the elements but from another, more sinister force?

Q

QUEENSFERRY

One of the burning issues of the last 30 years has been the question of extraterrestrial contact. Was the Earth visited in the past by beings from other worlds? Tales from the Bible and other ancient texts could be interpreted as referring to advanced flying machines, and an account from the Hindu Vedas tells how a priest called Ajamila boarded a 'golden plane' and 'flew through the airways' to met with Lord Visnu. More directly a collection of ancient Indian works, the *Samaranga*, are claimed to describe the building of an aircraft, including instructions that 'the iron engine must have properly welded joints to be filled with mercury' and 'the body must be strong and durable and built of light wood, shaped like a bird in flight with the wings outstretched.'

Much of this written evidence depends on translation of long-dead languages and how the phrases used are interpreted.

But are we missing more straightforward clues? Is there contemporary evidence from Scotland that Earth has been visited by extraterrestrials?

In order to place the Scottish evidence in context, let us first consider folklore from further afield—the strange case of the Kayapo Indians. First discovered in 1952, the Kayapo Indians of the upper Amazon in Brazil have a strange ceremony. Once a year, the leading men of the village wrap themselves in suits made of straw. Over their head and neck they place a helmet also made of straw, so that they are covered from head to foot in the strange garment. Moving awkwardly around the village in this all-enclosing costume they look for all the world like astronauts walking with difficulty in their padded suits on the bare rock of the moon.

And it would not be too far fetched to make the spaceman link—for that is exactly what the Kayapo themselves believe. According to legend the villagers saw earthquake and fire erupt on a nearby hill. When they went to investigate they met a stranger who appeared out of the fire. They attacked him with their primitive weapons, but these simply bounced off his strange clothes. Eventually, once they had overcome their fright, the stranger and the Kayapo became friends. He taught the tribe many things—including how to make wonderful medicines which cured illnesses they had come to accept as the inevitable penalty of their way of life. The villagers' name for the stranger was 'Bep Kororoti', which translates as 'I come from space'. One day Bep Kororoti left the village in his gleaming white suit to return 'home'. He was seen to disappear in a loud blast of smoke and fire.

It is hard to be sure that the account passed to us is correct, but a ritual very like that of Bep Kororoti can be found in the heart of Scotland. The village of South Queensferry on the Firth of Forth has an annual festival which includes an entity known as the 'Burry Man'. On the first Friday in August one of the villagers is dressed in a bizarre costume. He is covered with a coat of cloth to which are sown thousands of burr pods. At the end of the dressing, just like 'Bep Kororoti', the 'Burry Man' is covered from neck to shin in an all-enclosing garment. His head and face are protected within a helmet also covered with burrs except for small openings for his eyes and mouth. The Burry Man finds it very difficult to walk in his suit. Indeed the traditional costume may be deliberately designed to make it hard to move. So is it possible that the original Burry Man could have been an 'astronaut' from another world who struggled to adjust to our gravity? Or are we remembering in this strange ceremony something from our own past—that Mankind originated from space, and colonised the planet Earth?

A visitor from Brazil would be struck by the similarity between Bep Kororoti and the Burry Man. And it has to be asked whether it is simply coincidence that South Queensferry sits at the heart of the Falkirk UFO Triangle which stretches from Bonnybridge [qv] to West Lothian and across the Forth into Fife. And was it pure chance that, during the centenary celebration of the Forth Railway Bridge in 1990, a UFO was seen by several witnesses hovering over the structure? There is also the incident at Lochore Country Park only 20 miles away—a woman sitting in a car was approached by a giant figure wearing a one-piece silver suit which covered the strange entity from head to toe.

The jigsaw in Scotland is not complete, however. What we do not have is a tradition, like that in Brazil, which would link the Burry Man to the appearance of a stranger who actually claims to be from another world.

So other explanations also have to be weighed up. According to the official version, this unique festival is a relic of ancient pagan worship, a representation of the god of Vegetation or even the mysterious 'Green Man' [qv] himself. While this solution cannot be ruled out, it does not explain why the Burry Man and Bep Kororoti are so alike—even down to carrying long decorated poles. And these bizarre entities are not alone. Across the world figures dressed in crude replicas of astronaut-style space suits can be found taking part in strange ceremonies. The implication seems inescapable.

QUEEN VICTORIA

Mystery surrounds Queen Victoria's interest in the paranormal. There has been particular speculation regarding her involvement with spiritualists, with rumours circulating during her lifetime, and resurfacing periodically since, that after the death of Prince Albert, Victoria consulted mediums in order to contact the spirit of her dead husband.

It is easy to see how these rumours have developed. Spiritualism was growing in popularity during much of the period of her reign (1837–1901). Among high society, an evening with a medium was a fashionable way to pass the time. Well known psychics, like the Scots born Daniel Home [qv], became international celebrities who mixed with the aristocracy and became a part of their circle. Home may be an outstanding example of how, in the climate of the time, a medium might rise to the top, but society in general took up spiritualism with a lively interest.

Rumours, however, are not proof. Victoria was certainly familiar with the activities of mediums and 'table rapping', but there is no real evidence that she consulted psychic mediums or was ever present at a séance. Claims by relatives of Robert Lees, well known for his alleged vision of 'Jack the Ripper', that Victoria consulted him, even presenting him with a book as thanks, have not been substantiated. Nor have any other alleged incidents linking the Queen with mediums been proved.

Her controversial involvement with John Brown, her Scottish servant, might have arisen because of Brown's ability to communicate with the dead—in particular Victoria's husband. There is no doubt that the two had a close relationship, but did that extend to, or was it even based on, Brown's psychic power? At that time the Highlands were regarded as one of the mystic centres of the realm. Highland blood was seen as being especially potent in producing 'second sight'. So where Brown was concerned it is possible to suggest a link between his Highland background, the 'second sight', and Victoria's longing to contact Albert in the next world.

The documentary evidence to back this up is lacking—Brown's diaries were burned on his death, proof that the powers-that-be felt that whatever the diaries contained they would do Victoria's reputation no good. But did that include reference to psychic experiments? The truth is that we can only speculate as to whether or not Victoria used Brown as a medium. It would provide an explanation for Brown's relationship with Victoria, but that relationship could have been based on other mutual interests. The rumours refuse to go away but until real proof appears, Victoria's involvement with the paranormal will have to remain 'not proven'.

R

REINCARNATION

The idea of reincarnation, that we experience many lives, has not fired the Scottish imagination, though it is a mainstay of many Eastern religions. However, reincarnation is very much a part of the paranormal fringe. It is a commonplace among spiritualists and mediums, who will often talk of their experiences from past lives. The general public is by no means hostile to the idea of reincarnation but, because it is frowned upon by Christianity, it has not been taken particularly seriously. There are few people in Scotland who have become famous through publicly discussing a past life, and the Scottish media pay reincarnation little attention compared with ghosts and UFOs.

Western Christianity fell in line with pagan beliefs which were not linked to reincarnation. A kind of glorious after-life, like an uproarious Heaven, was what was expected—a reward for the trials and tribulations of one existence, not a return to Earth in another outward form to gain fresh experience. Although the Scottish occult in the 19th and 20th centuries encompassed many traditions, the acceptance of reincarnation seems to have been largely due to the influence of Eastern religions. Growing acquaintance with Hindu beliefs through contact with India, the rise of British Buddhism (a 19th rather than 20th century phenomenon), and the foundation of the Theosophical Society by Helena Blavatsky and her Great White Brotherhood of Mahatmas, all served to popularise the concept of reincarnation. However, reincarnation did not take the same hold on English and Scottish spiritualism as it did in France or South America, where reincarnation was an essential part of the 'Spiritist' movement.

Scotland's best known recent case of reincarnation involves both an English woman and a well known Scottish historical figure. Ada Kay (born 1929), an established playwright and scriptwriter, had been plagued for years by the feeling that she was somebody else. These feelings came to a head in August 1967 when she was staying in a house in Jedburgh. This house was close to the site of the Battle of Flodden, where James IV and the 'flower of Scotland' were slaughtered on 9th September 1314 in a disastrous confrontation with English forces commanded by the Earl of Surrey.

It is more than likely that Kay was well aware of the historical links with the area, but she had not connected these events with her own troubled thoughts. However, as she lay in bed one night she suddenly found herself transported back in time to the ancient battlefield. As Kay wrote of the experience: 'I seemed to be lying on my back staring up at a tunnel of staves and blades . . . beyond them [the] merciless faces of men intent on killing me. My left arm I raised to cover my head to ward off the blows . . . I howled a howl of pure animal terror as the blades thrust down upon me.' Ada Kay was convinced that this was not just a vivid dream, but a memory of an incident that she had lived through. That in a past life she had, in fact, been King James IV of the Stewart dynasty. (There is nothing strange in a woman having been a man in a past life, as the whole idea of reincarnation is that we experience different paths for our own long-term improvement.)

Although Kay's realisation of her previous existence had come in a dramatic moment, she had been through earlier experiences which convinced her that she had a special link with Scotland, even though she had been born in Lancashire. She had visited Edinburgh Castle to view the Scottish crown jewels and seen blood trickling down the royal sword—an incident visible to no one else. Another time as she walked through Edinburgh's Old Town she looked across the Firth of Forth and glimpsed a fleet of tall sailing ships, their wooden outlines matching perfectly images she had seen of vessels dating from the time of King James IV.

By the 1960s Kay had assumed the character of her past life, even taking to dressing in the clothes of the period, and changing her surname to 'Stewart'. Ada Kay was sincere in her belief that she had lived in an earlier age, but independent evidence to back up her case has been lacking. It remains, however, a dramatic example of the way in which reincarnation can impact on an individual life.

Ada Kay's case may reinforce the views of sceptics who

argue that those who claim past lives have always lived before as Cleopatra, Julius Caeser or somebody equally famous. In fact, that is far from being the case. Many who remember living before believe they have experienced quite straight-forward lives as servants, cooks and foot-soldiers. Andrew Hennessey, a theosophist, remembers quite clearly being given the opportunity to choose between several lives from different times and levels of society, none of which involved a famous person. He was given this chance to choose in order that he could learn from different experiences. This is seen as part of a long process of improvement, stretching through millennia, until in the end a person becomes almost god-like—there is nothing left to learn.

REPEATER WITNESS

Most of us expect to see a ghost or UFO at best only once in our lifetime. However, repeater witnesses—though rare—are more widespread than might be believed. It is certainly true that in most cases a witness to a UFO incident or a ghost has that experience as a one-off event. Bob Taylor, whose remarkable encounter in November 1979 on Dechmont Law made world headlines [see Livingston UFO], saw no UFOs before or after the incident. Pat Macleod, who had an amazing close sighting of a Saturn-shaped object only feet above a busy Edinburgh street in 1992, had no other experiences. And for Tom Coventry, who witnessed a UFO which looked like a railway carriage sailing 20 feet above his head in Glasgow, it was his only encounter.

Some individuals, however, have experiences on a regular basis. Rita Gould from Glasgow has seen several different types of UFOs over a number of years. John Adams, also from Glasgow, has been through a variety of psychic experiences. So why should some people have repeated encounters in this way?

In Scotland there are many individuals who have what we could call psychic ability. They see spirits or communicate with the 'other side' all the time. So it might be argued that people like John Adams are psychic even though they may not realise it. Or even if they do realise it, do not have control over it.

This is generally the answer favoured by psychics, but we cannot be sure that a person who suffers (as they usually feel it to be unpleasant) repeated incidents is experiencing an identical situation to that of a psychic. There will be different levels and different types of experience.

As regards control, the evidence that it is possible to learn to subject psychic manifestation to conscious will is not conclusive. Some people do manage to stop spirit intrusion by the simple method of telling a spirit to go away. With more intense activity, the evidence suggests that the person or persons at the centre of repeated events find it hard to control the situation no matter how they try, or how much support they are given by mediums. On the other hand, in an incident in a village south of Aberdeen a medium speaking over the phone was apparently able to stop poltergeist activity by the simple method of having the person involved visualise certain objects. That, however, may be an exception to the rule.

UFOs are a different area in the sense that no one is sure whether UFOs are a psychic phenomenon or solid 'nuts-and bolts' objects. If they are psychic in nature then the sightings of repeater witnesses might be more easily understood. If not, then it is hard to understand why a number of people have UFO sightings time and again. And these incidents might be separated by months or years. Andrew McMichael from Edinburgh had a sighting in 1976 and then again in 1996. Lyn Livingston first witnessed a UFO in 1958 in Edinburgh, then in 1990 over the Firth of Forth.

One possible answer would be that UFOs are solid objects, but that they exist in other dimensions. A repeater witness, such as Joyce Dyers [qv] from Moffat who reported dozens of sightings in the 1970s, could be explained as an individual who had the ability to see into those other dimensions. This immediately raises other questions—why should this happen to the witness only on some occasions and not all the time? Sceptics would argue that the more sightings claimed by a witness the more likely it is that the witness is fantasising or consistently misidentifying everyday objects. However, if paranormal phenomena are genuine, there seems no reason why a witness' experience should be a one-off. Perhaps closer investigation of the repeater witness phenomenon may provide key clues as to the real nature of the supernatural.

RERRICK POLTERGEIST

The case of the Rerrick Poltergeist, which began in 1690, remains one of the best documented, most intense, paranormal incidents to have occurred in Scotland. In the gradual build-up of incidents, the range of phenomena displayed and the dramatic finale, it is a classic of its kind. But we are still left wondering why these events took place at a collection of farm buildings miles from any centre of human habitation, and with no previous history of supernatural occurrence.

That something odd was going on, however, was confirmed by three separate families over a period of years. The farm-house around which the incidents were concentrated was built in 1667 and was called Ringcroft of Stocking, in the parish of Rerrick. There is no record of any problem till around 1690, when William McNaught took over the tenancy, and certain unrecorded incidents started to affect the lives of the McNaught family. We know this because William asked his son, David, to consult a white witch who lived nearby. On his way back to the farm, however, David met with an army recruiting party, enlisted and disappeared to Europe. Before he vanished into obscurity, David told a friend of the family, John Reddick, what the white witch had told him, and asked Reddick to pass the message to his father—under the threshold stone at the farmhouse door he would find a tooth. This tooth had to be burnt to lift a curse on the family.

But by the time Reddick got round to paying a visit, William McNaught had died, and a new owner, Thomas Telfer, was now living in the cottage. Having heard of the alleged curse, he lifted the stone, found the tooth and burned it. It flamed 'like a candle', though Telfer was convinced it was not made of wax. Telfer, however, decided not to stay on at Ringcroft farm. In early 1695 a new tenant, Andrew Mackie, and his family moved in.

They had not been there long when, one morning, Andrew discovered that cattle which had been tied up securely had broken free. The same thing happened the following night, although this was puzzling rather than disturbing.

Things soon took a turn for the worse. One night a pile of peat blocks stacked in the living room burst into flame, and the family only discovered the fire in the nick of time. Then showers of stones were thrown at the house—not just pebbles but boulder-sized blocks. People visiting the cottage would find themselves the target of the invisible stone thrower. Pots, pans and other kitchen implements disappeared, only to turn up in odd places, such as the loft. There were many witnesses from outside the family to these inexplicable incidents—on one occasion, when a group of neighbours tried to enter the house they were beaten back by a hail of stones and sticks. One local minister was cut on the head by a large rock.

The Mackies moved out and the trouble stopped. But as soon as they moved back in it started again with renewed and ferocious vigour. Huge balls of fire moved in and around the house. From nowhere a thick wooden cane was thrust straight through the stone walls of the cottage and shaken about. The presence of clergymen seemed to send the 'force' into an agitated spate of activity. On one occasion the whole house was shaken violently and a hole torn in the roof through which poured rocks of all sizes. The barn door was ripped from its hinges and the barn wall disintegrated to rubble.

A strange voice now began conversing with Mackie. The spirit behind the voice appeared to indicate it was on some kind of bizarre mission, claiming to be 'God's messenger' sent to urge repentance on Mankind. It warned that it would return with even more powerful spirits to plague the homes of families in the area, a threat which never seems to have been carried out.

Mackie continued to suffer, until events reached a crescendo with fires breaking out in all parts of the house, fires which the family were unable to control. The cottage simply burned to the ground, but the spirit was still not content and the barn roof also went up in flames. Soon after, the infestation came to an abrupt end. A prayer meeting was held in what remained of Mackie's barn. As they knelt in a circle a black cloud formed in one corner of the building, grew in size and created a whirlwind of mud and chaff. Some were gripped about the body so fiercely that they shrieked with pain, the marks being visible for days. But at least their anguish seems to have appeased their tormentor. When the black cloud vanished, the poltergeist had gone.

As Andrew Mackie ruefully remarked: 'If I should tell of this, I should not be believed.' There have been many since who have no wish to believe the events at Ringcroft farm. The account of the incident was written and published at the time by the Reverend Alexander Telfair. Telfair was the first minister of nearby Dundrennan Church, yet little is known about him apart from his involvement with the Mackie family. The accusation against him is that he exaggerated (perhaps even invented) events at the farm to attract attention to himself, or to counter growing scepticism about religious belief. Yet it is hard to see how Telfair could have fabricated the account when he lived and worked in the area. He would have been quickly exposed and ridiculed, whereas it is known that he continued as a minister till his retirement in 1731.

However, that he may have exaggerated events, in spite of naming several witnesses, cannot be ruled out. Although the events contain the classic elements of a poltergeist infestation, the intensity of the events has not been repeated since in Scotland. The destruction of a home signifies a major paranormal incident which goes far beyond anything recorded over the following centuries. In Telfair's defence it should be said that he did not make any telling religious points in his account of the case and, in his comments, appears as puzzled as everyone by Mackie's suffering. Centuries have passed since the incident ended, but as yet no one has been able to explain why this extraordinary eruption of the paranormal occurred.

ROSSLYN CHAPEL

Rosslyn Chapel in Midlothian is rapidly becoming one of the world's mystic centres, although at first glance it appears less than impressive. Over 500 years old, from the outside the chapel looks half finished, almost like a ruin—as if the masons involved in building it had been suddenly ordered to stop.

But we know that vast sums of money were spent, and lavish attention paid to its construction. Rosslyn Chapel was carefully planned down to the finest detail. According to the current Earl of Rosslyn's official guide to the chapel, what remains is 'only part of what was intended to be a large cruciform building with a tower at its centre', but when its founder, Sir William St Clair, Prince of Orkney, died in 1484, 'he was buried in the unfinished building and the larger building he had planned was never realised.'

However, others have taken a more mystical view of the chapel's design and origins. They argue that if it now appears half built then it was deliberately meant that way. The reason why was unclear until it was realised that the chapel is meant to look like King Solomon's Temple at Jerusalem. The logic behind this is St Clair's association with the Knights Templar [qv]. In the 13th century the Templars, it is claimed, discovered the Holy Grail, the cup or plate used by Christ at the Last Supper, when they excavated the site of Solomon's Temple during an invasion of the Holy Land. After the Templars were forcibly disbanded by King Phillip of France in 1307, the survivors fled to Scotland and legend has it that they secreted the Grail, with other religious artefacts, at Rosslyn. Within the structure of the building itself, later Templars left coded messages to future generations, so that they could discover this great secret for themselves.

In recent times it has been the vault beneath the chapel, rather than the chapel itself, that has been the subject of the greatest speculation, and it is here that the Holy Grail is said to lie hidden. A fragment of the Holy Rood, the actual cross of Christ, is also rumoured to have been secreted in the vault, but the vault has been sealed for more than three centuries, and the current guardians of the chapel, the 7th Earl of Rosslyn and his family, are said to have no plans to investigate these claims.

The chapel itself is full of strange carvings, many depicting Biblical themes—such as The Seven Deadly Sins and The Dance of Death. Others are clearly of pagan origin, and most numerous are those of the Green Man, the ancient god of fertility and vegetation. We probably know him better as Robin Hood [qv], ruler of the forest, who is just the green man in another guise. He was as popular in Scotland as England and the legend probably developed from the beliefs of our Celtic forefathers. At the base of one of the pillars can be found eight dragons, and from their mouths a vine emerges and winds itself around the stone support. There may be a link here to Scandinavian mythology, and the eight dragons of Neifelheim which were said to lie at the foot of Yggdrasil, the great ash tree which brought together Heaven and Earth. All of these carvings seem to have a tale to tell, but what exactly are they saying and why is all this pagan-influenced carving to be found here? It is a secret that has been puzzling investigators into the occult for many years. Is it really a cryptic message intended to reveal the location of the Holy Grail, or is there an even greater mystery?

One of the more sinister features is the 'Apprentice Pillar'. The pillar was carved by a young apprentice, whose talent was such that he is said to have been murdered in the chapel by his master in a fit of jealousy. At the south-west corner, high up on the wall, a carved head with a wound on its forehead is reputed to depict the murdered apprentice.

A recent theme of occult writers has been that, contrary to Christian teaching, Jesus of Nazareth was married and had several children who escaped to France after his crucifixion. Jesus' line, therefore, did not die with him but continued. The true succession, so it is said, does not lie with the Catholic Church and its offshoots but with the bloodline of Jesus whose descendants still live today. If Jesus had a wife and family it would rock the present Christian Churches to their foundations. If these secrets are encoded in the carvings at Rosslyn, they are a potential time-bomb for Christianity.

Against such a backdrop it is almost run-of-the-mill to learn that at Rosslyn Chapel you will find proof that a Scot, Henry Sinclair, Prince of Orkney, discovered America one hundred years before Columbus. The evidence comes again in the shape of those mysterious carvings, this time of an American cactus and Indian sweetcorn, made long before the 'New World' was reached and these plants made known to European society. Some say that Sinclair's journey across the Atlantic, funded by the Knights Templar, was not some whim, but a deliberate act to discover a hidden secret in the wilds of North America, perhaps among the native Indians. Or did he journey down into the South and meet up with the Incas and Aztecs? Their mythology is full of meetings with bearded white men whom they regarded as gods.

But the strange forces that drew the founders of Rosslyn Chapel to this location can still be felt today. Dowsing in the chapel has shown that the whole area is a cauldron of swirling energy, and that lines of some strange force run directly through the spot where the present altar is located. It is even claimed that an astral doorway is located in one corner which opens into other dimensions. There is no doubt that it is this focus of energies which has led to such an important religious site having been established here. Psychic mediums who have visited the chapel say that it somehow boosts the intensity of their contact with spirits.

Even UFOs are apparently attracted to this area, and there have been reports of strange sightings of every kind. Odd balls of light have been seen moving in the vicinity of the chapel itself, which is situated at the centre of a UFO triangle stretching from West Lothian to the Pentland Hills. Whatever the true nature of these phenomena, Rosslyn Chapel lies at the heart of a puzzle which brings together mysteries old and new.

S

SATANISM

Satanism is a phenomenon often talked about, though in practice rarely encountered. There are individuals in Scotland who could claim to be Satanists, but the key question is whether there exists a widespread and organised conspiracy. Is it true, as one Church of England cleric claimed on a television programme, that 'Satanism is growing'?

The evidence from Scotland to back this up is scant, which may be why Scottish Churches have been virtually silent on the matter. There is no organised Satanist Church, as there is in the United States, with its 'Church of Satan' based in San Francisco and founded by Anton La Vey. In Scotland, on the other hand, all we have are rumours. In occult circles gossip abounds, but even though Satanists by nature may prefer to avoid the limelight, there is not much to confirm the existence of Satanist practice in Scotland beyond a fringe of participants.

Even so, Scotland has not been free of 'satanic scares'. The most notorious took place in Orkney in the 1980s, when it was alleged that a coven of Satanists had been holding secret meetings and engaging in various kinds of bizarre practices, including animal sacrifice. The alleged events were eventually exposed as fantasy, products of the overwrought imagination of social workers and police, who had apparently been influenced by accounts of supposed satanic cults in the USA (all later revealed as fictional). The Orkney authorities' concern that the activities on their island were part of an international satanic conspiracy was also a factor. The only aspect missing from this 20th-century 'witch craze' was belief by the authorities that Satan really existed. Without that crucial piece of the jigsaw any allegation of Satanism is bound eventually to be exposed as false, as all have been, including Orkney's.

It is true that Satanism and witchcraft often seem to overlap, and the idea of Satanism as a religion distinct from witchcraft did not really exist before the 18th century. Before then, the (Christian) authorities viewed all followers of the Devil as witches, and all witches as followers of the Devil. They were out, according to witch-hunters, to destroy all good Christians. But modern witches (who prefer to be called Wiccans) see witchcraft and Satanism as two quite different 'religions'. Satanism is the worship of God's great enemy, Lucifer, the fallen angel, the entity who exults in evil. Satanists see themselves without any doubt as enemies of Christendom, and regard this enmity as the whole point of following Satan. Wiccans, on the other hand, believe themselves to be followers of an ancient pre-Christian tradition in which the old gods of nature, such as Pan, are worshipped. According to Wiccan belief, this old religion has a continuous history from the distant past right up to the present. Its followers were the alleged 'witches' hunted down during the medieval period. They were not 'anti-Christian', but simply followers of a different religion.

Admittedly, though, it is sometimes hard to see where some aspects of Wicca and Satanism are different in practice, when followers of these 'paths' use ritual magic for their own benefit.

Worship of Satan brings with it the belief that Satan's power can be used for the individual worshipper's own ends. Satan's power must exist, even if it is less than God's—it is even acknowledged in the Bible that he is a powerful figure. However, Satan uses his influence for selfish, evil ends. He is willing to use his strength to obtain what he wants regardless of how this impacts on people. Satan's aim is world domination and, as part of that, the destruction of the Christian way of life. He is not out to wipe mankind from the face of the Earth—in fact the control of mankind is a key part of Satan's strategy. So he desperately searches for followers to help him carry out his plans.

That is why Satanism is seen as essentially a mass conspiracy rather than a matter of individual conversion. So, in the USA above all, there have been claims that rock music lyrics are filled with 'satanic' messages. And that even major companies use the numbers '666', the 'Mark of the Beast', in their phone lines, product numbers, bar-codes and the like. This has been much less of an issue in Europe and so far no Scottish company has been accused of being in league with Satan.

While there are 'white witches' there are also 'black witches'. It is a major division within Wicca today, and those who follow the 'dark side' appear hard to separate from Satanists in practice. Both are intent on using the forces of the occult for negative ends—in other words, to benefit themselves. There are undoubtedly practitioners of black witchcraft in Scotland, although so far they have been at pains to distinguish their activities from those of Satanists. But to the public they probably appear as one and the same.

Since the 18th century, and the decline in the persecution of witches by the Christian Church, Scotland's Satanists have been allowed to go about their business in relative peace. However, they have yet to declare their allegiance publicly, and so the only conclusion that can be drawn is that they remain very few in number

SAWNEY BEAN

Tradition tells us that a family of vampires and cannibals roamed the west coast of Scotland two centuries ago. The leader of the family has come down to us as Sawney Bean, though his real name was Alexander Bane, which can be translated simply as 'Alex the killer'.

However, if 'Sawney Bean' was originally a Gaelic term it might refer to a group of fairy folk. Whatever the true origin, the tale connected with Bane is a bizarre one. With his family he is reputed to be responsible for the mysterious disappearance of hundreds of innocent travellers. Bane, however, was not killing for profit, but for food—he and his followers were allegedly cannibals and perhaps even vampires. One account describes how a man and woman were attacked and while the husband fought back, his wife was dragged from her horse and eaten before his eyes. Even as they stabbed her throat some of Bane's group gathered round to drink her spurting blood.

A dramatic story, but is it fact or fiction? Did Bane's family really engage in mass murder or were they simply convenient scapegoats? How reliable are the stories of his activities, and was it all simply black propaganda directed against a band of outlaws? If a serial killer really was on the loose, then clearly someone had to be found to take the blame. And it seems that strange incidents had created a 'death triangle', notorious throughout Scotland at that time. Over several years, in an area stretching south from Ayr to Ballantrae, many people taking the coast road mysteriously disappeared. During the same period, body parts were washed ashore along the whole length of the Firth of Clyde. Arms and legs were the usual grisly flotsam. Heads were never found, which has suggested to later investigators that they were being kept as trophies or being used for ritual purposes.

The authorities of the time were more concerned with stopping the murders than pinpointing motives. It was believed that all the deaths were connected and several suspects were arrested from the local area, convicted and hanged. But the killing went on, and it was clear that the wrong people had been executed. Suspicion eventually centred on Alexander Bane. A group of soldiers searched the cliff that ran for miles along the shore and claimed they had caught the whole Bane family in an enormous cave with pieces of human flesh suspended from the roof of their 'home'. Unfortunately, there are no written reports of this incident, nor have any details of the charges against the family survived, so we cannot be sure that the account was not simply trumped up to brand Bane guilty in the public's mind. Living in isolation with only his family for company, Alexander Bane would have been an easy target.

Reputedly born in Edinburgh, he had moved over to the west coast with his wife and apparently set up home in a cave, which by tradition is said to have been situated below Benane Head, just south of Girvan. But why would he choose to live in a cave? Was this the result of poverty, or were there more sinister motives behind his arrival in the area? Vampirism has in recent times become closely linked to Eastern Europe, but that was not always the case. Hundreds of years ago vampires [qv] were a well known danger in many parts of the British Isles—for example the Croglin vampire near Carlisle. And one of the centres of vampire activity was reputed to be the area in which Bane lived. Maybe Bane was aware of these stories, or perhaps he knew of a local cult which practised the drinking of human blood. Aristocrats engaged in all kinds of bizarre rituals at this time, as the activities of the Hell Fire Club in England show. In France the King's closest friends were practising Satanism [qv]. Maybe Bane supplied groups like these with human sacrifices.

Even those who accept that Sawney Bean was a real person argue that we cannot be sure that human agency was responsible for these deaths. Various kinds of suspects have been put forward as the possible murderer. Could 'he' have been a weird animal of an unknown kind—a 'monster'?

During the period of Bane's activity, the countryside in this area was reckoned to be as wild, remote and inaccessible as the Scottish Highlands. It was not easy to visit and there were large areas where very few people lived. The shoreline was riddled with caves, some of which ran hundreds of yards into the cliffs and were linked to each other by subterranean tunnels. It was a strange place for a human family to choose to live, but it could easily have provided a refuge for a large wild animal, or an unknown 'prehistoric' specimen which could have lingered on in an area like this. Loch monsters [see Morar, Loch; Ness, Loch] are regularly seen even today, as are phantom 'black cats' [see Phantom Pumas]. Can we dismiss the chance that in a more backward age a strange beast, perhaps a prehistoric survivor, prowled the area and attacked passing humans? A more obvious solution may lie in the fact that wolves survived in Scotland until 1746.

But perhaps Bane and his family were prehistoric survivors, the last members of an ancient tribe thousands of years old. Stone age people still survive in parts of the world today alongside more advanced societies.

It is certainly strange that Bane managed to escape for so long if he was the guilty party. His family group numbered several dozen, and it might be thought they would have been the first target of suspicion rather than the last. Another odd fact is that corpses and body parts are still washed up along the Solway coast. Lately these unsolved deaths have been attributed to the Irish troubles. But perhaps, as in the Sawney Bean case, the truth lies elsewhere.

The evidence for Sawney Bean's existence comes from written accounts published many years after the alleged events took place. Sceptics argue that it was all just a good story presented as fact in the style of writing at the time. Several centuries on, it is extremely difficult to disentangle the reality from the fiction, but the accounts of Bane's activities are too convincing to dismiss as complete fabrication.

SCEPTICS

Despite increasing public interest, the paranormal has not been without its critics. Steuart Campbell is Scotland's leading UFO sceptic, and his views have had a wide impact. Campbell was at one time the Scottish representative of the British UFO Research Association (BUFORA) and compiled their official report on the 1979 Livingston UFO incident [qv]. Although Campbell was convinced that 'something' had happened to Bob Taylor in Dechmont Woods, he ruled out any extraterrestrial involvement or indeed anything inexplicable. In his account, which formed the basis of all later writing on the event, he suggested that the Livingston encounter could be explained by Taylor having suffered an epileptic fit triggered by seeing a mirage of the planet Venus, a phenomenon which would have produced a bright object in the sky. As Campbell described the incident: 'Rounding a corner [Taylor] was confronted by a hemispherical enlargement of the image of Venus appearing to be in the clearing in front of him. . . . A combination of surprise, fear and the unusual sight may have been enough to trigger the epileptic seizure. Some of the images may have become distorted in the aural phase of the attack'. This view aroused controversy but Campbell was convinced that UFO sightings could be explained as misidentification of natural phenomena. In his book, *The UFO Mystery Solved*, Campbell argued that planet or star mirages were at the root of all UFO reports. Critics retorted that although this may account for unexplained lights in the sky it seems harder to apply this 'solution' where close encounters occur.

Campbell did not confine his scepticism to UFOs, and took on the 'Loch Ness Monster' mystery [*see* Ness, Loch]. In *The Loch Ness Monster: The Evidence* he examined the photographic evidence for Nessie. Those who believe that there is an unidentified creature in the loch argue that the sheer number of photographs prove that the waters really do hide something strange.

Campbell pointed out that, taken on its own, each photograph had a perfectly logical explanation. The alleged sightings of the 'monster' were in reality wave movement, known animals seen at a distance, floating logs, etc. In other words, as with UFO accounts, witnesses were simply misidentifying natural phenomena. So although there was superficially a large body of supporting evidence, Campbell's argument was that in effect it added up to nothing at all. It certainly did not prove that the monster was other than a figment of the collective imagination.

As yet, Campbell's criticism of the photographic evidence has not been effectively countered. And his transition— from involvement in BUFORA to outright rejection of all things paranormal—has made him a very effective critic of the 'inexplicable'.

SCHIEHALLION

A prominent mountain in Perthshire, it is perhaps better known these days outside rather than inside Scotland. That was not always the case. Its name is of Gaelic origin and has been translated as 'fairy hill of the Caledonians'.

Clearly at one time it was considered to have special mystical significance, perhaps because of its perfect cone-shaped appearance when viewed from the east. Many hills have a 'fairy knowe', so Schiehallion must have been regarded as a key place for communicating with the gods if it was the focus for a whole tribe. Its pagan past can be recognised in a sacred well which is still visited on May Day, and a phantom hound which is sometimes seen haunting its lower slopes—a memory perhaps of one of the many pre-Christian gods, as dogs were associated with Diana, known as Skadi in Norse mythology, the huntress of the forest, carrying her bow and a quiver full of arrows. Schiehallion will continue to attract the inquiring mystic as it did our pagan ancestors.

And, indeed, its great sanctity explains its continuing attraction for a variety of 'fringe' religious and occult groups today. It is seen as one of the legendary 'Omphalos'—a mystic place, one of the seven sacred spots on the planet where, in order to control the destiny of the Earth, ceremonies have to be held to placate the gods.

SCONE

Scone, situated outside the city of Perth, has played a key part in Scotland's history as the place where generations of Scottish kings were crowned, the last being Charles II in 1651. The site of the enthronement or 'coronation' ceremonies is still clearly visible today as a raised artificial mound or 'moot' located within the grounds of Scone palace. A replica of the coronation stone, the famous 'Stone of Destiny', stands on the mound.

A Christian chapel has been built on the moot but there can be little doubt that this site has a long tradition as a meeting place stretching back into pagan times. Indeed, the coronation ceremony of Scotland's kings included pre-Christian symbolism.

This site at Scone Palace may have been chosen because it is alive with earth energy. Dowsing [qv] has shown that a complex web of ley lines crosses at this point. It is true that key energy areas such as this can be found at various spots across Scotland so the Scone moot is by no means unique. But it may be that there were also traditions, now lost, linking it to the old gods, or even a standing stone circle which has simply disappeared. It may also be the case that the moot connects to other powerful energy points close by which have yet to be discovered. The city of Perth itself grew up around a sacred grove which, as Christianity took over, became connected to St John the Baptist. It should be noted that St John was closely linked to the Knights Templar [qv] whose activities and mystical beliefs are a continuing subject for specu-lation. The Templars certainly had close links to Scotland's rulers and would have been present, during the Middle Ages, at any ceremony anointing a new king.

Whatever the history behind the Scone moot it remains a site of powerful energy. A place any future monarchs of Scotland would do well to consider as the location for a coronation.

SCOTT, MICHAEL

Michael Scott was undoubtedly a real figure, well known as a philosopher who lived at about the same time as Thomas the Rhymer [qv]. However, Scott earned a reputation as a wizard who, among other things, split the Eildon Hills [qv] into three with the help of the Devil, and—also by magical powers— built Glenluce Abbey overnight (curiously also the location of Scotland's first documented poltergeist incident [see Glenluce Devil]).

History may have been unfair to Scott, as there is no evidence that, even if he was interested in the occult, he took it to the extent of magic-making. But Scott, perhaps through his interest in astrology, an interest shared at the time by many educated people, may have created the impression that he was dabbling in the black arts. That, at least, seems to have been the popular view.

STANDING STONE CIRCLES

In spite of years of investigation by amateurs and professionals, we are no nearer solving the mystery of Scotland's standing stone circles. Who built them and what purpose did they have?

According to archaeologists, they served a religious or ritual purpose—a convenient explanation which hides the fact that no one can be sure what our ancestors intended. Nor can we be sure of the dates of construction. Were the circles put up 3,000 or 10,000 years ago? The former date is usually believed to be nearer the mark, as the further back we go, supposedly the less organised and sophisticated the society. But without written records to rely on it is all ultimately guesswork.

One fact we can be sure about: at one time Scotland had a great many standing stone circles, of which those that remain are merely a small selection. Even so, what remains today is highly impressive. The Hill o' Many Stanes at Mid Clyth, Caithness, consists of 22 rows of small, low-set stones, some 200 in number, which were once part of a fan-shaped pattern running north-south down the south-facing slope. Six hundred stones may originally have been in place. The huge Ring of Brodgar in Orkney once had as many as 60 stones in its circle. The diameter of this perfect circle is more than 100 metres, and it has been estimated that building it, together with its ditch cut into solid rock, would have taken 80,000 man-hours.

Over the centuries, individual stones and whole circles have been removed for building or because they got in the way of farming arrangements. As recently as February 1992, a farmer removed five of the Garleffin stones from his fields beside the village of Ballantrae, on the grounds that if they were made a scheduled monument he would have been unable to plough the field without permission. So much for Scotland's heritage. However, it does emphasise the point that what we see today of stone circles is only a fraction of what we once had. There may well have been a network of stone circles stretching from the lowlands of Scotland up to the Shetland Isles.

Although the purpose of the circles may never be properly understood, there are a number of clues. One thing is clear: these structures were put up with the heavens in mind. Callanish [qv], like that other great monument, Stonehenge, works as a sophisticated astronomical calendar. It took the genius of Scot Alexander Thom to discover just how organised our prehistoric ancestors had been. Thom, an engineer, surveyed hundreds of stone circles, concluding that they were not a crude arrangement of individual stones, but set out to specific ground plans. Across Scotland a basic unit of measurement had been used in their construction—he christened it the 'megalithic yard', a measurement of 2.72 feet.

If the people of the time—the Neolithic Age, according to archaeologists—were operating to a more sophisticated plan than was previously thought, does that bring us any closer to understanding the reason why? If circles were used as calendars, then it would allow a check to be kept on seasons of the year—and much longer periods of time, as movements of the sun, moon and stars could be charted. However, why go to all the trouble of laying out stone monuments every few miles to achieve this end. Farmers certainly do not need a stone-built or even written calendar to work out the seasons of the year. There are plenty of other signs. Just watch the strength of sunlight in October compared with May. So although circles must have had a link with the heavens, this may have been more for religious than practical purposes.

Understandably, the mystery of the stones has led to those interested in the paranormal putting forward controversial solutions. Were our ancestors marking time till the return of craft from outer space? The pyramids at Giza were set up in a line to correspond with the arrangement of the Orion star system, as it was thousands of years ago. Was this simply because these stars could be clearly seen in the heavens? The Dogon tribe in Africa had intimate knowledge about the star system of Sirius—information which staggered the Europeans who made first contact. All over the world there are ancient tribal dances which seem to depict spacemen. And what of those strange carvings found on undatable stones throughout Scotland? Drawings which the experts call 'cup and ring' marks, but could just as easily be a crude depiction of a solar system with its central sun and rotating planets. It has also been noted that many standing stones are placed in a circular or oval formation—just like crop 'circles'. Often both are found close together. Were they built to mark the appearance of this mysterious phenomenon? Some argue that crop circles are UFO landing sites. So perhaps it all fits. . . .

It is all too easy to get carried away. Stonehenge and Callanish are distinctly visible from an overflying craft, but would the same be true of smaller versions. And why build so many? But if they were not crude beacons for UFOs, did they have a more mystic purpose? Ancient interdimensional contacts? Stone circles are often claimed to have a very powerful concentration of 'earth energy'. Were these circles constructed with this energy flow in mind? Could this build-up of energy have been used to contact spirits or other alien entities? It has been argued that the circles could be used today if we knew the right techniques. The pyramids may have been built with the same purpose in mind. Their very shape was designed to create a kind of energy box, it is said, supposedly preserving metal and even flesh for great periods of time. Standing stone circles do not form an enclosed space like the pyramids do, but it may be that they can form an enclosed sphere of energy, created by a process long forgotten.

Speculation on the true purpose of standing stone circles drives professional archaeologists to exasperation. But the truth is that our understanding of the circles may be hampered by the fixed attitude adopted by professional investigators, preventing the discovery of an important key to our past and future.

T

THEATRE AND CINEMA GHOSTS

Although it is understandable that the spirit of a dead person might want to remain close to the place it once lived, why should cinemas attract ghosts? The only actors found there are on reels of film, and audiences change from one day to another. Yet some bizarre incidents have occurred on cinema premises over the years.

Frank Mackay, working in the 1950s as a projectionist in the Realto cinema in Dundee, came to believe in the reality of ghosts after one particularly frightening incident. Frank explained: 'I was in the projection room splicing film. I had my back to the door and distinctly heard it open and then close. I was sure that my workmate had come into the room and I called out "I'll be with you in a minute." There was a definite presence behind me as if someone was looking over my shoulder. I turned round to say something, but I was stunned to find that there was no one there.'

That was not the only strange encounter Frank Mackay experienced at the Realto. 'There was a spiral staircase leading to the attic. As I was coming down the stairs I caught sight of a pair of legs rushing up towards me. I expected to see a woman, but you can imagine my astonishment when the two legs passed me by, visible to the thigh, but with no body above.' It seems odd that only part of the phantom should be seen, but such partial apparitions do occur—headless spirits are not uncommon, for example.

In fact the Realto was a former theatre, converted when films became more popular than live acting. Many features of the old theatre could be found there. So perhaps spirits of the acting fraternity were still hanging around.

The appearance of spirits at a venue in Stirling used for occasional theatrical performances might be related to its former history as a gaol. During one play, which dealt with the lives and deaths of former prisoners, the haunting seemed to reach fever pitch with unexplained drops in temperature, doors slamming shut for no reason, chairs moving position and voices heard singing at dead of night. Many of the former inmates went to the gallows, so restless spirits may well have been a factor. However, the actors' changing room was especially affected, so perhaps they were being pestered by a lover of the theatre. According to one source, a member of a travelling acting troupe who performed there was sub-sequently jailed and hanged for murdering his mistress. Perhaps it is this gentleman who is trying to make a comeback.

The Ramshorn theatre in Glasgow, located on the site of a former church, has suffered from similar types of disturbance.

A woman called Edie is said to haunt the toilets where the minister's vestry was once located. Strange footsteps have been heard and overpowering smells have invaded the air— the sort of activity that would usually be attributed to a poltergeist. The building was built over an ancient crypt, so it is unclear whether the ghosts are connected with the performing arts, or are spirits of those buried there long ago.

A Green Lady haunts the Citizens Theatre in Glasgow, and though the link to the acting profession might not be clear, it is worth remembering that green is the colour of the fairies, the inhabitants of 'other worlds'.

But the case of 'the great Lafayette' provides a more direct and obvious link. A famous conjuror, Lafayette was tragically killed in a fire at the Empire Theatre in Edinburgh in 1900. Strangely, over 90 years went by before his ghost made an appearance. In 1994 the Empire re-opened as a live acting venue again, now renamed the 'Festival Theatre'. Coincidence or not, a tall dark figure was seen soon after at the very spot where the fire that killed Lafayette started. The following year the tall dark figure was again seen, this time in the upper circle.

THOMAS THE RHYMER

Thomas 'the Rhymer' earns his place in the history of the Scottish paranormal as the first documented abductee [see Abduction]. In Thomas' case, however, it was fairies and not extraterrestrials who took him away. Thomas' experience is distinct from the abduction phenomenon as it developed in the 1980s and 1990s, with its sinister 'greys', but its tone of innocent adventure would not be out of tune with the 'contactee' spirit of the 1950s—a time when George Adamski allegedly met humanoid aliens who were remarkably friendly. However, not all fairies were of such a gentle nature, as other experiences confirm.

Thomas the Rhymer is believed to have been a real person, Thomas of Ercildoune, who came from the village of Earlston and lived from around 1210 to 1290. His abduction by the 'little people' is alleged to have happened on the Eildon Hills [qv] which have enjoyed a mystic reputation for centuries—either a remarkable coincidence, or further evidence that the Hills may be a gateway into other worlds. [*See also* Scott, Michael]

TOLLISHILL

Tollishill in the Lammermuirs is an intriguing place because there is a definite link between a standing stone circle to be found here and a folk legend. Only part of the circle now remains, although what is still standing seems to link to outlying stones across the valley, some of which are lying flat. Ordnance Survey refuses to recognise these stones for what they are, although dowsers can follow energy lines which link the remaining standing stones to these 'outliers'. The Tollishill circle is undoubtedy a focus for powerful energy, and the area is littered with remains of our prehistoric past, suggesting that this agriculturally poor area had a mystic attraction to our ancestors.

The folk tale associated with the site is a curious one and in its recent versions makes no mention of the actual stone circle. Thus, on the face of it, the stones and the story seem to have no connection. But there is an obvious link—this spot clearly had a strong mystical significance, as can be deduced from the presence of the stone circle, and the Tollishill site forms the central part of the story, as the characters involved lived at this lonely outpost.

In one typical early-20th-century version, the narrative concerns the actual mistress of Tollishill Farm, Maggie Hardie. The farm has fallen on bad times and Maggie goes to the local landowner from whom she and her husband are renting the farm, and asks if they can delay paying the rent. The Earl, John of Lauderdale, is described in terms reminiscent of the 'Black Man', a common term in times past for the Devil, not because of his skin colour, but because of his demeanour. John was 'a dark, pale-faced man, dressed in black. . . . Two black hounds lay at his feet'. John is far from sympathetic, but agrees to delay payment. However, he sets Maggie a seemingly impossible task as part of the bargain. He tells her: 'You and your husband shall remain at Tollishill secure until next midsummer, if in June you bring me, as payment, a ball of snow.' Maggie succeeds in this strange task by storing snow in a cave.

Clearly the story, however mangled and modernised it has become over the centuries, describes events which seem to defy the laws of nature. But on the other hand it does involve everyday natural phenomena, heat and cold, and above all the changing seasons. So perhaps the 'folklore' involved relates to the gods of nature, one of whom has become 'Lord John' in the modern version. This is confirmed by the timing of Maggie's meeting with him—in November, the month when in pre-pagan belief the forces of darkness were spreading across the world as winter set in. The combination of November and June in the accounts leaves little doubt that there is an underlying theme of mystic significance which has been gradually submerged beneath a modern fairy tale.

Perhaps 'Maggie' herself, with her almost magical ability to prevent snow melting, was a goddess of some kind, later transformed into a sanitised version of her former self. No doubt at one time the standing stones also played a part in the folk tale, but as the significance of the circle became lost, its link with the forces of nature gradually disappeared from people's consciousness. Tollishill, however, deserves to be recognised as one of Scotland's most mystical sites.

U

UFOs

Scotland experienced the UFO phenomenon within weeks of Kenneth Arnold's June 1947 sighting of nine shimmering discs over Mt Ranier in Washington State. Arnold's encounter, from which the term 'flying saucer' was coined, is usually accepted as being the trigger which sparked public interest in unidentified flying objects. As early as July 1947, Andrew Cherry saw a disc-shaped UFO with an occupant inside, hovering over the Portobello district of Edinburgh. In the 1950s UFO sightings were reported all around Scotland and considerable space was devoted by the newspapers to reporting the phenomena. Even George Adamski, the world's first celebrity 'contactee', visited Edinburgh for a public meeting held in halls in the Tollcross area of the city.

It appears that events did quieten down for a while thereafter. UFO societies such as the Scottish UFO Research Society, set up in the 1950s, did not survive into the 1960s, and for all the reports that emerged from north of the border, Scotland had not made world headlines. England, on the other hand, had the 'Warminster Mystery' during the 1960s—an alleged spate of sightings around the small Wiltshire town, which inspired several books and attracted intense interest. And by the late 1970s Wales had the 'Welsh Triangle'.

However, even though over a hundred sightings in a period of a few months were reported from the town of Moffat [qv] during 1978, these events failed to make any major impact outside Scotland. 1979 was a watershed, and two events were to have a long-term impact on Scottish ufology—the founding of Strange Phenomena Investigations (SPI) by Malcolm Robinson, and an incident which occurred on Dechmont Law near Livingston [qv]. On November 9th, forestry worker Bob Taylor had an experience during which he believed he encountered a spacecraft of some kind. The police were called in and the ensuing media speculation created a frenzy of interest. Taylor's encounter was widely reported and even featured on Arthur C Clarke's *Mysterious World* television series (and on many others since).

There was a further series of reports into 1980, but after that came a sharp decline. It was not for another decade that the UFO phenomenon in Scotland really hit the headlines once more. The 1990s saw a massive increase in the number of UFO reports, even before the emergence of the Bonnybridge [qv] 'hot spot'. Whatever the truth behind the number of UFO reports around the village, it succeeded in attracting world-wide attention to Scottish ufology. And the attention it aroused was undoubtedly largely due to the work of Malcolm Robinson and Councillor Billy Buchanan, the local representative for the area. It also, as Bob Taylor's encounter had, encouraged more people to join UFO societies and enter the controversial field of UFO investigation. However, disagreement soon arose among Scottish ufologists over the manner in which UFO reports were being handled, and this led to some embarrassing incidents. But by the end of the 1990s, thousands of new reports and been documented, many from earlier decades, and there was a thriving UFO network with several societies, magazines and websites. Curiously, though, a UK-wide phenomenon began to emerge—the decline in the late 1990s of the number of reported sightings. As the new millennium dawned, ufologists were beginning to wonder where all the UFOs had gone.

So how has Scottish ufology compared to the rest of the world? In theory there should be no difference. Why should Scottish UFOs be unlike those reported anywhere else on the globe? Yet in one significant respect Scotland has been in line with England and out of tune with the USA—in the area of abductions. There have been some fascinating Scottish cases—the A70 encounter [see Wood, Gary] and the experience involving a young witness with small entities in a wood near Meigle [see Abduction] are well documented events—but the number of reported incidents has been very low.

That contrasts with the vast number of Scottish sightings of strange lights in the sky and even reports of solid objects. UFOs have been described as shaped like discs, cigars, triangles, pyramids, the planet Saturn, a railway carriage and even a flaming globe of the world. There appears to be no rhyme or reason for this weird mixture. Some of the closest encounters produce the most bizarre sightings—like the flaming globe [see Orkney] and flying railway carriage [see Glasgow] which appeared within feet of the respective witnesses.

The Scottish UFO phenomenon seems to stretch into every aspect of our strange world. Spacecraft from other planets is only one among a number of solutions proposed by ufologists. Some claim that they have seen UFOs emerging from below the ground [see Underground], that UFOs have been involved in downing aircraft, that they are linked to the ancient Egyptians (a figure similar in appearance to the dog or jackal god Anubis has appeared to UFO witnesses on a number of occasions), and that they are connected to the world of spirits and fairies.

There is evidence to support one and all of these theories. However, all but the dogmatic will agree that in spite of 50 years of scrutiny the UFO phenomenon remains an enigma. One which is unlikely to be solved, though instances are reported somewhere in the world almost every day of the week.

UNDERGROUND

Where do UFOs go when they are not flashing across the sky? There is a school of thought which believes that they head underground. One witness claims to have seen spaceships burrowing into the ground on a mountainside near the village of Kinbuck. Abductee Gary Wood [qv] suspected that he was taken to an underground base somewhere below the

Lothians rather than to a spacecraft. Another victim of alien abduction has described finding himself inside a building of some kind. (Was it coincidence that this encounter also occurred in West Lothian?) The possibility that 'aliens' originate from below ground, rather than from other planets, cannot be ruled out.

The belief that strange entities live below the Earth has a long history. Fairies [qv] and other nature spirits were believed to have their homes underground, a fact made clear by the many hills which still today boast a 'fairy knowe' [qv]. The idea that the Earth is home to a secret group of beings has not gone away in our 'advanced' society—in fact the opposite has happened. During the 19th century, the occult writer Bulwer Lytton described in his book, *The Coming Race* (1871), an underground civilisation of a mystic nature who were masters of a strange force known as 'vril' power. H G Wells, in *The Time Machine* (1895), described a more brutal underground race, the Morlocks. They were, however, more technologically advanced than those who lived above ground.

These accounts were fictional though some believe that, at least in Bulwer Lytton's case, his account was based on fact. And that his information was gained not from distant and mysterious lands, but from Scotland, where rumours of subterranean tunnels such as those where the alleged 'cannibal' Sawney Bean [qv] lived were widespread.

And fairies living below ground should not conjure up quaint images. When the accused witch Isobel Gowdie [qv] confessed to meeting the fairy people underground, she mentioned the strange machinery she saw there which made a tremendous noise. Robert Kirk [qv], who met with the fairies near the town of Aberfoyle, described a whole civilisation of houses and workshops organised by the fairies in their underground cities. Perhaps H G Wells' account of the Morlocks was closer to traditional pre-Victorian views of fairies than might at first be thought.

By the 1950s the idea that the Earth was hollow had gained wide acceptance among occult circles. It was claimed that when the explorer Richard Byrd flew over the Arctic in 1926 he photographed a giant hole at the North Pole—the long-sought-after entrance to the subterranean world. According to occultists, this and other photographs have either been suppressed or altered to conceal the evidence.

More recently, underground bases have been linked to the Military establishment as places where alien craft have been stored and extraterrestrials are employed to produce advanced technology. It is said that the use of aliens was the main reason why the West won the space race and was way ahead of the Soviet Union. Area 51 in the United States has been most closely associated with the 'alien underground' scenario. Even Machrihanish [qv] on the Mull of Kintyre has been claimed as a likely location, though the evidence from individuals who have worked on the base is that the land on which it is built is not suitable for underground bunkers and therefore nothing could be hidden there.

A hidden underground system has also been used to account for the elusive nature of loch monsters. It is suggested that a series of deep channels allow 'Nessie' and 'Morag' (the inhabitant of Loch Morar) [see Ness, Loch; Morar, Loch] to move from loch to loch and, as they connect with the sea, even to leave the Scottish mainland altogether. Sceptics point out that, as the lochs are at different heights above or below sea level, such a system of passages simply cannot exist.

The idea of life below ground has a long history, stretching back to the darklands of the Greek Hades. As the interior of the Earth is yet to be explored, can we be so sure that no civilisation ever made it their home?

V

Vampires are not entities we usually associate with Scotland, although there is a connection with Slains Castle near Peterhead. It was the sight of this brooding ruin which inspired Irishman Bram Stoker to write *Dracula*, whose vision of the immortal being dependent for his continued existence on human blood has left an enduring legacy. Yet the idea of the vampire is not new. It is in fact hundreds of years old, and while it is now almost completely tied to Eastern Europe this was not always the case. If we go back several hundred years, the belief in vampires was widespread throughout Britain and there were certain parts of the country where vampires were especially active. South-west Scotland was viewed as a particular haven for the 'undead'.

In past centuries, vampires were seen as more like the zombie of Voodoo religion than the very human-looking

Dracula we think of today. They were, in a sense, restless souls who left their graves at night to walk among the living. However, the vampire tradition may explain the origins of the Sawney Bean [qv] legends. This family of alleged cannibals lived along Scotland's south-west coast and though branded as flesh eaters, which the 'undead' traditionally were not, some of the accounts of their murders describe the family drinking the blood of their victims—the classic behaviour of the vampire.

Then there is the case of the Croglin vampire in Cumbria, an area closely related to Scotland—it was once part of it—and just south of Galloway, a region intimately linked to vampire stories. In the Croglin incident, a woman staying at Croglin Grange was attacked one night by a strange-looking entity with a brown face and flaming eyes. The creature bit her on the throat, but ran off when she screamed. Some months later it appeared again at her window, and her brother shot the being in the leg. They watched it disappear over the church-yard wall into a family vault. When the vault was opened they found in one coffin a brown mummified figure with a recent gunshot wound on the leg.

A vampire? If so, where have they all gone? The Sawney Bean murders and the Croglin encounter took place centuries ago, so what about more recent times? The problem for those interested in the paranormal is that almost no one today believes in the existence of vampires. Blood-drinking exploits by mass murderers, most infamously Peter Kurten the 'Vampire of Dusseldorf', are enough to convince people that vampirism is the product of a diseased mind, and that anyone who even hints that it is a genuine phenomenon is not far behind. It is a view with which it is hard to disagree, given that there are no victims. Nor, in modern times, have any deaths ever been linked to such a creature.

Whilst the above is true of human vampirism, it is less true of incidents involving animals of which some reports do exist. In August 1976 John Stewart, a farmer from Ballageich Hill near Glasgow, found that overnight five of his geese had been mysteriously killed. Each one had on its body a number of puncture marks about one and a half inches deep, regularly spaced about four to five inches apart. The classic signs of a vampire death. Furthermore, there were no other apparent injuries. However, it is always difficult to be sure that any draining of blood has occurred in such cases unless a large amount has been removed.

There are also alleged cases from England. One was reported just south of the border, in Cumbria, where several sheep had their jugular vein severed, but no other injuries. And this took place as long ago as 1810. A similar incident, again involving sheep, took place in 1905.

It is certainly true that animals in Scotland have been attacked by mysterious intruders—there have been horse mutilations, savaged sheep, and cattle discovered with broken necks. Around Perth and Inverness, the police and the army have been involved in tracking these mysterious killers. So there is certainly something odd going on in the countryside, but not much that can definitely be tied to vampirism. And would anyone recognise the evidence even if they saw it? Probably not, especially if we are dealing with the vampire extraterrestrial suggested by some. But if vampires exist why would they attack only animals and not humans? Or given the many unsolved murders and disappearances, do their activities simply go unnoticed in an age when people no longer believe that such entities exist.

VIDEO EVIDENCE

The arrival of the camcorder has brought significant new evidence for those interested in the paranormal. The bulk of this new material has been on the UFO phenomenon. Some of the footage taken has received extensive publicity. An interesting aspect has been that a considerable number of the filmed incidents have been taken within the famous 'Bonny-bridge Triangle' [see Bonnybridge], an area stretching from West Lothian to the town of Stirling and northwards into Fife.

According to the *Falkirk Herald* one UFO was even captured on police video cameras, which filmed an object reported by Catherine Penman of Hallglen, near Falkirk. Her husband, Scott Penman, first spotted the UFO at around 10 p.m. According to Catherine: 'It was a really bright light which was down quite low. At first I thought it was a star, but it was ten times bigger than a star and was really close to the house. There is no way it could have been a helicopter or a plane because of the length of time it hovered in the air. I contacted the police because it was so unusual.'

Even greater publicity was given to video footage taken by 63-year-old Margaret Ross of Stenhousemuir. Her video of an object seen in May 1996 shows a bright light criss-crossed by stripes of different colours. Margaret and her husband Alex spotted the UFO as they were preparing for bed, and it appeared to them to be disc-shaped and brighter than a star. As they videoed it, the UFO appeared to zoom toward the house. There is certainly no doubting the unsettling nature of the couple's experience, although some UFO investigators believe that the camera may have unintentionally doctored the image of a natural object.

However, in October of the same year Margaret Ross caught another UFO on video. At first the white object which she was videoing to the south of her house pulsated for about 15 minutes. Then it gradually changed, transforming into a half moon shape with intensely bright diagonal bars and a glowing outer shell. Mrs Ross noticed the UFO after she had got out of bed at around 6 a.m. By a strange coincidence, her daughter Alison had also spotted the same object from her front room window a couple of miles away. She watched it for some time before ringing her mother at 7 a.m. to draw it to her attention. Mrs Ross, who had by then already been videoing the UFO for an hour, was delighted to have independent confirmation of what she had seen.

More remarkable video footage was taken in October 1996, this time by Hallglen resident Barry Macdonald. Barry was driving along Windsor Road in the Camelon district of Falkirk when he and his girlfriend Jane Adamson spotted a mysterious object hovering in the sky. It was around 6.40 p.m. when they stopped the car and got out to take a closer look. After they had watched the object for several minutes, Barry remembered that he had his video camera on the back seat. Barry is a keen angler and to prove the size of his catch he makes sure he has the evidence on tape. This time he was going to use his camera to even greater effect. Although he only managed to film the object for about 30 seconds before it disappeared, his footage was to cause a worldwide sensation, and appear on TV programmes across five continents. The UFO on his tape is an orange oval which seems to change shape, becoming a white disc—the classic 'flying saucer' shape. It seems to glow orange again, then turn white once more before disappearing. Whether it simply 'vanishes' or moves away at an incredibly high speed is impossible to tell—it is there one moment and gone the next. Checks with local airports indicated that no aircraft were in the vicinity at the time.

In November 1995, Brian Curran's home near Polbeth, Bathgate, was 'buzzed by a fireball UFO', according to *The Sun* newspaper. The report also claimed that 'the huge blazing craft appeared just yards from them as they cleared up after a party'. Although, in fact, the orange object remained some distance away in the night sky, the video footage clearly shows that something very strange took place. The UFO appeared as a bright orange disc and had the characteristics of a three-dimensional object. Its surface was ruffled—one commentator described it as like a baby's rusk. The most intriguing aspects of the mystery object were the two semicircular gaps, one at the bottom and the second on the lower right, which in the early frames look like monstrous bites out of a round cheese. It is as if a mechanism is in operation, and two smooth coated sections move out of the main body to fill the empty spaces. As Brian and his wife Shirley continued watching, the object disappeared, then reappeared, then shot off again at an amazing rate and vanished. Air Traffic Control at Edinburgh

Airport reported that there had been no unusual sightings that night.

Interestingly, in February 1996 a similar object was filmed over Inverness, and days before the Curran encounter an almost identical UFO was filmed over Norwich in England. In November 1996 Alec Bell of Fauldhouse in West Lothian captured a UFO on video which bore a striking resemblance to the one seen on the Curran video. Mr Bell observed the UFO for 30–40 minutes and his footage clearly shows a glowing disc-shaped object in the sky. Just as in Brian Curran's video, sections are missing from its rim.

These are only the highlights of a quite extensive collection of video evidence of UFO activity over Scotland. Controversy erupted when a video that has been described as the 'best piece of footage ever taken'—that of a triangular-shaped craft over Larbert—was whisked away to the USA. It has never been seen in Scotland, although no doubt even if it were screened here it would not be enough to convince the sceptics.

Perhaps the most intriguing material to have been filmed so far, however, does not involve UFOs. Extensive recordings of ghostly figures have been made by Warner Hall [see Paranormal Paintings] from Falkirk, with the footage seeming to show not only people from past centuries, but buildings and even battle scenes.

WEIR, THOMAS

The life and death of Thomas Weir (1600–1670) bring together all those elements of the paranormal which still puzzle us today. Was he a Devil-worshipper or a black magician? Did he meet alien entities? Or was he, and the society which executed him, simply deluded?

Weir was the man who notoriously blew tobacco-smoke in the face of John Graham, Marquis of Montrose, as Graham was on his way to his place of execution in May 1650. Montrose had fought on the side of Charles I in the English Civil War, while Weir was a committed Puritan. Later Weir became a magistrate and Captain of the Edinburgh City Guard. By the 1660s, he had also earned a reputation as a God-fearing citizen and a renowned preacher. Weir was particularly welcome in the homes of well-off citizens to lead them in prayer, and he was especially welcomed by the female sex, or so it was later said, though this could simply be colouring Weir's past with the benefit of hindsight.

So had Weir been living a double life for years? Or at some point did he and his sister with whom he lived simply go mad? Out of the blue, he confessed to having been for fifty years a servant of the Devil. But it was the details he gave that shocked Edinburgh society. He confessed to having sex, not only with his sister, admitting that they had lived together as man and wife, but with the wives and daughters of leading members of the city council, many of whom he knew as friends. He claimed he had done this by occult means, using a magic staff the Devil had gifted him, to appear in their bedrooms at dead of night. Most bizarre of all, he described how he had copulated with a horse in a farmer's field.

The first reaction of friends was that Weir had gone mad. But though they hoped that he would eventually shut up, the opposite happened. His protestations of guilt grew more vehement. Whenever he had the opportunity he denounced himself to anyone who would listen. Weir had become a scandal, and the city authorities were left with no other option but to arrest him, lock him in the Tolbooth and charge him with witchcraft.

An accusation of being a witch did not automatically bring a death sentence. In Scotland, uniquely in Europe, an accused witch had the right of having a lawyer to defend him or her. Most accused witches were set free. And even if a guilty verdict was returned a witch might not be sent to the bonfire. Society had a complex attitude to witchcraft. So, at this stage, Weir's fate was by no means set in stone. Had he begun to contradict himself, claimed that he had been seized by a fit of madness, or simply said no more, he would in all likelihood have been set free. But Weir would not play that game. He continued to announce his guilt, give details of the weird practices he had engaged in and describe his meetings with the Devil.

The authorities were being pushed into a corner, one from which there was no escape—especially when Weir's sister Jane began to confess to the same occult crimes. Weir was brought to trial, found guilty and executed, as was his sister. Curiously though, the witchcraft charge was dropped and Weir met his death on the grounds of 'incest, sodomy and bestiality'. It was Jane alone who was branded as the consulter of 'witches, necromancers and devils'. This was a calculated act—Weir's high-ranking friends had no wish to be linked to a servant of Satan, and rumours of a conspiracy were soon sweeping the capital. It was claimed that a secret group of wealthy men had forced a lookalike to take Weir's place and he had been seen, staff in hand, walking the streets of surrounding villages. Even at the time it was recognised that there was more to the case than met the eye.

So was it all in Weir's twisted mind? There are several puzzling features about his account. Sex with a horse seems on the surface the admission of a deranged mind. But on the other hand, this strange act was part of ancient pagan rites. The Kings of Ulster in past times ritually copulated with a mare to achieve long life. Weir had fought in 1641 with the Puritan army in Ulster against Royalist Catholics. By that time he had, according to his own account, already become a follower of Satan, but he may have learnt of this strange practice during this period. Furthermore, when we consider that horses were regarded as sacred animal by various occult groups, and add to that recent cases of horse mutilation, the episode becomes even more puzzling. And then there is Weir's description of a strange airborne machine. The 'flying chariot' sparking flames which carried him from Edinburgh to Dalkeith in broad daylight for a meeting with the Devil.

Clearly something had disturbed Weir's mind. But were these real events nevertheless? Had he become mixed up with strange entities of some twilight world? Although at first Weir talked freely about the Devil, in the later part of his time in gaol he became reluctant to describe Him though he still chatted unreservedly about his own crimes. Had he been warned to stay off the subject? Or did he realise that if he tried explain exactly who the 'Devil' was he simply would not be believed?

WITCHCRAFT

Is the power of witchcraft simply a figment of the imagination? Or does the Devil really exist? And are the sacred rituals witches practise truly capable of affecting the world around us? Before 1700 society seemed to have no doubt on the matter—witches existed, and there was a real problem in trying to stop them harming their fellow men. The belief ran from the top to the bottom of society. James VI believed, at least for a time, that there was an organised world of witchcraft, and wrote a book on the subject, *Demonology*. He accepted that his cousin, the Earl of Bothwell [qv], had used several witches including a well known healer, Agnes Sampson, in an attempt to murder him. James, in his thinking, was very much in tune with the people he ruled over.

Far from the rarefied atmosphere of court circles, at the village level, neighbours accused each other of casting spells and took direct action against those they suspected of engaging in the black arts. The Devil, in their view, was no phantom of the mind, but a flesh-and-blood figure who could appear in human guise, or take on whatever form He wanted. He could appear anywhere at any time, as He did in the Edinburgh Castle cell of accused witch John Cunningham. It was said that He was even able to murder those He wanted to keep quiet—the strangling of John Stewart in Irvine gaol, to stop him testifying against an accused witch, Margaret Barclay, was cited as evidence of this terrifying power. The Devil would try all sorts of tricks to prevent His followers revealing their involvement in His activities. So John Cunningham had a pin locked under his tongue as a magic ruse to stop him confessing, it was said.

It seems true that in Scotland, as throughout Europe, more women than men were accused of witchcraft, although both sexes were seen as potential malefactors. And the focus of all the evil activity was very much a male, the Devil himself.

There was clearly a sexual aspect to women's involvement with the Devil, and the confessions extracted from accused female witches contain frequent descriptions of sexual activity. Isobel Gowdie [qv] commented that the Devil's member 'was as cold as ice' inside her and, naturally 'much bigger than a normal man's'. He was also capable of satisfying a woman far above the usual. That was not always the case, though, and other witches confessed that sex with the Devil could be a painful experience. The detailed descriptions of sexual activity have encouraged some to believe that gatherings of witches did take place, that witches were organised into covens and that their faith was all based on the survival of a pagan cult. The 'Devil' was simply the local 'priest'—a man dressed up as a goat or other animal, to represent one of the ancient gods of nature.

To society, the account given by witches of their regular meetings at all kinds of venues—from North Berwick Kirk to the hills around Inverness, from Auldearn [qv] Kirk to an East Lothian beach—seemed to support the view that witches formed an organised secret group, serving an un-Christian entity, out to undermine society. Huge efforts were made to stamp out the evil practice, as confessions were forced out of suspected witches and 'witch prickers' moved from village to village looking for the 'Devil's mark'—a blemish on the skin where Satan marked his followers. If a pin was pushed into the spot, but the individual felt nothing, it was regarded as proof that he or she was a witch. Scottish 'prickers' were highly regarded in England, one of whom, John Kincaid, was much in demand in the north of the country.

By the early 1700s belief in witchcraft, at least among the educated ruling élite, had died out. Witchcraft charges were laughed out of court and those who assaulted witches were more likely to face the penalty of the law than the accused witch.

This modern view of witchcraft as a delusion may strike many today as a sensible approach. Those who most vehemently deny it was a delusion, and who believe the accounts of executed witches, are today's followers of Wicca, as witchcraft now prefers to be called. Since the 1950s there has been a revival in the 'craft' (another contemporary term for witchcraft) and by the 1990s Scotland had its own witch king. Today's Scottish witches claim a direct descent from those persecuted several centuries ago, and some say that their forebears were in fact practising witches. Incidentally, witches are not necessarily treated any better than in the past and Scotland's witch king, who lived in Paisley, did not find universal tolerance from the community.

Witches of the 1990s deny any link to the Devil. They see themselves as inheritors of an age-old pagan religion, worshipping nature gods, such as Pan. Wiccans feel that man has lost touch with nature, which explains why some Wiccans believe in naked dancing and even naked weddings, as this apparently allows better communication with the spirits of other worlds. And ancient spells are still cast. Wiccans believe that by using the right materials at certain times of the year, and performing the correct ceremony, it is possible to make spirits do as you ask. Wiccans stress that their 'magic' is only used to work good. But there is no doubt that some people practice black magic today, as it is said people did in the past. There are undoubtedly active 'dark side' covens in Scotland, out to use magic for their own ends. According to those involved, black and white magicians continue to engage in psychic battles.

So is there a rational explanation that accounts for witches' beliefs? Were witches early drug addicts who fantasised about their exploits? Various preparations were well known to people at the time and used as a means to kill pain or to induce a state of ecstasy. However, this answer does not apply to current witches, who see the power of witchcraft as flowing from the rituals they practise.

The followers of paganism, of which Wiccans form one branch, are increasing in number. There are several UK magazines catering for the pagan community, and Scotland has its own regular publication, *Sourcery*. However, followers of Wicca in Scotland number only a few hundred, with most covens located in and around Edinburgh. Leaders of the Scottish craft like Dougie Bain have been willing to promote their activities and argue for the positive side of Wiccan belief, yet it remains to be seen whether Wicca will achieve anything more than a minority following [*see also* Satanism]

WOOD, GARY

Although Scottish abduction incidents [*see* Abduction] have been rare, events on the A70 road in West Lothian have aroused considerable interest. It was not by any means Scotland's first abduction case, but it was the first to receive media attention. The event gained particular credibility because it involved more than one person which, at least in theory, meant that there was corroboration. However, although one of the abductees, Gary Wood, has talked extensively about his experiences, his fellow witness, Colin Wright, has been a lot less vocal. He does, however, back up Gary Wood's account of events.

Wood and Wright's ordeal took place on 17th August 1992 on an evening that started innocently enough. According to Wood's version: 'The receiver on my satellite dish blew and I rang my friend Ian Phillips out at Tarbrax village to see if he could help. Another friend Colin Wright arrived just as I was getting ready to go. We set off around 10 p.m. We came to a bend in the road, the A70 in West Lothian, and Colin pointed to something above us. The object was floating 20 feet above the road. It was black in colour, shiny and about 35 to 40 feet across. It looked metallic. It wasn't making a noise but on seeing it I got really frightened. The thought went through my head: "If I stop this car something will run up and grab me." I really felt as if my life was being threatened. I just wanted to get away. I accelerated under the object and I could see things hanging from it. A shimmering light came down, the exact width of the road. And then I wasn't in the car. I was thinking: "where's the car? Where's Colin?" I could see only blackness and really thought I was dead. Then I was back in the car on the wrong side of the road with Colin screaming "Did you see it?"'

Wood remembers driving at speeds of over 90 m.p.h. to Ian's house and hammering on his door. Then came the next shock. It was now 12.45 a.m. A journey which should have taken 45 minutes at most had inexplicably lasted three times as long.

For weeks after, Gary suffered nightmares. One morning he found himself nearly a mile from his house, half-dressed and dazed. Puzzled and worried, he tried to make sense of his encounter and why time was missing from his life.

The steps he took to solve the mystery have aroused controvcrsy but could be seen as understandable in the circumstances. He decided to undergo hypnosis [qv] to discover what had taken place in the time between seeing the UFO and landing back in the car. He underwent several hours of hypnotic regression and a bizarre tale emerged. Wood described the hidden memories that were brought back: 'I felt I was in my car and it was like being electrocuted, as if my muscles were being pulled in on me. I saw three wee men coming towards the car. Then there was a taller entity, six to seven feet, translucent like a grey white colour. It came close to me and said: "I've got a life like yours, but different." What it was trying to tell me was "look, I'm not a monster." There was also a brown-coloured being with a heart-shaped head and folds of skin, about four feet in height. It looked ancient.'

The entities also appear to have put Gary Wood through some kind of medical examination. 'I saw two objects go away from my chest. At the same time the entities were looking at my left leg. I couldn't move at all during this time. There was an object right inside my ear making a humming noise.'

Curiously, during the whole period of his ordeal, Wood had no sight of his friend Colin Wright, but he did see someone else. 'There was a naked female on the ground, in her early 20s with blonde hair. She was trying to cover herself up. She was very distressed. Her eyes were red with crying.' If that was bad enough what happened next must have been really frightening. 'There was a hole in the ground full of gel-like paste. There was something moving in it and then this thin grey creature rose out of it.'

Some say that hypnosis should not have been carried out as it has brought back unsettling memories, but Gary disagrees:

'Before the hypnosis I was scared to sleep at night. I realise now that whatever took me away wasn't going to hurt me and I learned that through the hypnosis sessions.'

It will not surprise students of abduction cases to learn that Wood has an unexplained incident from his childhood. 'I went missing for most of a day when I was just four years old and where I was during all that time has never been explained. I just have vague memories of playing with children in strange coloured sand.' There is no definite evidence that this was an early abduction experience and Gary Wood has an open mind on the incident. However, it does seem to fit into a pattern which, it is claimed, occurs in these cases. According to American abduction expert Bud Hopkins: 'we have learned that specific pairs of children have been repeatedly abducted over the years and brought together periodically in the same strange environment.' Hopkins is a firm believer in the use of hypnosis to recall hidden memories.

Whatever the reality behind Gary Wood's strange encounter, it has had a profound impact on his life. He explains it this way: 'The A70 incident has changed me. I appreciate my life more. We don't realise what we've got. I have also taken up UFO research to find out why these things happen to people.' However, Wood also has a word of warning: 'I'm quite happy that UFOs are still a mystery. I am worried about what might happen when we do meet these entities. The governments know what's going on, but they're only looking after their own interests. Sometimes change isn't a good thing. I would like there to be an answer, but I dread the day when it comes. We're the ones who'll cause the harm. Humans are a warlike race.'

There is no doubting Gary Wood's belief that the events he experienced actually happened, even though the alien encounter aspect was 'remembered' only under hypnosis. The use of hypnosis to recall allegedly lost memories is controversial in British UFO circles, and its use was banned by BUFORA. In Scotland there is less hostility and a more uncertain attitude towards its effectiveness. Wood underwent analysis by an independent psychologist as part of a television investigation into the incident. This analysis confirmed that he had experienced trauma, which supports the view that Wood and Wright confronted something strange on the night in question, even if the details remain controversial.

X-FILE SCOTLAND

The success of the television series *The X-Files* was a phenomenon of the 1990s. Did it stimulate interest in the paranormal, especially the abduction phenomenon? Or did its success arise from growing interest in unidentified flying objects and other unexplained incidents? It is noticeable that during the 1990s Scotland became a world UFO hot spot [qv], the centre being the village of Bonnybridge [qv]. But there is far more—in fact, Scotland is surely in the running as the world's X-File hot spot, as there is hardly a square mile about which there is not a bizarre tale to tell. With ghosts [qv], loch monsters [*see* Morar, Loch; Ness, Loch], poltergeists [qv], phantom pumas [qv], vampires [qv], haunted castles [*see* Castle Ghosts; Glamis] and fairy hills [*see* Fairy Knowe], we are far ahead of alleged centres of mystery like Tibet.

But why should Scotland be such a strange place? Whatever

the cause, it seems to have been around for a long time. There is plenty of evidence to suggest that King Arthur and his guide Merlin lived in Scotland rather than England. The island of Arran was regarded as Avalon, Arthur's final resting place, and his greatest battle may have taken place at Camelon near Falkirk. When that strange sect the Knights Templar [qv] were banned by the Pope for Devil-worship, many of them fled to Scotland. It is even argued that they brought the Holy Grail and Christ's head with them, and that both these objects lie buried beneath Rosslyn Chapel [qv] in the Lothians. Druids have an even longer history—the druids supposedly died out centuries ago, but Scotland has become a centre for a revival of this strange religion. It is said that Arran was once known as the Isle of Apple Trees, a fruit sacred to the druids, and Arran may have played a key role in a cult which predates the arrival of Christianity. Modern druids have made the island their home, and there is an active College of Druidism in Edinburgh.

Were druids responsible for Scotland's most enduring mystery? There are more standing stone circles [qv] here than anywhere else in the world, and one of the most complex of these is to be found at Callanish [qv]. Is this just chance or does it show that Scotland has forever been an area regarded as mystic? Were these enigmatic circles even set up as beacons to ancient visitors from deepest space?

The world's greatest medium, Daniel Home [qv], was Scottish. And one of the most famous paranormal incidents of recent times involved the prosecution of Callander-born Helen Duncan [qv] as a witch by a government concerned about her psychic visions. She had produced uncannily accurate information about a ship sunk by enemy action, an incident which the authorities in World War Two were trying to keep secret. And there is Carol Compton [qv] from Aberdeenshire, who in the 1980s was charged with using the 'evil eye' while working in Italy. We even have our own 'Nostradamus' in the 'Brahan Seer' [qv]. The most famous was Kenneth Or, whose prophecies are still respected today. The present Brahan Seer, Swein Macdonald, is consulted by people from all over the world.

There is no mysterious creature better known across the world than the 'monster' of Loch Ness [*see* Ness, Loch]. Research teams from as far away as the USA and Japan have come over to prove or disprove its existence. Scotland can even boast its own yeti [qv]. The 'Grey Man of Ben MacDhui' [qv] may not be the spirit of a dead climber as some claim, but an unknown animal which stalks the Cairngorms, hiding away from prying eyes.

Bram Stoker was inspired to write Dracula by seeing Slains Castle near Peterhead. But that is not our only link with vampires [qv]. In the past, south-west Scotland was seen as a centre of vampire activity.

It is strange too that Scotland earned a reputation as a centre of witchcraft [qv] activity at a time when these 'servants of the Devil' were being tortured and burned across Europe. Looking back it is said that our ancestors were just superstitious and created a great satanic conspiracy out of nothing more substantial than overheated imaginings. But when set against the many strange incidents that have happened here, can it be dismissed as mere imagination? [*See* Satanism]

Scotland's role as the home to the bizarre reached new heights with the remarkable success of the Findhorn [qv] Foundation.

Communication with plants and fairies [qv], and living in spiritual harmony with nature, turned out to be a way of life that attracted international attention and inspired millions of followers. From all over the world 'greens' and those who wanted to abandon the rat race flocked to Findhorn to find a new focus for their life. From a group of three, including Scot Robert Crombie [qv], living in a dilapidated caravan, it has grown to a centre that has influenced world opinion. Should we thank Scotland's nature spirits for this achievement?

More sinister, perhaps is the experience of Jenny Hill. In 1992 she had her car stolen from a Glasgow street and reported the theft to the Strathclyde Police. The following day two plain clothed individuals turned up at her work and asked to speak to Jenny. They were shown in to her office. She noticed that they were carrying with them a black plastic bag, and she wondered what the visitors wanted. She was surprised to learn that the two, a man and woman, were from the police. They knew about the theft of her car and claimed that they had found it. They told her that the plastic bag contained items from the vehicle and, without asking for permission, emptied the contents on to the floor. Jenny was dumbfounded at this act—and by what came tumbling out of the bag. She later reported: 'It was just rubbish. It had nothing to do with my car whatsoever. I couldn't understand what was going on. I asked them to clear up the mess and leave.' They did just that. But after they had gone Jenny found herself becoming more and more perplexed. What on earth had been going on? She decided to ring the police. They were just as amazed—they knew nothing of these individuals and could not understand what they had been up to.

So what conclusion can we come to? Is Scotland a vast window into another dimension? We know that over the centuries Scotland has witnessed paranormal 'hot spots' of all kinds—from UFOs [qv] to witch covens—and even in this modern age the unexplained events show no sign of ceasing.

Y

YETI

Tales of the yeti tend to be linked to far-away lands, but the 'abominable snowman', as he is popularly known, may perhaps be found no further away than the Cairngorms. That is an explanation for encounters with an entity of which the Grey Man of Ben MacDhui [qv] is the most famous example.

This being has usually been explained as a 'guardian spirit' of the mountain or the ghost of dead climbers. But the details given by Professor Norman Collie suggest that perhaps a flesh-and-blood being was involved. Collie described hearing 'a crunch and then another crunch as if someone was walking after me but taking steps three or four times the length of my own'. Decades after this incident another mountaineer Peter Densham told of a similar experience on the summit. 'I had the sudden impression someone was near me. . . . I stood up and was conscious of a crunching noise from the direction of the cairn on my left'. Like Collie before him, Densham experienced an overwhelming desire to leave the mountain and made the descent as quickly as possible.

However, an alleged encounter reported by a mountaineer is more detailed and specific. According to this account the witness saw 'about 20 yards away a great brown creature swaggering down the hill . . . [it] had an air of insolent strength about it . . . it rolled slightly from side to side, taking huge measured steps. It looked as though it was covered with shortish brown hair. Its head was disproportionately large, its neck very thick and powerful . . . it did not resemble an ape. Its hairy arms, though long, were not unduly so, its carriage was extremely erect'. Wendy Wood, better known for her political activities, was another visitor to the mountain who had no doubt that there were strange things going on. She later wrote of her encounter describing how she heard a loud voice right beside her, speaking what she thought was Gaelic, though she could not make out the sounds properly. She also had the sensation experienced by Collie and Densham that someone or something was following her.

These types of experiences are by no means confined to Ben MacDhui, but there has been a far greater concentration of incidents linked to the mountain. It could be argued that, unlike the Tibetan experience, there has been a lack of physical evidence such as snowprints. Snow, of course, does not lie here as it does in the Himalayas so what might be found instead is mud footprints although these do not last for any length of time in our damp climate. The truth is we are not geared up for searching for the creature. A yeti in Scotland seems to defy common sense. However, there are vast expanses of Scotland which are rarely visited, and the Highlands cover an area the size of Wales. We know that flesh-and-blood pumas [see Phantom Pumas] have hidden themselves in far more densely populated parts of the country. So why not a creature which possesses more cunning and intelligence, and perhaps wants to avoid direct contact with man?

Z

ZALUS

Zalus is without doubt one of the most bizarre entities to have been associated with the Scottish UFO scene—especially as it seems likely that he never existed. Was Zalus just the figment of someone's imagination, or did the whole affair conceal a more sinister secret?

In August 1995, when interest in the Bonnybridge [qv] UFO hot spot was at its height, a story appeared in several newspapers claiming that an entity called Zalus was going to put in an appearance at a UFO meeting to be held in Falkirk town hall. It was said that during the event an alien being would enlighten the audience as to the purpose of extraterrestrial contact and Earth's role in the evolution of the universe. It seemed an unlikely scenario and, as might be guessed, it turned out that there was no truth in the story.

Local councillor Billy Buchanan was alleged to have been

linked to Zalus. In fact, he had no connection with the supposed alien and was understandably upset that his name had been dragged into the affair. Councillor Buchanan had been working hard to establish Bonnybridge's reputation as a genuine UFO hot spot and felt that the Zalus story simply undermined his efforts.

Ufologists began to suspect it had all been part of a dirty tricks campaign deliberately intended to discredit ufology in general and the Bonnybridge hot spot in particular. The government and the Ministry of Defence may have become concerned about the extent of interest in UFO sightings in the area and decided to undermine the credibility of the phenomenon. This was the view of UFO expert Malcolm Robinson, who claimed that 'someone could be spreading disinformation on behalf of the government to take the heat away from sightings of military objects.' His comments were not taken seriously at the time, but perhaps they should have been.

It is true that the name Zalus originated from the magazine *Enigmas*, the publication of the UFO group Strange Phenomena Investigations (SPI), so it was not entirely a concoction of a government department. It was also the case that one of the speakers at the conference claimed that he would be imparting knowledge gained directly from the aliens. This, as it turned out, was the very human Geri Rogers from Edinburgh. Councillor Buchanan, according to the *Scotsman* newspaper, explained Mr Rogers' role in the affair: 'He told me he was part of a British group researching the "Council of Nine", and would be telling everyone what should be done to prevent catastrophe on a world scale. I couldn't understand much of what he was on about, but he deserves to be listened to.'

But why had the press played the affair for all it was worth? Was it simply a good story, or something altogether more sinister? Amid all the claims and counter-claims, it should be noted that at the time Councillor Buchanan was planning to organise a petition to put pressure on the government to investigate UFO incidents in the area. He had also been in touch with the local MP. Perhaps the authorities were becoming rather concerned about the Bonnybridge phenomenon and simply took action to extinguish this most inconvenient hot spot.

FURTHER READING

Adams, Norman: *Haunted Scotland*
(Mainstream Publishing, 1998)

Baigent, Michael: *Ancient Traces* (Penguin Books, 1998)

Baird, Robert: *Shipwrecks of the West of Scotland*
(Nekton Books, 1995)

Beaumont, Comyns: *The Riddle of Prehistoric Britain*
(Rider, 1946)

Binns, Ronald: *The Loch Ness Mystery Solved*
(W H Allen, 1984)

Bord, Colin and Janet: *The Enchanted Land* (Thorsons, 1995)

Campbell, Elizabeth Montgomery: *The Search for Morag*
(Tom Stacey, 1972)

Campbell, Steuart: *The UFO Mystery Solved*
(Explicit Books, 1994)

Campbell, Steuart: *The Loch Ness Monster* (Birlinn, 1996)

Compton, Carole: *Superstitions* (Ebury Press, 1990)

Cowan, David: *Ancient Energy of the Earth* (Thorsons, 1999)

Cyr, Donald L: 'King Arthur's Crystal Cave' (in *Stonehange Viewpoint*, Issue 108, 1997)

Devereux, Paul: *Earthlights* (Turnstone, 1982)

Dorward, David: *Scotland's Place Names*
(Mercat Press, 1998)

Dunford, Barry: *The Holy Land of Scotland*
(Brigadoon Books, 1996)

Gilbert, Adrian: *The Holy Kingdom* (Corgi Books, 1999)

Gray, Affleck: *The Big Grey Man of Ben Macdhui*
(Lochar Publishing, 1989)

Halliday, Ron (Ed.): *McX: Scotland's X-Files*
(B&W Publishing, 1997)

Halliday, Ron: *UFOs: The Scottish Dimension*
(Scottish Paranormal Press, 1997)

Halliday, Ron: *UFO Scotland* (B&W Publishing, 1998)

Harrison, Paul: *The Encyclopaedia of the Loch Ness Monster*
(Robert Hale, 1999)

Hawken, Paul: *The Magic of Findhorn*
(Souvenir Press, 1975)

Holmes, Richard: *The Legend of Sawney Bean*
(Frederick Muller, 1975)

Hough, Peter: *Supernatural Britain* (Piatkus, 1995)

Keay, John and Julia: *Encyclopaedia of Scotland*
(HarperCollins, 1994)

King, Dorothy: *Tales and Legends of Scotland*
(George G Harrap, 1927)

Kirk, Robert: *The Secret Commonwealth* (D S Brewer, 1976)

Love, Dane: *Scottish Ghosts* (Robert Hale, 1995)

Macdonald Robertson, R: *Highland Folktales* (House of
Lochar, 1995)

McLeish, Norrie: *The Haunted Borders*
(Alba Publishing, 1997)

Miller, Hugh: *My Schools and Schoolmasters*
(B&W Publishing, 1993)

Miller, Hugh: *Scenes and Legends of the North of Scotland*
(B&W Publishing, 1994)

Moir, Helen: *Larkhall* (Tempus, 1998)

Pennick, Nigel: *Dragons of the West*
(Capall Bann Publishing, 1997)

Randles, Jenny: *The Paranormal Year, 1993*
(Robert Hale, 1993)

Robbins, Russell Hope: *The Encyclopaedia of Witchcraft and Demonology* (Hamlyn Publishing, 1959)

Robertson, James: *Scottish Ghost Stories* (Warner, 1996)

Strachan, Gordon: *Jesus the Master Builder* (Floris, 1998)

Watkins, Alfred: *The Old Straight Track* (Abacus, 1974)

Whittaker, Terence: *Scotland's Ghosts and Apparitions*
(Robert Hale, 1991)

FURTHER INFORMATION

If you have had a paranormal experience, UFO encounter, or have video footage or photographic evidence that you would like to report, please write to Ron Halliday at:

SEMR, 35 Fountain Road,
Bridge of Allan, FK9 4AU.

If you would like details of *Phenomenal News*, the magazine of SEMR, please write to:

SEMR (PN), 35 Fountain Road,
Bridge of Allan, FK9 4AU.

INDEX